Part of the One Church?

Part of the One Church?

The Ordination of Women and Anglican Identity

Roger Greenacre

Edited by
Colin Podmore

CANTERBURY
PRESS
Norwich

Copyright in this volume © The Estate of Roger Greenacre, 2014

First published in 2014 by the Canterbury Press Norwich
Editorial office
3rd Floor, Invicta House
108–114 Golden Lane
London EC1Y 0TG

Canterbury Press is an imprint of Hymns Ancient &
Modern Ltd (a registered charity)
13A Hellesdon Park Road, Norwich,
Norfolk NR6 5DR, UK

www.canterburypress.co.uk

British Library Cataloguing in Publication data

A catalogue record for this book is available
from the British Library

978 1 84825 627 9

Typeset by Manila Typesetting Company
Printed and bound in Great Britain by
Ashford Colour Press Ltd

Contents

Acknowledgements

The cover photograph is used with permission of the Pontifical Council for the Promotion of Christian Unity.

An extract from the transcript by Fr Patrice Mahieu of his conversation with Roger Greenacre on 19 March 2010 is included in the Introduction by kind permission of Fr Mahieu.

Chapter 4 was first published in *One in Christ*, 21 (1985) and is reproduced by kind permission of the Editor.

Chapter 5 was first published in *The Messenger of the Catholic League*, 229 (May 1986) and is reproduced by kind permission of the General Secretary of the Catholic League.

The Open Letter republished in Chapter 7 was first published in the booklet *Lost in the Fog? The Lesson for Ecumenism of Lambeth 1988*, the text of which is copyright © The Church Union 1989. It is reproduced by kind permission of the Chairman of the Church Union.

Chapter 8, a lecture given at the Centro Pro Unione, Rome, on 2 May 1990, was first published in the *Bulletin 'Centro Pro Unione'*, 39 (Spring 1991), 4–10. The Centro Pro Unione is a ministry of the Franciscan Friars of the Atonement. Published with permission.

The speech which forms Chapter 11 was first published in the *Chronicle of the Convocation of Canterbury* (July 1992) and is reproduced by kind permission of the Synodical Secretary of the Convocation.

Chapter 13 and the articles which form Chapter 17 were first published in *The Month* in March 1993 and February 1995. They are reproduced with the permission of The Trustees for Roman Catholic Purposes.

The article republished in Chapter 14 was first published in the *Church of England Newspaper* for 8 October 1993 and is reproduced by kind permission of the Editor.

The speech which forms Chapter 15 was first published in the *Report of Proceedings* of the General Synod (November 1993).

Chapter 18 is an English translation of an article first published in French in *Unité des Chrétiens*, 99 (July 1995) and is included by kind permission of the Editor in Chief.

The letter included in Chapter 19 was first published in the *Church Times* on 3 November 1995. It is reproduced with gratitude to the *Church Times*.

Chapter 20 was first published in *The Server*, 17, no. 11 (Autumn 1997) and is reproduced by kind permission of the Secretary-General of the Guild of the Servants of the Sanctuary.

Chapter 23 was first published in *New Directions* in July 1999 and is reproduced with permission.

The Editor is indebted to Roger Greenacre's friend and executor Canon Jeremy Haselock for his encouragement and judicious editorial advice.

Foreword
by Geoffrey Rowell

It is a privilege to be asked to contribute a Foreword to this significant collection of papers by the late Canon Roger Greenacre.

Roger and I first came to know each other when we worked together on the Church Union Theological Committee, which was the context of some of the papers published here, as well as being responsible for two symposia on sacramental theology, *Confession and Absolution* (1990) and *The Oil of Gladness: Anointing in the Church* (1993). When I was appointed to a Wiccamical Prebend of Chichester Cathedral – one of four canonries founded by Bishop Robert Sherburn 'to increase the learning of the Chapter', it was good to be part of the General Chapter of the Cathedral of which Roger was Canon Chancellor. Like so many others I profited from his gift of friendship, shown in his generous hospitality. When I became Bishop in Europe, I was delighted to find Roger, having retired from his Chichester canonry, serving as Chaplain of Beaulieu-sur-Mer on the Côte d'Azur. This had brought him back to his beloved France, and enabled him to have a significant pastoral and ecumenical ministry far beyond the three years which were initially envisaged.

We owe Dr Colin Podmore, as Roger Greenacre's literary executor, a great debt for gathering these papers together, ordering them, and preparing them for publication. As his introduction to this collection makes clear, the ordination of women to the priesthood – and even more the ordination of women to the episcopate – raises sharp and significant questions about

Anglican identity, and it is important that these questions are properly understood, both by Anglicans in the Catholic tradition and more widely. Underlying differences of ecclesiology, largely unacknowledged, can mean that those holding different positions on the presenting issue can be like ships that pass in the night.

As is made clear time and again in these papers, Roger was not an impossibilist in the matter of the ordination of women, but he was rightly concerned about the authority of the Church of England (or indeed the Anglican Communion) to make a change in the historic apostolic ministry of the Church, which Anglicans claim to share with the historic churches of Christendom both East and West, without greater ecumenical consensus and without a clearly articulated theology of development.

These papers are written always with a properly challenging yet creative courtesy, and at times an inevitable sadness as Roger reflects on the ecumenical consequences of a unilateral decision. Their clarity will surely assist those who are concerned that there are real questions about these issues which still have to be asked. For those for whom this is unfamiliar and even puzzling territory, given the new situation in which the Church of England finds itself, they should serve as a reminder that there is a wider context in which questions of faith and order must be asked and answered than the parochialism of the English context. We are, after all, as the Declaration of Assent puts it, only 'part of the One, Holy, Catholic and Apostolic Church'.

✠ *Geoffrey Gibraltar:*
The Rt Revd Dr Geoffrey Rowell
Bishop of Gibraltar in Europe, 2001–13

Feast of St Augustine of Hippo, 2013

Introduction
by Colin Podmore

In the articles and addresses that make up this book Canon Roger Greenacre presents – to Anglicans and to ecumenical partners – a classical understanding of the Church of England's identity and its place within the Church Catholic. The ecclesiological and ecumenical issues that he addresses are not just relevant to the debate on women's ordination but have much broader significance. They include issues of unity and diversity, of 'uniatism' and of 'Anglican patrimony'; of the relationship between the local and the universal, and the distinction between independence and interdependence; of 'reception', and of decision-making in a divided Church. The frame of reference is wide: Roger's thinking and writing were informed both by the Anglican tradition (and especially the seventeenth-century Caroline Divines) and by the French Catholic tradition with which he was so familiar; by the thought of John Henry Newman and of the Second Vatican Council; by current debate within the Roman Catholic Church; and above all by the Anglican–Roman Catholic ecumenical dialogue that was of such importance to him.

A Positive Vision

This volume gathers together lectures, speeches, sermons and articles that Roger wrote in the last quarter of the twentieth century, between 1975 (when he returned from ten years in

Paris to become a residentiary canon of Chichester Cathedral) and 2000, when he retired from Chichester and returned to France for a further ten years of ministry on the French Riviera. Not all of them focus directly on the issue of the ordination of women to the priesthood, but each is relevant in one way or another to that theme.

None of the chapters is hostile to the ordained ministry of women, which Roger supported, as indicated by his choice of a female deacon for the mass that marked the golden jubilee of his priestly ordination in 2005. Only one (Chapter 6 – 'The Bishop as Icon of Christ') sets out arguments against the ordination of women to the priesthood and episcopate in the universal Church, a possibility to which Roger remained open in principle throughout his life. Roger wrote the paper which forms that chapter reluctantly, setting out the arguments 'not as the statement of a theological position but as a possible starting point for reflection and discussion'.[1]

The vision that unites the chapters of this book is not a negative but a positive one – of a Church of England fully conscious of its place and role as 'part of the One, Holy, Catholic and Apostolic Church', rejoicing in its catholic heritage, and bringing its distinctive Anglican tradition (not only of liturgy and spirituality but also of theology and ecclesiology) into communion with a reformed Roman Catholic Church under a reformed papacy. It is a vision which, in the middle years of Roger's life (roughly between 1960, when he was 30, and 1985, when he was 55), he – in common with many others – believed the fruits of the Second Vatican Council and the work of the first Anglican–Roman Catholic International Commission (ARCIC I) might bring to fulfilment in his lifetime.

All but two of the chapters were written after that quarter century of hope, in the eight years before and the eight years after 11 November 1992, when the General Synod of the Church of England gave final approval to the legislation

---

1 See Chapter 6, p. 56.

permitting the ordination of women to the priesthood – a period in which developments in the Roman Catholic Church also tended to militate against fulfilment of the ecumenical vision. Some chapters focus directly on the consequences of the 1992 decision, while others look at Anglican ecclesiology and Anglican–Roman Catholic relations more generally. In many of those written after 1992 hope remains – rekindled first by the Episcopal Ministry Act of Synod 1993, which kept alive the vision of the Church of England's place within the Church Catholic, and then in 1999 by the ARCIC II report *The Gift of Authority*.

In the last four chapters of the book Anglican–Roman Catholic dialogue comes to the fore, with a reflection on the dysfunctionality that Roger identified in both churches and then, in Part 4, three presentations of the 1999 ARCIC II report *The Gift of Authority*, which allow the book to end on a note of renewed – if cautious – hope. In fact, of course, in 2003 the Anglican Communion was plunged into an even deeper ecclesiological crisis which effectively placed Anglican–Roman Catholic dialogue 'on hold' for the rest of that decade. That crisis, and the attempts to address it – ultimately through the Anglican Communion Covenant – placed the earlier ecclesiological crisis over the ordination of women in the shade.

Aspiration and Obligation

In addition to its wider significance, the book fulfils one of Roger Greenacre's aspirations as his life drew to a close. As Roger prepared to retire in 2010 from his chaplaincy on the French Riviera to the London Charterhouse, in his eightieth year, he conceived three retirement projects. The first was a study of the correspondence between Bishop George Bell of Chichester (of whose cathedral Roger had been a residentiary canon for the last quarter of the twentieth century) and the Belgian ecumenist and liturgist Dom Lambert Beauduin (in whose honour he had taken the name Lambert as his name in religion when he became an oblate of the Abbey of Notre-Dame du Bec in 1982). The second was a book which would draw together his study and writing on the Blessed Virgin Mary in the Anglican tradition. The third was an Open Letter about the implications of the ordination of women to the priesthood and episcopate for the Church of England's self-understanding as, in the words of the Declaration of Assent, 'part of the One, Holy, Catholic and Apostolic Church'.[2] Sadly, he fell ill not long after his arrival at Charterhouse and died on 30 July 2011, before any of these projects could be completed – or, in two cases, even begun.

As Roger's literary executor, I have felt an obligation to fulfil his aspirations for the publication of his work as far as possible. We had gathered copies of the Bell–Beauduin correspondence from various archives before his retirement, but he had not begun work on it, so there was nothing from his pen to publish. Although he had not commenced work on the book about Mary either, he had written, lectured and preached on that subject over many years. This made possible the publication in January 2013 of a collection entitled *Maiden, Mother and Queen: Mary in the Anglican Tradition*.[3] An account of Roger's life is offered in the first part of that book, together with the addresses given at the requiems celebrated for him in London and Chichester; a bibliography of his publications concludes the volume.

To Roger the third aspiration was by far the most important. At Charterhouse he began work on his Open Letter and, despite his illness, he made some progress. Among the papers in his apartment when he died were some notes, an outline and a complete draft of the first section. Looking through Roger's publications and his unpublished lectures, I realized that in them he had in fact addressed or at least touched upon most of the themes that he was hoping to cover in the Open Letter. Publishing them in this book, prefaced by the draft of the first

---

2 Canons of the Church of England: Canon C 15, para. 1(1).

3 R. T. Greenacre, *Maiden, Mother and Queen: Mary in the Anglican Tradition*, edited by C. J. Podmore (Norwich: Canterbury Press, 2013).

section of his Open Letter and his outline for the rest, goes some way towards fulfilling the aspiration for his retirement work that was closest to Roger's heart. Inevitably, there are overlaps between some of the chapters; these have been left, so that each chapter retains its own integrity.

Between Memory and History

The fulfilment of an aspiration and an obligation is not in itself sufficient justification for publishing a book, however. As already indicated, this publication aspires to serve wider and more important purposes. Over 20 years have elapsed since November 1992. For Anglicans who are over 40, the debate that led up to the 1992 vote has become a distant memory; for most who are younger (including a whole generation of priests), it is not even that, having occurred before they had reached adulthood or even (as for most current university undergraduates) before they were born. On the other hand, the time is not yet ripe for writing the history of the debate. Some of its participants are still members of the Synod; they are figures of the present, not yet of history. Moreover, this book has been compiled before the new synodical process, begun in 2013, to permit women to be consecrated as bishops is concluded. Only when that definitive decision about women's ministry in the Church of England has been taken and the necessary canon has been promulged can the debate that led up to it be treated as a matter of history.

In this interim period, when memory is lacking or dim yet definitive history remains unwritten, many find it difficult to understand why 20 years ago so many opposed the ordination of women to the priesthood in the Church of England – or, indeed, why so many of us cannot in conscience receive the ministry of women so ordained. One of the purposes of this book is to begin to bridge the gap between memory and history, and in doing so to offer some explanation.

Reasons for Opposition

There are, broadly, three types of reason which required Anglo-Catholics to oppose the ordination of women to the priesthood in 1992 and which give rise to a continuing inability to receive priestly ministry from women:

- ❖ 'Ecumenical reasons' relate to the effect of ordaining women to the priesthood on the prospect of restoring communion between the Church of England and the Roman Catholic and Orthodox Churches which make up by far the greater part of historic catholic Christendom.
- ❖ 'Ecclesiological reasons' concern the effect of such ordinations on the self-understanding of the Church of England as being only 'part of the One, Holy, Catholic and Apostolic Church' and therefore not having the right to arrogate to itself decisions that can properly be made only by the Church as a whole.
- ❖ 'Opposition in principle' relates to the nature of priesthood and the roles of men and women in relation to it.

Until the Measure had been approved there were also other types of reason for opposition:

- ❖ Some argued against the terms of the legislation (most of which consisted of provisions for those who would remain opposed).
- ❖ Some held that the legislation was 'inopportune' – i.e. that the time was not right (for example because, though there was a substantial majority in favour, that majority did not amount to the consensus within the Church of England that such a significant change demanded).

Different reasons, or combinations of reasons, carried different weight with different people, as is still the case.

Opposition in Principle

Today, most Anglo-Catholics who oppose the ordination of women to the priesthood do so primarily for reasons of principle concerning the nature of priesthood and the roles of men and women. That is probably especially true of younger Anglo-Catholics, whose opinions have been formed in the 1990s and in the first decade of the present century.

A number of explanations may be advanced for this. One is that many of those who opposed the legislation because of its terms, because it was inopportune, for ecumenical reasons or even for ecclesiological reasons accepted the ordination of women to the priesthood once the General Synod had approved it. Roger found acceptance by those who argued that 'the Church has decided' and they should therefore accept the decision difficult to understand: they had themselves advanced the ecclesiological argument that the Church of England is not 'the Church' but only part of it, and as such had no moral right to decide.

Another reason is that the process of reflection did not cease in 1992. The Episcopal Ministry Act of Synod 1993 stated:

> The General Synod regards it as desirable that . . . all concerned should endeavour to ensure that . . . discernment in the wider Church of the rightness or otherwise of the Church of England's decision to ordain women to the priesthood should be as open a process as possible.[4]

In such a process a doctrine proposed by a Synod (in this case, a doctrine together with actions already taken on the basis of it) may be received or rejected by the faithful who were represented in the Synod concerned and by the wider Church. A significant instance of non-reception came on 22 May 1994 (that this was just ten weeks after the first ordination of women to

---

4 The Episcopal Ministry Act of Synod 1993, s. 3(a)(i): www.churchofengland.org/media/35648/episactofsynod.rtf

the priesthood in the Church of England can hardly be a coincidence), when Pope John Paul II made a definitive statement on the subject in his Apostolic Letter *Ordinatio Sacerdotalis* ('On Reserving Priestly Ordination to Men Alone'):

> . . . in order that all doubt may be removed regarding a matter of great importance, a matter which pertains to the Church's divine constitution itself, in virtue of my ministry of confirming the brethren (cf. Luke 22.32) I declare that the Church has no authority whatsoever to confer priestly ordination on women and that this judgment is to be definitively held by all the Church's faithful.[5]

Since 1994 Anglo-Catholics have engaged in a process of reflection, notably in the preparation of and reflection upon the 2004 report *Consecrated Women?*[6] (the report of a 'shadow working party' established by Forward in Faith at the suggestion of the then Archbishop of Canterbury, George Carey, to produce a counterpart to the official 'Rochester report' *Women Bishops in the Church of England?*[7]). This has led many who in 1992 had an open mind on the principle of ordaining women to the priesthood, and many who have only begun since 1992 to consider the question at all, to conclude that the ministerial priesthood is an intrinsically masculine role and that consequently women cannot be ordained to it.

Ironically, this conviction has developed at precisely the same time as social and political thinking in the United Kingdom has come to be dominated by an 'Equalities' agenda which considers women and men to be not only equal but also in all respects interchangeable. According to this view, there

---

5 http://www.vatican.va/holy_father/john_paul_ii/apost_letters/documents/hf_jp-ii_apl_22051994_ordinatio-sacerdotalis_en.html

6 J. Baker (ed.), *Consecrated Women? A Contribution to the Women Bishops Debate* (Norwich: Canterbury Press, 2004).

7 *Women Bishops in the Church of England? A report of the House of Bishops' Working Party on Women in the Episcopate* (GS 1557) (London: Church House Publishing, 2004).

is no role whatsoever that cannot be undertaken by either sex; 'motherhood' and 'fatherhood' are collapsed into 'parenting' and the roles of 'wife' and 'husband' into 'partnership' – with the corollary that the institution of marriage must be opened to partners of the same sex. Equality is confused not only with interchangeability but also with identity (sameness), so that 'discrimination' (drawing distinctions), and not just 'unfair discrimination', is believed always to be wrong.

In such a context, many people find it impossible to understand opposition to the ordination of women to the priesthood as resting on any principle other than support for inequality (prompted, they presume, by mindless conservatism if not outright misogyny). Recognizing this, Archbishop Rowan Williams told the General Synod in his Presidential Statement on 21 November 2012, the day after the failure of the original Women Bishops legislation:

> A great deal of this discussion is not intelligible to our wider society. Worse than that, it seems as if we are wilfully blind to some of the trends and priorities of that wider society. We have some explaining to do. We have, as the result of yesterday, undoubtedly lost a measure of credibility in our society.[8]

He recognized, however, that 'the ultimate credibility of the Church does not depend on the good will of the wider public' and that 'we would not be Christians and believers in divine revelation if we held that'.[9] For opponents of ordaining women to the priesthood, 'credibility' is not to be sought at the expense of truth. But it is salutary to note that the reasons of principle (concerning the essentially masculine nature of priesthood and the distinctiveness of certain roles of men and women – notably in relation to fatherhood, motherhood and priesthood) that are at the forefront of the minds of most Anglo-Catholics now

---

8 General Synod, *Report of Proceedings*, 21 November 2012, pp. 158–9.
9 *Report of Proceedings*, p. 159.

are precisely those which people whose minds are formed by secular society in the early twenty-first century find the most difficult to engage with. Many may find the ecumenical and ecclesiological arguments with which this book is overwhelmingly concerned easier to accept.

Ecumenical and Ecclesiological Reasons

Back in 1992, as Roger Greenacre repeatedly reminds us in this book, the majority of Anglo-Catholics who opposed the ordination of women did so primarily for ecumenical and above all ecclesiological reasons. The House of Bishops' *Second Report* on the Ordination of Women to the Priesthood, published in 1988,[10] made it clear that some of the bishops were 'opposed on theological grounds' (which the report detailed at length), but many participants in the debate tended not to use these arguments – perhaps, in many cases, because they had yet to come to a conclusion about the issue of principle.

Furthermore, in the *Second Report* the question was repeatedly stated as being that of whether the Church of England *should* ordain women to the priesthood, not whether it *could*. The theological grounds were treated as reasons for not ordaining women to the priesthood and not necessarily as reasons why such ordinations would, sacramentally, be of no effect. Perhaps it was this impression of argument against ordaining women as distinct from argument that ordaining women was impossible that led Archbishop Runcie, in presenting the report to the General Synod, to comment, surprisingly, 'Despite the divisions in the House of Bishops, I was encouraged that not one bishop appears to consider it absolutely impossible.'[11]

The final approval debate that November saw the two sides arguing past each other – one arguing that women should

---

10 *The Ordination of Women to the Priesthood: A Second Report by the House of Bishops of the Church of England* (GS 829) (London: General Synod, 1988).

11 General Synod, *Report of Proceedings*, 4 July 1988, p. 427.

be priests and the other arguing (for the most part) not that women should never be ordained to the priesthood and still less that they definitely could not be (opposition in principle) but that whether they should or could be was not a question that the Church of England was competent to answer (opposition on ecclesiological grounds).

In February 1992 Roger numbered himself among those who were 'agnostic or even marginally in favour of the proponents on the strictly theological question as to whether women can become priests' – but yet could not 'recognize that any province of the Anglican Communion . . . or indeed even the Anglican Communion as a whole . . . possesses the necessary authority to resolve this question'.[12] Responding to another speaker in the debate on the Episcopal Ministry Act of Synod in November 1993, he commented,

> The vast majority of those opposed do not recognize themselves in either of the two categories that he has mentioned: those who oppose because they doubt the wisdom of the legislation or perhaps its timing, and those who are impossibilists. The vast majority, I believe, of those who voted against fall into neither category. They are not impossibilist; they are simply unable to recognize the authority of this Synod or of a purely national body to define a question which remains for them open.[13]

Four years later, in November 1997, he told sixth-formers at Worth School,

> I am not an 'impossibilist' with regard to the ordination of women to the priesthood. In other words, although the theological case against this innovation is undoubtedly serious, I do not think that either side has yet provided an overwhelmingly convincing and conclusive case. It is possible, therefore,

---

12 See Chapter 10, p. 96.
13 See Chapter 15, p. 150.

that at some point in the future (not, admittedly, the very near future) both the Roman Catholic Church and the Eastern Orthodox churches may decide (perhaps even jointly) that the Church's practice may be changed without betraying the teaching of Scripture and Tradition. I do not say that I think this probable, only possible.[14]

However, addressing a Sacred Synod of Anglo-Catholic clergy towards the end of the decade, in October 1999, Roger for the first time felt obliged to recognize that his own position was by no means shared by all Anglo-Catholics. He referred to 'our stand' but then immediately qualified that as the position of only some Anglo-Catholics:

the stand of those of us who have always affirmed that our fundamental objection to the ordination of women to the priesthood and the episcopate is that we cannot accept the authority of a part of the Church . . . to make a unilateral change in the historic ministry of the universal Church of this kind . . .[15]

Roger always approached the question in the context of the quest, to which he was deeply committed, for the restoration of communion between the Church of England and the Roman Catholic Church. His thinking was informed by the fruits of ecumenical dialogue – especially the successive reports of the first and second Anglican–Roman Catholic International Commissions. The Church of England's decision to ordain women to the priesthood was wrong because, as the Director of the Holy See Press Office said in response to it, it constituted 'a new and serious obstacle to the entire process of reconciliation' with the Roman Catholic Church.[16] But Roger's reasons for opposing it – and, crucially, for being unable to concelebrate with

14 See Chapter 21, p. 196.
15 See Chapter 24, p. 231.
16 Vatican Information Service (www.vis.va): Holy See Statement on Anglican Vote for Women Priests, Vatican City, 12 November 1992.

or receive communion from women priests after the decision had been taken and acted upon – were in the end not ecumenical but ecclesiological. His primary concern was the impact of ordaining women to the priesthood not on the Church of England's ecumenical relations (or even on the unity of the Anglican Communion and the Church of England) but on the Church of England's identity and self-understanding.

As already mentioned, only Chapter 6 of this book rehearses arguments of principle against ordaining women to the priesthood. Otherwise, only the ecclesiological arguments against ordaining women to the priesthood in the Church of England are set out. Roger Greenacre was one of the leading exponents of those arguments, and (not least because, due to his ecumenical profile in France, he was called upon to expound the Church of England's identity more frequently than most) he advanced them more often and over a longer period than many. These factors combine to give his articles and papers on the subject an especial significance – another reason for collecting them together in this volume.

Essentially, as Roger told the Convocation of Canterbury in July 1992, the ecclesiological arguments concerned the need for

obedience to a strong and ancient strand in Anglican self-understanding which has tried to make us sharply aware that we do *not* constitute the whole Church but only a fragment of the *Una Sancta*, and that a fragment of a divided church does not have the right to act as if it were the whole.[17]

It is that thought that gives this volume its title. Does the Church of England still see itself as merely 'Part of the One Church', and if so, is it willing to behave accordingly?

The ecumenical argument carries less weight now that the Church of England has ordained women to the priesthood (the ecumenical damage has been done), but the ecclesiological argument that ordaining women to the priesthood conflicts with

---

17 See Chapter 11, p. 100.

the Church of England's self-understanding continues to have force. If arguments relating to the distinctiveness of men and women are difficult for those who have been formed by the modern secular context described above to engage with, it may well be that they will find the ecclesiological arguments concerning the Church of England's identity and authority more accessible.

The most frequent response to the eccclesiological argument – that the Church of England need not worry about changing the Orders it claims to share with the Roman Catholic Church because Rome does not recognize that claim – is misconceived. The Church of England's self-understanding is that it is part of the catholic Church and that it ordains to a threefold ministry which (like, for example, the Nicene Creed) it shares with the whole Church. The Church of England's identity is undermined when it acts in a way that conflicts with its self-understanding, regardless of whether that understanding of its identity and actions is shared by other churches.

An Ecumenical Vocation

If the ecclesiological argument – that the Church of England needed to resist the ordination of women to the priesthood and episcopate in order to be true to its own identity – was intellectually paramount for Roger, the ecumenical argument was at least as important to him emotionally. In November 1992 he was 62. Inspired by the prominent presence in the Community Church at Mirfield, where he trained for the priesthood, of the tombs of Bishops Charles Gore and Walter Frere, who had participated in the Malines Conversations of the 1920s, he had given the best years of his life to the cause of the restoration of communion between the Church of England and the See of Rome.

He spent the academic year 1961–62 at the Catholic University of Louvain as the Archbishop of Canterbury's priest student. As Chaplain of St George's, Paris, from 1965 to 1975, he quickly became the Church of England's leading representative in France, lecturing on Anglicanism at the Ecumenical Institute of the Institut catholique de Paris, attending meetings of the French Bishops' Conference as the Anglican observer, and serving as one of the founding Co-Chairmen of the French Anglican–Roman Catholic Committee (French ARC). After returning to England he served as a member of English ARC from 1981 to 1996. As such he co-authored English ARC's study guide to the *Final Report* of the first Anglican–Roman Catholic International Commission (ARCIC I)[18] and played an important part in the negotiation of the important (but now little known) agreement, adopted by the English House of Bishops and the French Bishops' Conference, on eucharistic hospitality in the context of twinnings and exchanges.[19] In 1982 he sealed his ecumenical commitment by becoming an oblate of the Abbey of Notre-Dame du Bec in Normandy. His monograph *The Catholic Church in France: An Introduction*, which was published by the Church of England's Council for Christian Unity in 1996, served as a guide to the Church of France for English Anglicans – especially those involved in the numerous diocesan, civic and parish twinnings with French dioceses. During his quarter century at Chichester and indeed after his return to France in 2000, Roger continued to be one of the principal exponents of the Anglican tradition to an ecumenical audience in France and Belgium.

Of the papers collected in this volume, 'Anglicanism and Confessional Identity' (Chapter 4) was given in French at a conference in the Benedictine monastery of Chevetogne, Belgium, in 1983 and first published in its journal *Irénikon*. 'Diversity in Unity: A Problem for Anglicans' (Chapter 8) was given at the *Centro pro Unione* in Rome in 1990. 'The Communion Between and Within Our Churches: The Anglican Experience of its Fragility' (Chapter 18) was published in French in the

---

18 [R. T. Greenacre and D. Corbishley] Anglican–Roman Catholic Committee, *Study Guide to the Final Report of the Anglican–Roman Catholic International Commission* (London, 1982).

19 *Twinnings and Exchanges: Guidelines Proposed by the Anglican–Roman Catholic Committees of France and England* (London: Church House Publishing, 1990).

ecumenical periodical *Unité des Chrétiens* in 1995. Roger also published articles in the French ecumenical journals *Istina* and *Unité Chrétienne* and gave papers at conferences in Salamanca and Czestochowa.

It is no accident that someone so ecumenically active should have written so much in the last quarter of the twentieth century about Anglican ecclesiology. Nor is it surprising that so much of that writing should have included significant comment on the crisis of Anglican ecclesiology sparked during those years by the prospect and reality of the ordination of women to the priesthood and episcopate in the Anglican Communion. Those called upon to engage in ecumenical dialogue about the Church, and to expound the Anglican tradition to others, are obliged to reflect upon Anglican ecclesiology more than most, and ecumenical dialogue is one of the main contexts in which ecclesiological reflection and writing occurs. Roger's understanding of the Church of England and its place in the wider Church was also informed by history in general and church history in particular – having read first history and then divinity at Cambridge, he remained first and foremost a church historian rather than a theologian.

The Second Vatican Council and the ARCIC Vision

During his year in Louvain, Roger had got to know the Belgian theologians who were to be so influential on the course of the Second Vatican Council, which opened in October 1962. Back in London from 1962 to 1965, he followed the progress of the Council closely. By the time it ended, he had moved to Paris, and it was from there that he watched the implementation of its teaching. As a member first of French ARC and then of English ARC, Roger paid close attention to the work of ARCIC.

Roger's ecumenical vision was of a communion of churches under the primacy of a Bishop of Rome who would exercise his office collegially with his fellow bishops, as envisaged by the Council and by ARCIC. It was of a communion of reformed

INTRODUCTION

churches under a reformed papacy, and certainly not of the absorption of the Anglican tradition into an only partially reformed Roman Catholic Church. Someone as ecumenically experienced as Roger, in frequent contact with Roman Catholic ecclesiologists who were as critical of their own church as Roger was of his, could never fall into the trap of comparing the Church of England as it is with an idealized vision of Rome that bears little relation to reality. Having spent so many years as a guest on the other side of the fence, he knew that the grass there was no greener.

Roger's sorrow at the way that history unfolded after the heady days of ecumenical advance that he experienced in Paris in the late 1960s and early 1970s was directed at both churches. If the Church of England had betrayed the ARCIC vision in 1992 by what Geoffrey Rowell called 'a unilateral step of divergence',[20] so too had the Roman Catholic Church. The failure to publish its Official Response to the work of ARCIC I before 1991, nine years after the *Final Report* appeared, the Response's substantially negative tone, and the fact that it ignored the positive responses of those national episcopal conferences that had studied the *Final Report* (thereby throwing the Vatican II and ARCIC understanding of episcopal collegiality into question), were not only disappointing. They also rendered implausible the ecumenical argument that the Church of England should not ordain women to the priesthood because this would prevent progress towards a restoration of communion with Rome that would otherwise be in prospect. Given that, if two members of the General Synod's House of Laity had voted differently, the legislation to permit the ordination of women to the priesthood would have been rejected, it is not too much to claim that had Rome's response been more timely and more positive, the Church of England's betrayal of the ARCIC vision would not have happened when it did. But Roger knew that two wrongs

20 D. G. Rowell, 'The Church on the Cross': unpublished sermon preached at All Saints', Margaret Street, 22 November 1992. For other quotations from this sermon, see pp. xxxiii–xxxiv and 116–17.

do not make a right. Roman betrayal of the ARCIC vision could never justify Anglican betrayal.

What Roger found impossible to understand, and increasingly difficult to accept, was the fact that those who urged the General Synod to ignore the pleas of Rome and vote for divergence, and those who, after the decision had been taken, not only accepted it but (as bishops) implemented it by ordaining women to the priesthood, included some of those who were or had been leading participants in ARCIC's work. Most notable among these was Bishop Mark Santer of Birmingham who, speaking in the Final Approval Debate as Co-Chairman of ARCIC II, encouraged the Synod not to heed the repeated warnings from Rome that if the mother church of the Anglican Communion ordained women to the priesthood that would place a serious obstacle in the way of the restoration of communion between the two churches.[21] Christopher Hill, who had been the Anglican Co-Secretary of ARCIC I and ARCIC II from 1974 to 1991, supported the ordination of women to the priesthood in principle, but was opposed to its enactment in the Church of England on ecumenical grounds. However, having been consecrated as Bishop of Stafford in February 1994, he ordained women to the priesthood – even though, in a diocese with four bishops and as bishop of an episcopal area with many Anglo-Catholic parishes, it would have been easy for him not to do so. As Co-Chairman of French ARC and then as a member of English ARC, Roger had spent more than two decades expounding and promoting ARCIC's work without being called upon to participate in it himself as a member of ARCIC. That those who had been given that privilege,

---

21 Bishop Santer said that he was speaking 'as co-chairman of ARCIC, to say something about the ecumenical implications of the decision that lies before us today, especially from the point of view of the Roman Catholic Church'. Having explained 'the official view of the Roman Catholic Church' he went on to explain why, in his view, the Synod should ignore it (General Synod, *Report of Proceedings*, 11 November 1992, pp. 727–9) and voted in favour of the legislation. He did not resign as Co-Chairman of the Anglican–Roman Catholic International Commission.

to whom he had looked up as leaders of the ecumenical cause to which he had devoted his life, acted in ways that could only serve to negate that life's work, and encouraged others to do so, was a bitter disappointment.

Roger's inability to understand this was part of the reason why he set out to write an Open Letter on the subject to Christopher Hill (by then Bishop of Guildford), and why he accorded it the highest priority among his retirement projects. As he explained, the Letter was intended to be 'not so much an attack ("J'accuse!") as a search for the basic causes of our disagreement': 'What I need above all to do is to *understand* how this has happened.'[22] No more is the publication in this volume of the outline and opening section of the Open Letter an attack on its addressee. Its publication should be seen as framing and setting in context the chapters that follow.

Debate about Women Priests in the Church of England, 1978–92

Roger Greenacre's first substantive treatment of the ordination of women came in April 1978, when he gave an address on the subject at the Loughborough Conference on Catholic Renewal, republished here as Chapter 3. That summer, the 1978 Lambeth Conference passed an extraordinarily lengthy resolution on 'women in the priesthood' which filled two pages of the Conference report. It made no comment on the substantive issue, but merely acknowledged 'the autonomy of each of its member churches, acknowledging the legal right of each Church to make its own decision about the appropriateness of admitting women to Holy Orders' and also 'that such provincial action in this matter has consequences of the utmost significance for the Anglican Communion as a whole'.[23]

---

22 See p. 4 below.

23 *The Report of the Lambeth Conference 1978* (London: Church Information Office, 1978), pp. 45–7.

In the Church of England's General Synod that November a motion calling for legislation to remove the legal barriers to the ordination of women to the priesthood and episcopate, moved at the invitation of the House of Bishops by the Bishop of Birmingham, Dr Hugh Montefiore, was defeated in the House of Clergy.[24] It was not until six years later, in November 1984, that the General Synod passed a resolution calling for the introduction of 'legislation to permit the ordination of Women to the Priesthood in the Provinces of Canterbury and York'. In July 1988 the Synod debated the *Second Report* of the House of Bishops on the issue – a substantial (140-page) document which set out in detail the theological arguments for and against ordaining women to the priesthood. The Synod went on to give 'general approval' to the draft legislation, committing it to a revision committee.[25]

Back in 1985 a commission had been appointed to examine the theological issues bearing on the ordination of women to the episcopate, with a view to the Church of England's contribution to the 1988 Lambeth Conference, which was bound to address the subject. Roger Greenacre was chosen as one of its members and the paper which forms Chapter 6 of this volume was one of his contributions to its work. In 1986 the Commission's remit was extended to embrace a general study of the nature and function of episcopal ministry, and its report was not published until 1990.[26]

By then the 1988 Lambeth Conference had passed a resolution which similarly recognized that individual churches of the Anglican Communion could ordain women to the episcopate but made no comment on the substantive issues involved, and

---

24 See J. Field-Bibb, *Women Towards Priesthood: Ministerial Politics and Feminist Practice* (Cambridge: Cambridge University Press, 1991), pp. 141–9.

25 For an overview the process from 1984 to 1988, see C. J. Podmore, *Aspects of Anglican Identity* (London: Church House Publishing, 2005), pp. 125–7. For detailed summaries of the reports and debates, see Field-Bibb, *Women Towards Priesthood*, pp. 162–75.

26 *Episcopal Ministry: The Report of the Archbishops' Group on the Episcopate* (London: Church House Publishing, 1990).

the first woman had been elected and consecrated as a bishop in the USA. The same Lambeth Conference that effectively ended hope of the restoration of communion between the Anglican Communion and the Roman Catholic Church by acquiescing in the ordination of women to the episcopate also passed a resolution recognizing the first two ARCIC Agreed Statements and their elucidations as 'consonant in substance with the faith of Anglicans' and those on Authority in the Church as 'a firm basis for the direction and agenda of the continuing dialogue on authority'. That irony was the subject of an article by the Canadian Roman Catholic ecumenist Fr Jean Tillard, to which Roger responded in an Open Letter. The article and the Open Letter were published as a booklet by the Church Union Theological Committee, which Roger chaired (see Chapter 7 of this volume).

In the Church of England, the General Synod revision committee having done its work, the legislation for the ordination of women to the priesthood returned to the floor of the Synod in November 1989 for revision in full Synod. In 1990 it was referred to the diocesan synods, because under the Synod's Constitution legislation providing for permanent changes in the services of Baptism or Holy Communion or in the Ordinal must be approved by the houses of clergy and laity of a majority of the diocesan synods before the General Synod can consider it for final approval. The diocesan synods were encouraged in turn to consult the deanery synods, and had until 30 November 1991 to respond. Thus, for the best part of two years, both the principle of ordaining women to the priesthood and the particular legislation drawn up to permit it were debated throughout the Church of England.

In February 1992 the Synod debated the Standing Committee's report on the reference to the dioceses. This marked the beginning of the final run-up at national level to the decision to be taken in November that year.[27] Legislation 'touching doctrinal formulae or the services or ceremonies of the Church

---

27 For details, see Podmore, *Aspects of Anglican Identity*, pp. 127–9.

of England or the administration of the Sacraments or sacred rites thereof' can only be submitted for final approval in terms previously approved by the House of Bishops and the Convocations of Canterbury and York (the synods of the Church of England's two provinces) and the General Synod House of Laity can require that it be referred to them for approval before the General Synod gives it final approval. The House of Bishops approved the legislation in June, and the Convocations and House of Laity in July.[28] Roger Greenacre's speech in the Convocation of Canterbury forms Chapter 11 of this volume.

On 11 November 1992 the General Synod gave final approval to the Priests (Ordination of Women) Measure. The voting was: Bishops: 39 (75%) – 13; Clergy: 176 (70.4%) – 74; Laity: 169 (67.3%) – 82. The Measure had been approved by the narrowest of margins; had two lay members (or five bishops) voted differently, it would have been defeated. Outside, supporters of the legislation celebrated jubilantly, while opponents slipped away into the night.[29]

After 11 November 1992

Looking back over a decade later, Fr David Houlding recalled the aftermath of the vote:

> The next evening, I remember saying Mass at All Hallows for our regular Thursday evening celebration. I could hardly get through the eucharistic prayer. It seemed to me that everything I believed about the priesthood had been destroyed. Everything I believed I stood for had been removed. I felt desperate.
>
> I suspect that this experience was true for very many. It was not so much a question of whether a woman could or could not be ordained to the priesthood, as we might

---

28 See Podmore, *Aspects of Anglican Identity*, p. 129.

29 For a fuller account, see Podmore, *Aspects of Anglican Identity*, p. 130.

have discussed from time to time, but rather how could the Church of England make this decision; what authority did this General Synod have; how could a number of votes sway our particular part of the Church to depart from the received tradition of the Church Universal? It was a crisis of authority. It was in every sense as if a death had occurrerd . . . a bereavement. We were all in a state of shock, incredulous at what had happened, and we went through many of the feelings that bereavement brings. We were bewildered and disillusioned. We were upset and broken. We were afraid and lost. And we were angry . . . It is easy for us, when we look back, to forget how deep the hurt went and how immense was the damage.[30]

In his powerful sermon 'The Church on the Cross', preached at All Saints', Margaret Street, in London on 22 November, the Feast of Christ the King, just 11 days after the vote, Dr Geoffrey Rowell (then Chaplain of Keble College, Oxford) spoke of the damage – both ecclesiological and personal – that it had inflicted:

I believe I can understand something of the pain that would have been occasioned to women deacons seeking a fuller ministry if the legislation had been defeated. But that pain would not have been the deep grief which is now being experienced by many faithful priests and laypeople of the Church of England. You grieve when you are bereaved and that would not have been the position of women seeking ordination. That would have been a hurt no less real, but of another kind. It does no service to speak in a generalized way about pain. The whole Church of England has to see that grief for what it is, to recognize it as a deep trauma of bereavement, and to know what the grieving is for.

---

30 D. Houlding, 'The Crisis of 1992 and its Aftermath: A Personal Reflection', in *In This Sign Conquer: A History of the Society of the Holy Cross (Societas Sanctae Crucis), 1855–2005* (London: Continuum, 2006), pp. 196–217 at pp. 198–9.

I have contact with many parishes of which my college is patron, parishes which stand mostly within the catholic tradition. Many priests young and old and a number of laity have sought my advice. I have spoken to many others, priests and some bishops who have likewise been endeavouring to respond to the consequences of the Synod vote. Words like 'bereavement', 'divorce', 'semi-divorce' occur time and again. There is a deep sense of loss and bewilderment and numbness. There have been many tears. Many of those to whom I have spoken, including some who supported the Synod decision, confess to their surprise at how deeply they have been affected. I share many of their feelings myself. There is a sense – quite understandable in the light of Anglican ecclesiology – of the shattering of a whole way of understanding the Church of England. The blow has been struck on one small corner of the glass, but the fissures and cracks run wild.[31]

Roger Greenacre recognized the importance of this sermon in setting out the way in which the decision involved 'a radical departure from the classical Anglican appeal to Scripture and the Primitive Church'.[32] His own first sermon after the vote, delivered not in a prominent Anglo-Catholic church like All Saints' but in Chichester Cathedral on the First Sunday of Advent, was necessarily more muted, but its theme – the light of the Christian hope burning in the darkness – gave a strong indication of his feelings about the context in which he was now called upon to proclaim the Christian faith. It forms Chapter 12 of this volume.

In the week after the vote, Roger had already begun to compose an article-length 'Open Letter to some Roman Catholic Friends', one purpose of which was to help him explore 'the painful dilemma in which so many catholic-minded Anglicans now find themselves'. It was eventually published, under the title '*Epistola ad Romanos*', in the Jesuit periodical *The Month* for March 1993

---

31 For a further quotation from this unpublished sermon, see pp. 116–17 below.
32 See Chapter 13, p. 116.

and forms Chapter 13 of the present volume. In it, Roger recorded the huge change in attitudes to the Roman Catholic Church on the part of Anglicans in general and catholic-minded Anglicans in particular that first the Second Vatican Council and then the ARCIC process had brought about. He bewailed the 'betrayal' of the ARCIC process on the part of both churches and then set out both the positive reasons for remaining an Anglican and the difficulties of the 'so-called "Roman Option"'.

In the latter context he made observations that would come to have even greater significance nearly two decades later, in the context of the Apostolic Constitution *Anglicanorum Coetibus*, which made provision for personal ordinariates for groups of former Anglicans within the Roman Catholic Church:

The question of a rite in the narrow sense of a particular liturgical tradition is secondary ... As a certain kind of 'Uniatism' has shown only too clearly, it is no use preserving artificially an Eastern rite unless there is a genuinely Eastern character to the theology and spirituality which accompany it. If nothing of Anglicanism is to survive within the Roman Communion but some elements of its liturgy, then some of the most tragic and divisive features of 'Uniatism' will be perpetuated and the lessons of history ignored.

In a paper I gave at Chevetogne in September ... I was asked to reflect on the difficult problem of the Eastern Catholic Churches (the theme of the Colloquium) from the perspective of Dom Lambert Beauduin's famous Malines thesis of 1925, '*L'Eglise anglicane unie non absorbée*' ... I argued that ... Anglicanism ... 'could not be reduced to a tradition of liturgy, spirituality and practical organization without theological content' and that 'concessions limited to the domain of liturgy and discipline would constitute an absorption scarcely concealed by a skin deep make-up'.[33]

33 See Chapter 13, pp. 128–9 below. The quotation is from R. T. Greenacre, 'La signification des Églises orientales catholiques au sein de la communion romaine dans la perspective de "l'Église anglicane unie non absorbée"', *Irénikon*, 65 (1992), 339–51 at p. 350.

The fact that Roger shared the theological and ecclesiological vision of his own bishop (the Bishop of Chichester, Dr Eric Kemp) was an important consideration leading to his provisional conclusion:

> For the time being . . . until or unless I am persuaded to the contrary, it seems to be my clear and imperative duty to stay with my bishop and give him my fullest support. The study of church history, moreover, clearly demonstrates that synodical or conciliar decisions are rarely the final word in doctrinal controversy; they have often proved to be the beginning, rather than the end, of a long and painful period of conflict and debate.[34]

The latter remark proved to be prophetic. In the run-up to the 1992 decision many supporters of the ordination of women to the priesthood expected that within 20 years opposition to the innovation would virtually disappear, but that has not proved to be the case. Nonetheless, hundreds of priests and a significant number of laypeople did leave the Church of England, most of them becoming Roman Catholics. Those who went included many of Roger's friends, as documented by letters from them that he retained among his papers. The grief of bereavement at the loss of a whole way of understanding the Church of England's identity was compounded by the parting of friends.

In the interval between the Measure receiving Final Approval from the Synod and gaining approval from Parliament and Royal Assent, attention was focused on working out a way of living together that would limit the number of opponents who would leave and provide more fully for those who would stay.[35] A start was made by the House of Bishops, meeting in Manchester with the rest of the bishops in January 1993. In June it went on to approve with only one abstention (by Bishop John Austin Baker of Salisbury, who was about to retire) arrangements that were

---

34 See Chapter 13, p. 127.
35 See Podmore, *Aspects of Anglican Identity*, pp. 130–2.

published in a document entitled 'Bonds of Peace', to which was appended a draft of what became the Episcopal Ministry Act of Synod 1993. It was accompanied by another document, entitled 'Being in Communion', which set out the theological rationale which underpinned it.[36]

Though the Act of Synod was pragmatic and pastoral in conception, it rests on a vital ecclesiological premise. The Church of England claims to ordain to a ministry that is universally valid. If that is so, then the ancient canonical maxim applies: 'quod omnes . . . tangit, ab omnibus comprobetur' – that which affects all must be approved by all. For the Church of England to change unilaterally something that it claims to share with the whole Church undermines the self-understanding whereby it is merely part of the whole Church. The justification for doing so, set out in the Act of Synod, was that the change would be subject to an 'open process' of 'discernment in the wider Church of the rightness or otherwise of the Church of England's decision'. It would remain provisional until such time as it was affirmed or indeed rejected not just by the Church of England as a whole but by the Church Catholic. Therefore, the stated purpose of the Act of Synod was not simply to offer pastoral accommodations, but rather 'to make provision for the continued diversity of opinion in the Church of England as to the ordination and ministry of women as priests'. It is in pursuance of that end that it stipulates that 'the integrity of differing beliefs and positions concerning the ordination of women to the priesthood should be mutually recognized and respected' and furthermore that there should be no discrimination against candidates for ordination or senior appointment on the grounds of their views about this issue.[37]

The Act of Synod's further provisions regarding appropriate episcopal ministry for parishes whose communion with their bishop would be impaired by his ordination of women to the

---

36 *Ordination of Women to the Priesthood: Pastoral Arrangements – Report by the House of Bishops* (GS 1074) (London: General Synod, 1993); *Being in Communion* (GS Misc 418) (London: General Synod, 1993).

37 See P. Avis (ed.), *Seeking the Truth of Change in the Church: Reception, Communion and the Ordination of Women* (London: T&T Clark, 2004).

priesthood was of no relevance to Roger Greenacre, who never served or lived in a diocese whose diocesan bishop ordained women to the priesthood. But its recognition that definitive decisions about the ministry of the universal Church cannot be taken by its individual parts was crucial in enabling him to remain in the Church of England with integrity. When he met Fr Jean Tillard in Paris in May 1993 he was still undecided about whether to stay in the Church of England or leave for the Church of Rome.[38] However, by August the draft Act of Synod had given him hope. In a further Open Letter, addressed to the Archbishop of York, Dr John Habgood, who had chaired the group that drew up the House of Bishops' proposals, which was published in October (Chapter 14), Roger set out the negative implications of the new situation for relations between bishops and their dioceses, but also how the 'theology of reception' enshrined in the draft Act of Synod had given him hope that 'it may yet be possible for those who saw the November decision as destructive of the catholicity of the Church of England to regard the Church of England as still "part of the One, Holy, Catholic and Apostolic Church" . . . [and] to make the Declaration of Assent without too queasy a conscience'.[39] As he explained in his speech in the General Synod's debate on the Act of Synod in November 1993 (Chapter 15),

> What is at stake in this debate is not merely the acceptance or the refusal of the draft Act of Synod but our whole understanding of the place of the Church of England within the One, Holy, Catholic and Apostolic Church of Christ.[40]

The Act of Synod was duly approved on 11 November 1993, the anniversary of the Synod's approval of the women priests legislation, by overwhelming majorities in each House (Bishops: 39–0; Clergy: 175–12; Laity: 194–14).

---

38 See p. 134 below.
39 See p. 143 below.
40 See pp. 149–50 below.

A Personal Dilemma

By August 1994, when Roger set out in a lecture published here
for the first time (Chapter 16) both 'the case for a move' and
'the case for staying', he had reached the settled conclusion that
'I stay where I am until and unless I have to move'.[41] Over the
next few years he continued to reflect on the implications of
what had happened both for Anglican ecclesiology and for the
quest for the visible unity of the Church to which he remained
committed, for example in the texts that form Chapters 17–22
of this volume. With the publication in May 1999 of the third
ARCIC Agreed Statement on Authority in the Church, *The
Gift of Authority*, there was at last a positive development to
weigh in the balance with the negative developments of the
preceding decade.

But from 2005 onwards the looming decision about the
ordination of women to the episcopate posed a fresh dilemma
that gave rise to Roger's intention to compose the Open Letter with which this volume begins. As Roger had indicated in
a number of the chapters written in and after 1993, he feared
that such a decision would represent a definitive end to any
realistic prospect of achieving, within the foreseeable future,
the ARCIC vision, place a question mark much more definitively against the Church of England's claim to be 'part of
the one Church', and require the abrogation of the Episcopal
Ministry Act of Synod which had enabled him to remain with
integrity in the Church of England after the decision to ordain
women to the priesthood. This renewed dilemma formed part
of the background to his planned Open Letter.

As already indicated, the Open Letter was a device that Roger
had used before in the context of debate about women's ordination and its consequences. His Open Letter to Fr Jean Tillard
in response to his reflections on the 1988 Lambeth Conference
forms Chapter 7 of this volume; his 'An Open Letter to some
Roman Catholic Friends' in response to the General Synod's

---

41 See p. 160 below.

approval of the Women Priests legislation forms Chapter 13; and his Open Letter to Archbishop Habgood of York on the proposed Episcopal Ministry Act of Synod forms Chapter 14. In the latter, incidentally, he quoted Christopher Hill, describing him as 'a better theologian and more experienced ecumenist than myself'.[42]

Like its predecessors, the Open Letter with which this volume begins was therefore, to a significant degree, directed not at its addressee or to its wider audience but to Roger himself. As is demonstrated by another set of notes, also printed in Chapter 1, he intended to look not only backwards at the causes of the divergence of view between himself and his addressee but also forwards, to the dilemma that he would face when the Church of England decided to ordain women to the episcopate.

He had referred to that future (but not necessarily imminent) dilemma in conversation with Fr Patrice Mahieu, a monk of Solemnes who interviewed him in March 2010 about the ARCIC process as part of his doctoral research, saying: 'When the Church of England ordains the first women bishops, which will not perhaps happen soon, I will have a very difficult decision to take.' He was still agnostic on the principle but clear on the ecclesiological issue:

My present bishop, the Bishop of Gibraltar in Europe, does not ordain women priests, and my former bishop, Eric Kemp, did not either. The ordination of women to the priesthood was understood as a provisional experiment. But when the Church of England starts ordaining women to the episcopate, the provision made for those who disagree will not work any longer. The Church of England will then sever itself from the Church Catholic. I don't know what the final answer will be on this topic in the Church Catholic. But I don't think we may take such a unilateral decision. If we believe that the Bishop of Rome has a primacy of responsibility for the

---

42 See p. 144 below.

unity of the Church, we must acknowledge that he has a right to say 'no' until everybody can say 'yes', and a right to be obeyed.[43]

Though he faced 'a very difficult decision', it was by no means clear-cut. As Roger said in his notes for his final Open Letter, he had 'continuing "difficulties" with Rome'. It would be 'hard to leave' (a phrase he underlined) and 'lose the riches of the Anglican tradition'. The Ordinariate that was established in 2011 within the Roman Catholic Church for former Anglicans, which had drawn in a small number of Anglican laypeople and Anglican priests (many of them retired), including some of Roger's friends, held no appeal for Roger. His ecumenical vision had always been that of Beauduin: 'The Anglican Church united, not absorbed' – the restoration of communion between the Church of England as a whole and the See of Rome, not the conversion to Roman Catholicism of individuals or groups. He could not see in the Ordinariate the fulfilment of this vision.

To the notes, written in November 2010, that Roger left for the writer of his obituary he added – in a spidery hand and thus clearly not long before he died – two things that he had 'once said': 'The only thing I can boast of are an audible voice and a legible handwriting' and 'If the Lord is kind, he will take me before the first woman bishop is consecrated in the Church of England.' That second comment was one that he had made to me more than once while he was still living on the Riviera; on one occasion he indicated that, although it was said as a *bon mot*, it was also meant seriously. His death in July 2011 delivered him from the dilemma that he feared.

---

43 Extract from the transcript, by Fr Patrice Mahieu, of his conversation with Roger on 19 March 2010, as corrected by Roger, who indicated that at that time he did not want this postscript to it to be published 'as it stands', because 'I do not want at this stage to unsettle the faithful in my church.' The transcript is published with the permission of Fr Mahieu.

Present and Future

As it transpired, the legislative process in which the Church of England was embroiled at the time of Roger's death had already failed to deliver a way forward which was capable of fulfilling its twin aims of admitting women to the episcopate of the Church of England and making provision for those who would be unable to accept that as a legitimate development. In consequence, when the legislation was presented to the General Synod for final approval in November 2012 it failed to secure the necessary two-thirds majority in the House of Laity.

The new legislative process that began in 2013 involves a House of Bishops' Declaration which includes the following as one of its 'five guiding principles':

> Since it continues to share the historic episcopate with other Churches, including the Roman Catholic Church, the Ortho-dox Church and those provinces of the Anglican Communion which continue to ordain only men as priests or bishops, the Church of England acknowledges that its own clear decision on ministry and gender is set within a broader process of discernment within the Anglican Communion and the whole Church of God.

Like the Episcopal Ministry Act of Synod which the Declaration replaces, this principle effectively reaffirms the Church of England's place within the One, Holy, Catholic and Apostolic Church and sets its decision to ordain women to the episcopate within a 'broader process of discernment' within the universal Church – features of the Act of Synod which had enabled Roger to remain in the Church of England. Many catholic-minded Anglicans – grouped in Forward in Faith, of which Roger was a founding member – are committed to remaining within the Church of England in order to point to its ecumenical vocation as 'part of the One, Holy, Catholic and Apostolic Church'. They are determined to keep alive within it the structured tradition – with a succession of bishops whose episcopal ministry the faithful can receive with confidence – that will make that possible.

In May 2011 a third Anglican–Roman Catholic International Commission (ARCIC III) began its work – laying foundations for an ecumenical future that, humanly speaking, now seems to have receded over the horizon to a point beyond the lifetimes of all concerned. Its programme of work includes the understanding of the Church as communion and the relationship between the local and the universal Church. Once again its membership includes no representative of traditional Anglo-Catholicism.

Some Anglicans may still enter as individuals or groups into communion with the See of Rome, but many will remain committed to the original vision of the Oxford Movement which began the Catholic Revival in the Church of England – recalling the Church of England to its catholic identity and bringing it, when God wills, to corporate reunion with the rest of the Western Church.

PART I

An Open Letter

I

An Open Letter to Bishop Christopher Hill (2011)

We took sweet counsel together:
and walked in the house of God as friends.
(Psalm 55.15 – Prayer Book Psalter)

Dear Christopher,

It was the work of ARCIC I (the first Anglican–Roman Catholic International Commission) that first brought us together soon after your appointment to Lambeth in 1974 and my move from St George's, Paris, to Chichester Cathedral in 1975.[1] Over the next eighteen years or so we met often in England and in France and our shared commitment to the work of ARCIC led to real friendship, a friendship shared with other friends, among whom I would single out Fr Ted Yarnold SJ[2] and Père Jean-Marie Roger

---

1 Christopher Hill was on the Archbishop of Canterbury's staff at Lambeth Palace for 15 years, from 1974 to 1989, as the Archbishop's Assistant Chaplain on Foreign Relations (1974–81) and the Archbishop's Secretary for Ecumenical Affairs (1981–89). He was subsequently a residentiary canon of St Paul's Cathedral, London (1989–96), Bishop of Stafford (1996–2004) and Bishop of Guildford (2004–13). He was the Anglican Co-Secretary of the first and second Anglican–Roman Catholic Commissions (ARCIC I and II) from 1974 until 1991 and has been a member of ARCIC III since its inception in 2011. He chaired the Church of England's Council for Christian Unity from 2008 to 2013 and has been President of the Conference of European Churches since 2013. Roger Greenacre was Chaplain of St George's, Paris, from 1965 to 1975 and a residentiary canon of Chichester Cathedral from 1975 to 2000.

2 Edward Yarnold SJ (1926–2002) was Master and then Tutor in Theology at Campion Hall, Oxford. He was a member of ARCIC I and II from 1970 until 1991.

Tillard OP[3] (of blessed memory) and also Suzanne Martineau[4] of Poitiers for special mention. I was very much a junior partner in this work, for I have never been either a professional theologian or a professional ecumenist; all my different jobs in the Church of England have had at least a strong, if not dominant, pastoral character. I was, however, while in Paris not only a lecturer at the Institut Supérieur d'Études Oecuméniques but also the first Co-Chairman of what is now French ARC, and then back in England a member for fifteen years of English ARC (ARCs being national Anglican–Roman Catholic Committees set up to bring the insights and achievements of ARCIC to bear on their particular national contexts). You were at the very heart of the work of ARCIC I and later of ARCIC II. But, although our participation in what I would call the ARCIC process was at different levels, we were at one in our commitment to its 'reception' in world Anglicanism.

But after 1992 our paths diverged. You are now a committed supporter of the ordination of women to the priesthood and episcopate in the Church of England, while my continuing loyalty to the texts of ARCIC has led me, as I will seek to explain in this letter, to oppose these developments. What I need above all to do is to *understand* how this has happened. This letter is not so much an attack ('J'accuse!') as a search for the basic causes of our disagreement.

---

3 Jean-Marie Roger Tillard OP (1927–2000) was a professor of dogmatic theology at the Dominican College of Philosophy and Theology in Ottawa from 1957, a member of ARCIC I and II from 1970, a member of the Faith and Order Commission of the World Council of Churches from 1975 and a vice-moderator of it from 1977 – in each case until his death.

4 Suzanne Martineau (1918–2012) was one of the few women to attend the Second Vatican Council – as a consultant and a translator for the Anglican observers. She later served with Roger Greenacre on the French Anglican–Roman Catholic Committee (French ARC) and wrote *Les Anglicans* (Éditions Brepols, 1996) – the counterpart of Roger's *The Catholic Church in France: An Introduction* (London: Council for Christian Unity, 1996). In his obituary for her, Christopher Hill described her as 'the grande dame of French ecumenism' (*Church Times*, 2 November 2012, p. 29).

The Collapse of Traditional Catholic Anglicanism

Though this letter will focus principally on the present crisis in the Church of England it will also need to take into account the crisis in world Anglicanism – the near collapse of the unity of the Anglican Communion and the controversy over an Anglican Covenant – for the two are intimately related. The crisis in the Communion apparently finds its defining issues in questions relating to homosexuality,[5] whereas that in the Church of England is apparently concerned with the question of women bishops. The word 'apparently' is crucial here, for I will seek to show (though I'm sure you for one are fully aware of this) how the fundamental difference is one of ecclesiology – our understanding of the nature and essential structures of the Church of Jesus Christ. I would want to single out two particular aspects of ecclesiological theology which are crucial to the present situation, the Development of Doctrine and the question of Subsidiarity.

The Development of Doctrine

Fundamental to the understanding of Anglican identity which I was brought up to accept (and, I suspect, you were too) were the conviction that the Church of England and indeed all the churches of the Anglican Communion were true parts – but only part – of the One, Holy, Catholic and Apostolic Church (there is surely no need to quote the familiar Preface to the Declaration of Assent[6]) and the claim that the English Reformation was grounded theologically on an appeal to Scripture and the Tradition of the Early Church.

Hence we have in classical Anglicanism a refusal to countenance innovation (as distinct from restoration and renovation) in faith and order – indeed, the accusation that both 'Papists' and 'Puritans' were equally guilty of innovation (by addition

---

5 In his outline for the Open Letter Roger wrote, 'Major factors include "gay marriage" and gay bishops (*sic*).'

6 Canons of the Church of England, Canon C 15.1(1): 'The Church of England is part of the One, Holy, Catholic and Apostolic Church . . .'

or subtraction), while the Church of England was faithful to the doctrine and practice of the early Church. So King James I, in a significant seventeenth-century use of the word 'novelist', could affirm: 'But if the Roman Church hath coined new Articles of Faith, never heard of in the first 500 years after Christ, I hope I shall never be condemned for an heretic, for not being a Novelist.'[7]

At the heart of classical Anglican apologetic was the appeal to the so-called Vincentian Canon of the fifth-century St Vincent of Lérins: 'Quod semper, quod ubique, quod ab omnibus creditum est' (what is always, everywhere and by all believed). The most difficult of these to be verified was 'semper', and Vincent himself did sketch out an early version of a doctrine of development. However, the classical Anglican theologians like Bishop Bull[8] believed strongly in the verifying authority of history; in this they had much in common with the Gallican theologians in France. So the celebrated Bossuet, Bishop of Meaux (who died in 1704), could argue: 'There is no difficulty about recognizing false doctrine; there is no argument about it: it is recognized at once, wherever it appears, merely because it is new . . .'[9] There is more need, in this view, of reliable historians than of an authoritative magisterium.

A revolution occurred in 1845 when John Henry Newman published his *Essay on the Development of Doctrine* and became a Roman Catholic on completing the book. His argument that there has, demonstrably, been and still is growth and development in Christian understanding of the meaning and necessary consequences of the original deposit of Revelation was accompanied by the (surely) inevitable corollary that there need to be

---

7 James I, *A Premonition to All Most Mighty Monarchs, Kings, Free Princes, and States of Christendom* (1609), quoted by P. E. More and F. L. Cross, *Anglicanism: The Thought and Practice of the Church of England, Illustrated from the Religious Literature of the Seventeenth Century* (London, SPCK, 1951), pp. 3–8 at p. 4.

8 George Bull (1634–1710), Bishop of St David's (1705–10).

9 Quoted by W. O. Chadwick, *From Bossuet to Newman* (2nd edn, Cambridge: Cambridge University Press, 1987), p. 17.

within the Church organs which can in the end discern authoritatively true from false developments. 'If', he wrote, 'the Christian doctrine, as originally taught, admits of true and important developments . . . this is a strong antecedent argument in favour of a provision in the Dispensation for putting a seal of authority upon those developments.' 'This', he affirmed, 'is the doctrine of the infallibility of the Church.'[10]

Newman's doctrine of development provoked enormous hostility in both Anglican and Roman Catholic circles: it can claim finally to have achieved full recognition in the Roman Catholic Church, thanks to the influential contribution of Yves Congar,[11] in the Second Vatican Council's Constitution on Revelation, *Dei Verbum*, where it is clearly stated:

> This tradition which comes from the Apostles develops in the Church with the help of the Holy Spirit. For there is a growth in the understanding of the realities and the words which have been handed down.[12]

Classic Catholic Anglicanism never identified the Church (and hence any infallibility attributed to the Church) with the Roman Catholic Church and with the See of Rome. Without excluding from ecclesial realities the churches of the Reformation, this tradition gave a privileged position to the witness of those churches which had preserved and continued the threefold apostolic ministry of bishop, priest and deacon. Here the testimony of Viscount Halifax, theologically literate but no professional theologian, writing to a fellow Anglican layman, is instructive:

10 *An Essay on the Development of Doctrine* (8th edn, London: Longman's, Green and Co., 1891), pp. 78–9: ch. 2, sections 2.5, 2.4.

11 The French Dominican theologian Yves Congar (1904–95) was made a Cardinal by Pope John Paul II in 1994.

12 'Dogmatic Constitution on Divine Revelation' (*Dei Verbum*), 8, in W. M. Abbott and J. Gallagher (eds), *The Documents of Vatican II* (London: Geoffrey Chapman, 1967), p. 116.

As I grew older and was brought face to face with the fact that Christians were divided on matters of faith, I do not think I asked myself whether this or that commended itself to my judgment, or might seem to be the more probable view, but I endeavoured to make sure what it was that the whole Church had taught on the subject, what were matters of faith, what, however good and true in themselves, were only matters of opinion, what, in regard to such latter matters, had been the generally accepted belief and practice of the Church; and where I found the whole Church had definitely spoken, or that this or that was the generally accepted rule of the Church, *there*, as far as I was concerned, the matter ended. Where the Church had not so definitely spoken, the matters stood on a different foundation, and whatever I might think about them, or be inclined to think about them, came under a different category and could not claim the same authority.[13]

The question therefore arises: how can Anglicans say that the ordination of women to the presbyterate and the episcopate is a clearly God-given development of Christian faith and order when the official voices of the Roman Catholic and of the Eastern Churches have affirmed the contrary? There are not uninfluential theologians in these churches who support the arguments in favour of such ordinations and who also argue that, for example, Rome's clear, repeated and authoritative declarations that she has no authority to go against the Tradition fall short of an infallible judgement.[14]

---

13 From a letter to Lord Wolmer of March 1919 reproduced in J. G. Lockhart, *Charles Lindley, Viscount Halifax* (London: Geoffrey Bles, 1935–36), vol. 1, p. 82.

14 If he had lived to revise his draft, Roger would doubtless have added a concluding sentence to this paragraph, showing why this admitted view on the part of some Roman Catholic theologians did not justify the Church of England's action in ordaining women to the priesthood. The earlier set of notes for the Open Letter printed below indicates that he had also intended to make the point that the present position was the reverse of that in earlier centuries, whereby Roman Catholics were arguing for a development of doctrine and Anglicans were refusing 'novelties'.

If we turn for a moment to the question of homosexuality – the major point of division in the wider Anglican Communion – we find both similarities and differences. The similarities arise because in both cases serious challenges to formerly safe assumptions based on apparently unequivocal evidence from Scripture and Tradition have been posed and because both challenges have resulted in the 'impairment' of full communion within the Anglican Communion. A further similarity would occur in those extreme cases (e.g. the situation in at least one of the Porvoo churches, the Lutheran Church of Sweden) where the marriage service is rewritten to accommodate a union of partners of the same gender. The vital difference is that ordination is an ecclesial act involving ecclesial recognition; what two persons of the same gender may do in privacy is a personal decision even when it involves conscientious dissent from official teaching – as in the case of practising Roman Catholic married couples who practise contraception. The unduly neglected Agreed Statement of ARCIC on moral questions, *Life in Christ* (1993), offers a serene discussion of a number of ethical issues, including also abortion, divorce and remarriage, where there are differences (judged not insurmountable) between the positions adopted by each communion. At present, the differences within the Anglican Communion would seem to be harder to resolve. Moreover, there is surely a lack of ecclesiological seriousness within Anglicanism when each constituent church of the Anglican Communion is permitted to make its own decision about the ordination of women as bishops and priests but a common position is demanded with regard to homosexuality. Respect for 'provincial autonomy' in the first case has made it difficult to refuse it in the second.

To return now to my main problem, the ordination of women to the ministries of priest and bishop, and to the second string of my case – the principle of Subsidiarity . . .

Here Roger's text breaks off. Roger had sketched out the rest of the Open Letter as follows:

Subsidiarity

- ❖ Collapse of the Anglican Communion's unity.
- ❖ Weaknesses of Rome and Canterbury on this subject.
- ❖ What is beyond competence of national synods to decide.
- ❖ My remaining difficulties shared by many Roman Catholics.
- ❖ *Apostolicae Curae.*

Petrine Ministry

- ❖ Is failure to accept the warnings of the Pope (and of the Orthodox) tantamount to a rejection of ARCIC I's and ARCIC II's work on Roman primacy?
- ❖ A minimal reading of Petrine ministry is one of maintenance of communion between local churches, unity in truth.
- ❖ A necessary element of 'conservatism'.

The Ordinariate?

- ❖ 'United not absorbed.'
- ❖ Anglican patrimony?

Although Roger was not able to write these three further sections, most of the themes he intended to cover had been addressed in earlier writings which are included in this book.

Women Bishops

Among Roger's papers is another (probably earlier) sheet of notes towards this Open Letter. It is headed 'Epistola Secunda' – a reference to his 'Epistola ad Romanos', published in March 1993 (Chapter 13), in which he considered his position after the General Synod's final approval of the legislation for the ordination of women to the priesthood. After references to the opening sections of the Open Letter (see above), the sheet continues with comments in note form (expanded slightly here) on the ordination of women to the episcopate and the dilemma with which it would confront Roger.

The ordination of women to the episcopate: why it is more serious than ordination to the presbyterate. Disintegration of Anglicanism.

Since 1992, the ARCIC texts *The Gift of Authority*[15] and *Mary* have been published. These are helping Anglicans to move from 'semi-papalism' (as described in the *Epistola ad Romanos*[16]) or even from an Erician position ('shy . . .')[17] to acceptance of Roman Catholicism. Ordination of women to the episcopate will mean saying No to *The Gift of Authority*. If the ordination of women to the episcopate is not a matter for the ministry of the Bishop of Rome in maintenance of the unity and communion of the churches, *what is*?

Our continuing 'difficulties' with Rome – the exercise of papal authority, birth control, the hard line on divorce and gays, communion in one kind – are shared by many Roman Catholics. These do not warrant separation; they can change. But the introduction of women bishops is almost certainly irreversible, and it

---

15 See Part 4 of this book.

16 See p. 131.

17 The reference is to the Rt Revd Dr Eric Kemp (1915–2009), Bishop of Chichester from 1974–2001, whose memoirs were entitled *Shy But Not Retiring* (London: Continuum, 2006).

is structural. If one cannot be in communion with Canterbury, then one must be in communion with Rome.

The Anglican Communion has thrown away the chance of sharing in the dialogue between Rome and Orthodoxy on the primacy of Peter.

What to do about 'fault lines'? *Apostolicae Curae*.

There is a distinction between being 'open' to change on women in the priesthood and on homosexual relations and taking unilateral action on such issues – for example, the consecration of Gene Robinson as Bishop of New Hampshire which, as Mary Tanner put it,

> flew in the face of a Resolution of the college of Anglican bishops at the Lambeth Conference, which was subsequently affirmed by the Primates' Meeting, and was contrary to the express advice of the Archbishop of Canterbury. In other words, it flew in the face of all the instruments of Anglican Communion at the world level.[18]

I have a personal vocation, not invented but conferred by the Church of England, to dialogue with Rome (I was sent as the Archbishop of Canterbury's Priest–Student to the Catholic University of Louvain, appointed to membership of French ARC and English ARC, awarded a Lambeth DD for my work on Anglican–Roman Catholic relations, and commended for it by Archbishop Rowan Williams).

It would be *hard to leave* and lose the riches of the Anglican tradition.

Schism is the breaking of an already existing unity. But perhaps it is also the breaking of a wound that was in the process of being healed (as betokened by Paul VI's gift of his episcopal ring to Archbishop Ramsey, and Cardinal Willebrands'

---

18 M. Tanner, 'Anglicans, ARCIC and Ecclesiology', in J. Baker and W. Davage (eds), *Who is This Man? Christ in the Renewal of the Church* (London: Continuum, 2006), pp. 53–62 at p. 58. Dame Mary Tanner (b. 1938) was General Secretary of the Church of England's Council for Christian Unity (1991–98) and European President of the World Council of Churches (2006–13).

initiative on the recognition of Anglican Orders, etc.).[19] From the beginning of ARCIC – from Paul VI and Michael Ramsey in 1966 – there has been a 'covenant' of searching for unity.

The dividing line is not so much between those who believe women may and should be admitted to the priesthood and episcopate and those who believe they cannot and should not, as between those who believe the ordination of women is so urgent to the truth and justice of the Kingdom that no delay is tolerable (and therefore, in principle, no concessions to opponents either) and those who believe that unity and communion are absolute priorities. Analogy of apartheid (Dutch Reformed Church in South Africa).

Resolution of the schisms with the non-chalcedonian churches (the schisms resulting from Ephesus and Chalcedon) is now easier than resolving the schism that we now face.

---

19 See p. 50 below.

PART 2

Before

2

The Ordination of Women:
What is at Stake?
Letter to *The Times* (August 1976)

Introduction (2013)

On 30 November 1976 Pope Paul replied to a letter from Archbishop Coggan, in which he reported the General Synod's belief that 'there are no fundamental objections' to ordaining women to the priesthood and its invitation 'to share in the urgent re-examination of the theological grounds for including women in the Order of Priesthood, with particular attention to the doctrine of Man and the doctrine of Creation'.[1] The Holy Father wrote:

> Your Grace is of course well aware of the Catholic Church's position on this question. She holds that it is not admissible to ordain women to the priesthood, for very fundamental reasons. These reasons include: the example recorded in the Sacred Scriptures of Christ choosing his Apostles only from among men; the constant practice of the Church, which has imitated Christ in choosing only men; and her living teaching authority which has consistently held that the exclusion of women from the priesthood is in accordance with God's plan for his Church.[2]

1 General Synod, *Report of Proceedings*, 3 July, 1975 p. 606.
2 *Women Priests: Obstacle to Unity? Documents and Correspondence, 1975–1986* (London CTS Do 576, 1986), p. 47.

Referring to the work of the Anglican–Roman Catholic International Commission, he added:

> We must regretfully recognize that a new course taken by the Anglican Communion in admitting women to the ordained priesthood cannot fail to introduce into this dialogue an element of grave difficulty which those involved will have to take seriously into account.[3]

At the 1968 Lambeth Conference, Coggan (then Archbishop of York) had been the leading advocate of the ordination of women to the priesthood. In his address to the opening plenary session and again in introducing the report of the Committee on Women and the Priesthood, which he had chaired, he is reported as having said that 'the Conference was not to be insulted "with silly arguments about our Lord having no women in the Apostolic Twelve"'.[4] In February 1976 he replied to Pope Paul's letter, suggesting that the visible unity of the Church 'will be manifested within a diversity of legitimate traditions' and that the ordination of women was an example of an issue in respect of which 'what seems to one tradition to be a genuine expression of such diversity will appear to another tradition to go beyond the bounds of legitimacy' – and nevertheless expressing the belief that 'in the power of the Spirit Christ's High Priestly prayer for unity will be fulfilled'. This drew a further reply from Pope Paul, in which he commented:

> Our affection for the Anglican Communion has for many years been strong, and we always nourished and often expressed ardent hopes that the Holy Spirit would lead

---

3 *Women Priests: Obstacle to Unity?*, pp. 47–8.

4 J. B. Simpson and E. M. Story, *The Long Shadows of Lambeth X: A Critical Eye-Witness Account of the Tenth Decennial Conference of 462 Bishops of the Anglican Communion* (New York, 1969), p. 190.

us, in love and in obedience to God's will, along the path of reconciliation. This must be the measure of the sadness with which we encounter so grave a new obstacle and threat on that path.[5]

Publication of the correspondence in July 1976 generated some discussion in the letters column of *The Times*. One of the letters was from the then Dean of Liverpool, Edward Patey.[6] Having expressed his own view that 'the admission of women to the priesthood of the Church of England at the earliest possible opportunity is required both by theological truth and practical necessity', he went on to suggest: 'The argument from ecumenism comes easily to those who (usually for quite other reasons) are opposed to changes in the ecclesiastical *status quo*.' His letter concluded thus:

> True unity comes as we hold on to our convictions in a spirit of mutual trust and love. If the ecumenical argument must be used, I would claim that those of us who advocate the ordination of women because this is the truth as we understand it are making a real contribution to that unity of all Christian people which must be based on truth as much as on love.[7]

It was in response to this letter that Roger Greenacre, who had returned to England from France the previous year, made his first contribution to the debate on the ordination of women to the priesthood, in a letter to *The Times*.

---

5 *Women Priests: Obstacle to Unity?* p. 50.
6 Edward Patey (1915–2005) was Dean of Liverpool from 1964 to 1982.
7 *The Times*, 9 August 1976, p. 11.

The Ordination of Women: What is at Stake?[8]

From the Chancellor of Chichester Cathedral

Sir, The Dean of Liverpool appears to suggest (August 9) that the recently published letter from the Pope to the Archbishop of Canterbury will only be heeded by those who are already opposed to the ordination of women. If this is so – which I would contest – then it does not speak very highly for the ecumenical sensitivity of Anglicans.

For surely it is possible to be agnostic on the purely theological issue as to whether the priesthood could be open to women, or even to be moving, as are many Roman Catholic theologians today, towards an affirmative answer, and yet draw back from an action that would without any doubt have the gravest adverse effects on our relations with the rest of Catholic Christianity, notably with Rome and with the Orthodox, and undo much of the real progress so hardly won over the last decade or so.

'The argument from ecumenism', writes the Dean, 'comes easily to those who (usually for quite other reasons) are opposed to changes in the ecclesiastical *status quo*.' It is accusations like this that can turn a serious theological debate into a *dialogue des sourds* [dialogue of the deaf].

I would ask the Dean and those who think like him to accept the fact that there exists a large number of Anglicans who have not closed their minds to the theological argument, but who are genuinely convinced that it would be wrong in principle for the Anglican Communion (or part of it) to force through a unilateral decision on so vital a matter until there has emerged much more of a consensus among those churches which have retained the historic threefold ministry of bishop, presbyter, and deacon. What is at stake is more than the doctrine of the ministry; it is our whole understanding of the exercise of doctrinal authority within the Church.

Yours faithfully,

ROGER GREENACRE

---

8 *The Times*, 11 August 1976, p. 13.

Further Correspondence

Published alongside Roger's letter was a letter from Canon John Austin Baker, later Bishop of Salisbury,[9] in which he asked 'Take away the primitive superstition that women must not approach the altar because menstruation makes them unclean (an argument which modern opponents presumably do not wish to use), and what rational objection remains?' His letter concluded thus:

> In fact, as regards the hard graft of commending the faith and helping people, women are already doing the same work as men. All that is being denied them is a kind of sacral status, partly because some men, consciously or not, want to keep for themselves a numinous 'power' and 'authority', and partly because many women church members, again for unconscious psychological reasons, can project such 'authority' only onto men.

This drew a response from Robert Runcie (then still Bishop of St Albans), suggesting that in arguing for women's ordination on the basis of 'current practice in the Church of England, some snide remarks about primitive superstition and sacral status, and his own opinion about the psychology of those who wish to maintain the unbroken catholic tradition of the presidency of the Eucharist' Baker had illustrated Roger's point that, in reaching decisions about ordaining women, Anglicans should be sensitive to relations with the Roman Catholic and Orthodox Churches. He concluded by asking:

> Is is surprising that Anglicans engaged in ecumenical dialogue sometimes have difficulty in convincing others of our theological principles or of our respect for the theological convictions of others?[10]

---

9 John Austin Baker (b. 1928) was a Canon of Westminster Abbey (1973–82) and then Bishop of Salisbury (1982–93).

10 *The Times*, 16 August 1976, p. 11.

This letter was published together with one from Mrs Jean Mayland[11] (a member of the Central Committee of the World Council of Churches), in which she argued that 'churches which have accepted the principle of the ordination of women should go ahead and ordain them' and 'should not be held back by ecumenical considerations but should go ahead and continue to explore the matter further'. These letters closed the correspondence.

---

11 Jean Mayland (b. 1936) was a member of the General Synod of the Church of England from 1970–90. She was ordained deacon in 1991 and priest in 1994 and served on the staff of the Council of Churches for Britain and Ireland (1996–99) and Churches Together in Britain and Ireland (1999–2003).

3

Christian Unity and the Ordination of Women: A Statement to the Loughborough Conference (Easter 1978)

At the Loughborough Conference on Catholic Renewal 'Risen Life in Christ', held in Easter week 1978 (a significant event in the history of Anglo-Catholicism in the latter part of the twentieth century),[1] Roger was asked to read a paper at the beginning of a session devoted to issues of current interest. His statement was subsequently published as a booklet by the Church Literature Association.

First of all, let us remember the warning that was given to us last night by Fr Richard Holloway:[2]

> I have a fear lest the tensions within the Church will simply tear the Church apart because we will each go our own way, not Christ's; and there is no human agent that can bring all this together. I fear lest we start playing church politics, adopting pressure group tactics, start throwing down gauntlets.

---

1 For this see P. Corbett and W. Davage, *Defend and Maintain: A History of the Church Union, 1859–2009* (London: Tufton Books, 2009), pp. 86–8.

2 Richard Holloway (b. 1933) was Rector of Old St Paul's Church, Edinburgh from 1968–80. As Bishop of Edinburgh (1986–2000), he was one of the founders of the liberal catholic movement 'Affirming Catholicism' in 1990. After his retirement he described himself as a 'Christian agnostic'.

And then he reminded us of how the Evangelical Revival killed itself by turning into a negative campaign.

Secondly, I have been asked to speak on one issue, or one and a half, but it is important to say that there are many other issues. Some raised are of a moral character, some relate to crises within our society, some relate to other issues facing the Church – the nature of doctrinal authority for example. The issue that I have been asked to introduce is not necessarily the most important, but potentially perhaps it is the most destructive – destructive of ourselves and of our spiritual renewal. It is therefore all the more important that we approach it *theologically*, with our minds and hearts cleared from emotional and polemical reactions of aggressive militancy, fear, or prejudice.

What is first of all at stake, not just in these questions, but perhaps in a wide variety of questions that you would like to discuss later, is the whole nature of theological investigation. What are the criteria – the tools – with which we work to discern God's will for his Church? This point was made very pertinently by the Bishop of Chichester[3] in the General Synod debate on the ordination of women in 1975, when he pointed out that we are confronted by a whole school of theologians who say that 'we can have little certainty what our Lord said, did, or intended', and that even attitudes clearly taken by the historical Jesus do not necessarily have binding authority upon us today.[4] As Dr Rowan Williams[5] asked in an article in *Christian* called 'The Possibility of Theology':

---

3 The Rt Revd Dr Eric Kemp.

4 General Synod, *Report of Proceedings*, 6 (1975), 550–1 (speech reprinted in *Church Observer*, Autumn 1975.

5 Rowan Williams (b. 1950) lectured at the College of the Resurrection, Mirfield (1975–77), at Westcott House, Cambridge (1977–80) and in the University of Cambridge (1980–86), latterly as Dean of Clare College (1984–86), before becoming Lady Margaret Professor of Divinity at Oxford (1986–92), Bishop of Monmouth (1992–2002), Archbishop of Wales (2000–02) and of Canterbury (2002–12). In 2013 he returned to Cambridge as Master of Magdalene College. In 1990 he was one of the founders of Affirming Catholicism, having given an address ('Affirming Tradition') at the original day conference held in London on 9 June 1990. In 1999 he chaired its 'millennium appeal' for funds, but he later distanced himself from it – presumably because he found it insufficiently catholic or insufficiently liberal, or both.

If this is so, what kind of theology is possible? If there are no points of reference – whether in the historical Jesus, or in Scripture, or in the doctrinal tradition – where can the theologian begin? And what precisely is he talking about?[6]

The danger, as he goes on to point out, and as Dr Mascall[7] has also pointed out, is that the vacuum is filled with arguments based only on 'human experience' or 'expediency' or 'appropriateness'.[8]

Equally important, and this is the theme I want to develop, there is at stake the question of the nature and the limitations of the ecclesial authority of the Anglican Communion, and of the particular national and provincial churches which make up that communion. I personally am convinced that we dare not and cannot say that the ordination of women is impossible. It is still a perfectly valid question for theological speculation and exploration: the debate must, and no doubt will, continue, however much we might wistfully long for it to go away and to stay away. Though we may have been arguing about it for years, we must remember that this is still a very new question for some other parts of Christendom, and we must give them time to ponder it and work out their attitudes. For there is a tendency on the part of many Anglicans to ignore or play down the undeniable fact that the churches which share with us the common inheritance of the Catholic ministry of bishop, priest and deacon have formally declared their opposition to the ordination of women on grounds of fundamental theological principle.[9] Within the Orthodox churches such opposition is almost unanimous, and within the Old Catholic churches

6 R. D. Williams, 'The Possibility of Theology', *Christian*, vol. 4, no. 1 (1977), 11–19 at p. 11.

7 The Revd Prof. Eric Mascall (1905–93) was Professor of Historical Theology at King's College, London, from 1962–73.

8 *Cf.* E. L. Mascall, *Theology and the Gospel of Christ* (London: SPCK, 1977).

9 *Cf. The Replies of the Leaders of Certain Churches to Letters from the Archbishop of Canterbury* (London: CLA, 1976).

there is only one bishop in favour.[10] In the Roman Catholic Church, although there is known to be a considerable movement in favour in a number of countries, the voice of authority clearly says no, and goes on to indicate that the ordination of women in churches of the Anglican Communion constitutes a barrier of the very gravest nature to the successful pursuit of that 'restoration of complete communion of faith and sacramental life', to which our two communions were solemnly pledged in March 1966 by the Common Declaration of Pope Paul VI and Michael, Archbishop of Canterbury.[11]

Now when I say that the voice of authority has spoken clearly, I realize that this needs to be qualified. The Pope himself has spoken, and so has the Sacred Congregation for the Doctrine of the Faith;[12] but I am aware that the authority of this Congregation is a subject of disquiet to many Roman Catholic theologians and that the Roman Catholic Church has not yet pronounced on this subject in an authoritative, conciliar, collegial, or final fashion. Nonetheless, it is clear that the Roman Catholic Church's opposition is, in part at least, motivated by a genuine ecumenical concern for its own dialogue with Eastern Christendom. It is also clear that if there has been no direct Roman Catholic intervention in the processes of Anglican decision making (for quite proper considerations of ecumenical tact and propriety), there is a clear, even an urgent, appeal from the Roman Catholic Church that we should hold back.

Let me remind you of Cardinal Hume's delicate but unambiguous warning to General Synod in February:

---

10 Women are now ordained to the priesthood in the Old Catholic churches of Germany (since 1996), Austria (since 1998), the Netherlands (since 1998), and Switzerland (since 2001).

11 Cf. A. C. Clark and C. Davey: *Anglican/Roman Catholic Dialogue* (London: Oxford University Press, 1974).

12 Cf. Sacred Congregation for the Doctrine of the Faith, *Inter Insigniores: Declaration on the Question of the Admission of Women to the Ministerial Priesthood* (London: CTS, 1976), republished in *Women Priests: Obstacle to Unity? Documents and Correspondence, 1975–86* (London: CTS Do 576, 1986), pp. 3–19.

May I suggest that we must not only listen to each other, but together listen to what the Spirit may be saying. There is an ancient practice in the Church of God whereby the faith and its formulation, tradition and ministries are matters to be decided in consultation with other local churches. Now that our dialogue is progressing, and as we move in the direction of closer collaboration on the basis of this mutual communion between the Churches, it would be – to take one important example – a matter for deep concern were the Anglican Communion to proceed further with the ordination of women without taking very seriously the position of the Roman Catholic Church, our brothers of the Orthodox Churches and of the Old Catholic Churches regarding so momentous a change. Now, you could rightly rejoin 'The same principles of mutual consultation should apply in respect of yourselves, the Roman Catholics'. Let me say that I look forward to the day when such consultation will be normal practice.[13]

The sad thing is that so many people have been hearing the warning in that statement, that they have failed to note the immensely encouraging and novel promise that from now on consultation and, by implication, deference to strongly held conviction shall be a mutual process. Now I believe that this promise of the Cardinal's is of immense importance, because it shows that our appeal to catholic consensus is no longer a chimera but a real possibility.

Let us look back for a moment at the Oxford Movement in the nineteenth century. There had been and still survived at that time a High Church tradition, and to this tradition the movement was the heir, but with one very important qualification. The earlier High Church tradition had been insular and triumphalist. Not only was the Church of England a true part

---

13 General Synod, *Report of Proceedings*, 1 February 1978, p. 141. The full text was published in *The Tablet* of 4 February 1978.

of Catholic Christendom, but it was the best, and purest and most truly reformed part of it.

This note of arrogance and complacency is totally lacking from the Fathers of the Oxford Movement. They were strongly convinced (and none more so than Dr Pusey) that the Church of England in her separation had been seriously diminished and weakened in her catholicity, and that the right attitude of Catholic Anglicans was one of penitence, of prayer for the restoration of what had been lost, and of humility rather than criticism before the so-called 'unreformed' churches of East and West. It was this deeply spiritual attitude that inspired the ecumenical zeal of such pioneers as John Mason Neale and Charles, Viscount Halifax. They had a vision of Christendom reunited, but one which the majority of their fellow Anglicans of their own generation could only see as a subject for derision and mockery: 'What is the use of appealing to the Orthodox? They aren't interested! What is the use of appealing to Rome? Every time you knock on that door it will be slammed with peremptory violence in your face!' It needed then men of heroic faith, unquenchable hope, and supernatural vision to persevere doggedly and dauntlessly in the face of repeated setbacks. And *now*? Now that attitudes have changed so radically, and in Rome more than anywhere else in Christendom, are we tragically going to be the ones who slam the door on the way that leads to reconciliation and unity?

We are not simply *Inopportunists*, that is to say, people fighting a tactical battle and saying 'This may be the right thing, but this is not the right moment', in a parody of S. Augustine's famous prayer, 'Lord, make me chaste, but not yet.' No, a deeper theological principle is at stake.

Anglicans cannot live their particular and specific witness (which, let us remember, includes a witness before the rest of Catholic Christendom to all the positive insights of the Protestant Reformation) in unquestioning and unconditional dependence on, and imitation of, Rome. On some issues it has been our vocation to give a lead; we gave it in the past, and we may still be able to do it now. A certain independence on some issues is our positive duty in the dialogue with Rome and with the East. The best Roman Catholics (I learnt this during the ten years I spent living in a state of 'partial communion' with the Church of France) do not want us to be just faded carbon copies of themselves. But though we can and should pioneer and take risks in some avenues of exploration, we cannot do so on issues which affect the basic, given, sacramental structures of the Catholic Church. In this field, the principle of *tutiorism* (in any doubt stick to the *safest* course) must apply. Consultations are now in process with our Roman Catholic, Old Catholic, and Orthodox brethren on this very issue. One between Roman Catholic and Anglican theologians was held at Versailles in March in the hope of untangling a knot that defies untangling, and is indeed a problem for us within the Anglican Communion: 'To what extent and in what ways churches with women priests and churches without women priests can be reconciled in sacramental fellowship.' This report is not yet published and I cannot therefore comment on it. In July of this year, just before the Lambeth Conference, there is to be an Anglican–Orthodox consultation in Athens. But not even the most sanguine optimist can imagine that the combined verdicts of Versailles and Athens, when we learn them, will give us a green light to go ahead without risk to our relationships with Rome and Constantinople.

To sum up then: We simply have no right to alter the received practice of the universal Church until, or unless, there is a clear and morally unanimous consensus of the whole body of Catholic Christendom. This applies not only to the ordination of women, but, I would argue, to Proposition 6.[14] I hope we all sincerely want the dialogue with the member churches of the Churches'

---

14 The Churches' Unity Commission, *Visible Unity: Ten Propositions* (London, 1976), Proposition 6: 'We agree to recognize, as from an accepted date, the ordained ministries of the other covenanting Churches as true ministries of word and sacraments in the Holy Catholic Church, and we agree that all subsequent ordinations to the ministries of the covenanting Churches shall be according to a Common Ordinal which will properly incorporate the episcopal, presbyteral and lay roles in ordination.'

Unity Commission to go on, and if so, the Ten Propositions will surely have to serve as a basis for that continuing dialogue. But though we should be ready to recognize, in a spirit of generosity, and indeed of penitence for the negativeness of our past attitudes, the substantial ecclesial reality of the Free Churches, their sacraments and their ministries, we cannot and need not do this by abandoning or betraying our belief in the God-given character of the threefold Apostolic ministry, and our longing to convey it in all its fullness to those who presently lack it.

The Anglican Communion has never claimed to be the *whole* Church, and so we have always felt bound (to quote the Preface of the 1662 Prayer Book) to reject such alterations as were of dangerous consequence 'as secretly striking at some established Doctrine, or laudable Practice of the Church of *England*, or indeed of the whole Catholick Church of Christ'.

This surely is the standpoint we must adopt when these questions come up for debate and resolution in our diocesan synods and in the General Synod. We are not fighting *against* anybody. Certainly not against women, or a better deal for women in church and society, nor against our fellow Anglicans, nor against our brothers and sisters in the Churches of the Reformation; nor even, in the last analysis, against the possibility that women may one day, by the authentic voice of true catholic consent, be called to the priestly ministry. If we are fighting at all – and we need to be very careful about the spirit in which we go to battle – we are fighting *for* a principle and *for* a priority: the principle of loyalty to 'the whole Catholic Church of Christ', and the overriding priority of catholic unity.

Postscript[15]

The foregoing Statement was read to the Loughborough Conference by Canon Roger Greenacre as the introduction to a discussion of topics of current interest. Later in the afternoon

---

15 This Postscript was appended to the published text of the statement.

it was decided not to take any vote – it was felt that the spirit of division was contrary to the spirit of Loughborough.

On the following day the Abbot of Nashdom,[16] in the course of some routine announcements, referred to the previous afternoon's discussions. Describing himself as a 'court jester' he said of Canon Greenacre's words:

> It seemed to me – and I am only speaking (of course) as a fool – that was a superb statement. [Applause] It may well be that you are only clapping my folly, but I think that that statement represented the view of many of us here. I would even dare to say, the majority; I would even dare to say the largest possible majority of us here. I say this simply as the court jester but . . . [it] seems to me that what Canon Greenacre said could well be an expression of the majority of this Conference.

The Abbot's words were received with a prolonged standing ovation by the great majority of those present.

---

16 Dom Wilfrid Weston (b. 1937) was Abbot of Nashdom from 1974–84, when he was secularized. As Canon David Weston, he was a residentiary canon of Carlisle Cathedral from 1994–2005.

4

Anglicanism and Confessional Identity (1985)

Roger read this paper in French to a gathering at the Benedic-
tine monastery of Chevetogne, Belgium, in August 1983. The
French text was published in Chevetogne's ecumenical journal
Irénikon in 1984[1] and Roger published this English translation
in One in Christ *in 1985.[2]*

Many Anglicans imagine rather naively that the claims which
they put forward on behalf of their own Communion are characterized above all by humility and modesty: they would find
it hard to imagine that often what strikes their non-Anglican
brethren and risks driving them to the point of exasperation
is rather a certain air of complacency, self-satisfaction and
euphoria. No Anglican, it is true, claims that the *Ecclesia angli-*
cana is quite simply the Catholic Church or the only authentic
Church; obviously it is only a portion, a part – a rather small
part, as it happens – of the *Una Sancta*. All the same, some
of the apologias for Anglicanism made by Anglicans – even
recently – possess a resonance which is not calculated to reassure
our brethren.

A first example is a statement by Dr Geoffrey Fisher (Archbishop of Canterbury, 1945–61): 'We have no doctrine of our
own – we only possess the catholic doctrine of the Catholic
Church enshrined in the catholic creeds, and those creeds we

---

1 *Irénikon*, 57 (1984), 163–75: 'L'identité confessionnelle et les "traditions"
de la Communion anglicane dans la quête de l'unité de tous'.

2 *One in Christ*, 21 (1985), 121–30.

hold without addition or diminution.'[3] This statement is very typical; one could easily find many other examples of the same genre.[4] But the question which it provokes me to ask is the following: is its fundamental emphasis one of moderation – the modest disavowal of any specifically Anglican confessionalism – or is it rather one of triumphalism – the accusation (or at least the suggestion) that all the other churches have either added something to, or subtracted something from, catholic doctrine which the Anglican Communion alone has preserved in all its purity and integrity?

The Anglican Communion has no doctrines or dogmas of her own. Has she on the other hand a theology of her own? Does she have – to put the same question in other words – an identity which can in the strictest terms be described as confessional? If we put this question to Anglican experts of the twentieth century, we discover that the majority of them energetically deny that there exists a system of Anglican theology or an Anglican systematic theology. Let us listen to William Temple, later to become Archbishop of Canterbury but at that moment Archbishop of York, writing in his introduction to the 1938 report *Doctrine in the Church of England*:

A systematic theology proceeds from premises regarded as assured, and from these builds up its fabric by continuous reasoning. There are systems of Catholic Theology and of Protestant Theology. To them we have, of course, owed much. But there is not, and the majority of us do not desire that there should be, a system of distinctively Anglican Theology. The Anglican Churches have received and hold the faith of Catholic Christendom, but they have exhibited a rich variety in methods both of approach and of interpretation.[5]

---

3 From a speech delivered at the Central Hall, Westminster, in January 1951, *cf.* (Dom) Anselm Hughes, *The Rivers of the Flood* (London: Faith Press, 1961), p. 50.

4 Some of these have been surveyed more recently in C. J. Podmore, *Aspects of Anglican Identity* (London: Church House Publishing, 2005), pp. 38–41.

5 *Doctrine in the Church of England: The Report of the Commission on Christian Doctrine appointed by the Archbishops of Canterbury and York in*

In 1978 Stephen Sykes (at that time Van Mildert Professor of Divinity at Durham University and Canon of Durham Cathedral[6]) published a little book with the title *The Integrity of Anglicanism*. It was a severe, mordant, powerful, even polemical, work; a criticism of a certain style of Anglican thinking which he judged to be confused, lazy and complacent. According to him the Anglican Church possessed – at least until the crisis of the nineteenth century – a theology and a theological position which could be called distinctively Anglican. Commenting on this judgement of William Temple he asks,

> And why should we not . . . speak of Anglican theology as both catholic *and* distinctively Anglican? Why should Anglicans be shy of actually having something identifiable in their approach to the truth of the Christian faith? Once it becomes obvious that there is no one Anglican systematic theology, any more than there is one Lutheran or Calvinist, one Greek Orthodox, or even one Roman Catholic, then nothing is lost if non-Anglicans discover that Anglicans do, as a matter of fact, bring a rather distinctive approach or group of approaches to questions of theological discussion.[7]

Sykes pursues his argument by analysing a distinction which has been proposed by two Anglican theologians of great distinction, Dr Michael Ramsey (Archbishop of Canterbury 1961–74) and Dr Henry McAdoo (Archbishop of Dublin and Co-Chairman of ARCIC I).[8]

1922 (London: SPCK, 1938), p. 25; *cf.* S. W. Sykes, *The Integrity of Anglicanism* (London and Oxford: Mowbray, 1978), p. 28.

6 Stephen Sykes (b. 1939) was subsequently Regius Professor of Divinity at Cambridge (1985–90), Bishop of Ely (1990–99) and Principal of St John's College, Durham (1999–2006).

7 Sykes, *The Integrity of Anglicanism*, p. 59.

8 Henry McAdoo (1919–98) was Bishop of Ossory, Ferns and Leighlin (1962–77) and Archbishop of Dublin (1977–85).

In 1945 Dr Ramsey, who at that time held the same chair at Durham that Canon Sykes held when he published his book, wrote:

> There *is* such a thing as Anglican theology and it is sorely needed at the present day. But because it is neither a system nor a confession (the idea of an Anglican 'confessionalism' suggests something that never has been and never can be) but a method, a use and a direction, it cannot be defined or even perceived as a 'thing in itself', and it may elude the eyes of those who ask 'What is it?' and 'Where is it?' It has been proved, and will be proved again, by its fruit and its works.[9]

Michael Ramsey wanted to show that if we did not have the right to speak of a *system* of Anglican theology we could certainly speak of a method of Anglican theology; a method which has had such exemplary practitioners as Hooker in the sixteenth century and F. D. Maurice in the nineteenth century and whose essential characteristic is a certain way of appealing to Scripture, tradition and reason as the authoritative sources of Christian doctrine. Today, he continued, this same method is still valid; the appeal to Scripture however must recognize the work of critical scholars, the reference to tradition cannot be content with a static appeal to the undivided Church but must be an appeal to a more universal Christian experience, and in the appeal to reason we must underline the need to accord the theologian a certain freedom over against the legitimate but not unlimited claims of ecclesiastical authority.

The Archbishop of Dublin has expounded his position in a small book aimed at a wide public, *Being an Anglican*, published in 1977, and in a larger volume, *The Spirit of Anglicanism* (with the subtitle *A Survey of Anglican Theological Method in the Seventeenth Century*), published in 1965. In the first of these he wrote:

---

9 A. M. Ramsey, 'What is Anglican Theology?', *Theology*, 48 (1945), 2–6 at p. 2; *cf.* Sykes, *The Integrity of Anglicanism*, p. 63.

To return then to what is distinctive in the Anglican tradition: the distinctiveness lies not in the content of the faith but in the method by which the Churches of the Anglican Communion make sure that what is being taught and proclaimed at any stage of history is authentic Christianity, 'the faith once for all delivered' . . . The method applies a three-fold criterion by appealing to Scripture, to tradition and to reason.[10]

In the second book he wrote:

Anglicanism is not a theological system and there is no writer whose work is an essential part of it either in respect of content or with regard to the form of its self-expression. Richard Hooker has some claim to be the greatest Anglican writer, but his work was to state a method in theology rather than to outline a system . . . The absence of an official theology in Anglicanism is something deliberate which belongs to its essential nature, for it has always regarded the teaching and practice of the undivided Church of the first five centuries as a criterion . . . The distinctiveness of Anglicanism proceeds not from a systematic theology but from the spirit in which theological questions are handled.[11]

Towards the end he added:

Seventeenth-century Anglicanism, taking it by and large, saw no solution to the problem of authority which did not admit of the mutually illuminating relationship of Scripture, antiquity and reason, and refused any solution which insulated authority against the testing of history and the free action of reason.[12]

---

10 H. McAdoo, *Being an Anglican* (Dublin: APCK and London: SPCK, 1977), p. 13.

11 H. McAdoo, *The Spirit of Anglicanism: A Survey of Anglican Theological Method in the Seventeenth Century* (London: A. & C. Black, 1965), p. v.

12 McAdoo, *The Spirit of Anglicanism*, p. 410.

Professor Sykes sets out a very critical analysis of Dr McAdoo's position. He believes that the Archbishop is trying to make four affirmations:

1 that there is no specifically Anglican corpus of doctrine
2 that Anglicans have no master theologian to compare with Calvin
3 that Anglicans do not try to stress specific doctrines (such as predestination)
4 that Anglicans do not try either to tie their theology to any specific philosophic system such as Thomism or nominalism.

Professor Sykes pursues his course by criticizing these four points:

1 He argues that it is possible to say that there is a *specifically* Anglican corpus of doctrine without saying that it is *uniquely* Anglican.
2 He argues again that the fact that Anglicans have no master theologian is irrelevant; in any case they tend to exaggerate the influence of Luther and Calvin on the Evangelical and Reformed churches.
3 He argues too that to underline or emphasize one specific doctrine is not characteristic of a systematic theology. What is more, it is far from evident that the systems of Calvin or Barth are constructed around a central doctrine.
4 He argues finally that an exclusive link with a particular philosophy is not a necessary element in systematic theology. He might have added that such a link is no longer characteristic today of Roman Catholic theology.

It is time now to try to give a résumé of Sykes's own position; after which I shall try – like some audacious David confronting a Goliath of theology – to express the reservations and the disagreements which his thesis provokes in me.

For Professor Sykes there does exist a characteristically Anglican theology, a characteristically Anglican corpus of doctrine, an Anglican ecclesiology. He agrees with Ramsey and McAdoo in their analysis of a theological method, but – for him – the existence of such a *method* implies necessarily the existence of a *content*.[13] Until the nineteenth century the comprehensiveness of the Anglican Church did not pose too many problems: the theological pluralism which had existed since the sixteenth century was clearly limited by a common recognition of the supreme authority of the Bible and of the normative authority of the Creeds and the definitions of the first ecumenical councils, by the obligation on the clergy to subscribe to the Thirtynine Articles, and by the universal recognition of a distinction between the fundamental articles of the faith and secondary or non-fundamental elements (*adiaphora* – indifferent). Sykes attributes what he sees as the disintegration of classical Anglicanism to the following factors:

1 The theological evolution of Newman: his exposé as an Anglican theologian of the theology of the *via media*, followed so shortly by his renunciation and criticism of that *via media* and his replacement of it by the idea of the development of doctrine.

2 The polarization between Anglo-Catholics and Evangelicals in the aftermath of the Oxford Movement, driving the two groups towards more extreme and more clearly contradictory positions.

3 The rise of the 'Broad Church' party – later to be known as 'liberals', 'modernists' or 'radicals'. According to Sykes, the Broad Church party is not (as has too often been asserted) the legitimate successor of the tendency called 'Latitudinarian' in the seventeenth and eighteenth centuries. The Latitudinarians accepted without equivocation the distinction between fundamental and non-fundamental articles of the faith; the representatives of the Broad Church tendency, by extending their critical method to the Bible and the Creeds, destroyed one of the essential bases of classical Anglicanism.

---

13 For a more recent discussion of this issue, see Podmore, *Aspects of Anglican Identity*, pp. 38–9.

4 Finally, Professor Sykes launches an attack on the nineteenth-century theologian F. D. Maurice, and on his theory that Anglicanism is not a middle way of compromise and moderation between two extreme positions or – to use his own term – 'an invisible equatorial line between Romanism and Protestantism',[14] but rather a union of opposites with the vocation of effecting a synthesis or reconciliation between positions which at present appear contradictory but which in reality are complementary – that is to say that it is a question of 'reconciled diversity' – or rather of 'reconciled opposition'.

Professor Sykes has helped Anglicans to make their own self-criticism and examination of conscience and they should indeed be grateful to him for that. Nonetheless I find it hard to digest all his argument and I must now try to set out the four reasons for my own disagreement with him.

First, I cannot believe that his vision of Anglicanism is in total conformity with the very complex history of our church. He fails in my view to give due weight to the long Protestant and Evangelical tradition in Anglicanism and – which is perhaps more serious – he does not come to terms with the fact that the theological justification of a 'de jure' *via media* came after the establishment of a 'de facto' *via media* of which one is forced to admit that its original character seems above all to have been dictated by political considerations. Moreover there does seem to be a fatal imprecision in the very notion of the *via media*. For a long time we have assumed that it refers to a *via media* between Rome and the Continental Reformation; but for Elizabeth's bishops (almost all of them disciples of Heinrich Bullinger of Zurich) it was rather a matter of a *via media* between Rome and the Anabaptists.[15]

---

14 Sykes, *The Integrity of Anglicanism*, p. 16, quoting F. D. Maurice: *The Kingdom of Christ* (Everyman Edition, London: J.M. Dent & Co. [1906]), vol. 2, p. 311.

15 *Cf.* N. T. Wright, 'Doctrine declared', in *Believing in the Church: The Corporate Nature of Faith. A Report by the Doctrine Commission of the Church of England* (London: SPCK, 1981), pp. 109–41 at p. 120.

Second, I agree with him when he affirms that the positions of radical scepticism advanced by certain contemporary Anglican theologians go beyond what ought to be tolerated in the name of comprehensiveness, and I also agree that we need to distinguish between strong official pronouncements on the teaching of our church, which are often necessary, and ecclesiastical sanctions against individuals, which are always dangerous: 'There is thus nothing anomalous in a situation in which a body both insists that it has a definite teaching, and also is tolerant of a free discussion of that teaching.'[16] But in spite of the presence of very questionable ideas in F. D. Maurice's theology, I believe that his vision of a *union of opposites* destined to be reconciled is worthy of our most serious attention. In the first place the idea of an invisible equatorial line between Rome and Protestantism has no attraction for me personally and is devoid of ecumenical interest. I believe rather that our actual *via media* is to be seen neither as a negative judgement upon the Roman Catholic Church and Protestantism nor as a claim to a successful achievement: it is no more than a somewhat blind act of hope, a fairly desperate effort to hold together elements that men have separated and opposed to each other. The Anglican Church is a church which is still seeking, and I can only identify myself with the *cri de coeur* of Michael Ramsey in a passage from *The Gospel and the Catholic Church* which Sykes himself quotes:

While the Anglican Church is vindicated by its place in history, with a strikingly balanced witness to Gospel and Church and sound learning, its greater vindication lies in its pointing through its own history to something of which it is a fragment. Its credentials are its incompleteness, with the tension and the travail in its soul. It is clumsy and untidy, it baffles neatness and logic. For it is sent not to commend itself as 'the best type of Christianity', but by its very brokenness to point to the universal Church wherein all have died.[17]

---

16 Sykes, *The Integrity of Anglicanism*, p. 44.

17 A. M. Ramsey, *The Gospel and the Catholic Church* (London: Longmans, 1936), p. 220; *cf.* Sykes, *The Integrity of Anglicanism*, p. 3.

I would like to add to this Anglican testimony that of a French Catholic philosopher, Etienne Gilson, quoted by Fr Yves Congar in his book *Chrétiens en dialogue*:

> Adversaries whose conclusions are in conflict must be allowed time to understand each other better, to understand themselves better, and to be reunited with each other again at a point still undetermined but certainly situated beyond their present positions.[18]

Gilson was writing on the subject of the philosophical opposition between Thomism and Augustinianism: Congar applies it to ecumenical work in general and to the ecumenical work of a Catholic in particular; I would want to apply it to Anglicanism and precisely to that union of opposites of which Maurice spoke.

Third, if Professor Sykes does not denounce he certainly does not welcome the new formula of subscription imposed in 1975 upon the clergy of the Church of England. Until the nineteenth century the formula imposed upon the clergy at their ordination and renewed on the occasion of any canonical installation (it is worth noting that subscription was not required of the laity) contained the phrase: 'I . . . do willingly and from my heart subscribe to the Thirty-nine Articles . . .' In 1865 the formula became less rigid:

> I, A.B., do solemnly make the following declaration: I assent to the Thirty-nine Articles of Religion, and to the Book of Common Prayer and of the ordering of bishops, priests and deacons. I believe the doctrine of the (United) Church of England (and Ireland) as therein set forth, to be agreeable to the Word of God.

---

18 Y. M.-J. Congar, *Chrétiens en dialogue* (Paris: Cerf, 1964), p. 102. Cf. Y. M.-J. Congar, *Dialogue between Christians: Catholic Contributions to Ecumenism*, tr. P. Loretz (London: Geoffrey Chapman, 1966), p. 128.

In 1888 a resolution of the Lambeth Conference of undeniable importance declared that newly constituted churches of the Anglican Communion 'should not necessarily be bound to accept in their entirety the Thirty-nine Articles of Religion': consequently many of the provinces of the Anglican Church have either quite simply dropped the Articles or modified their formulas of subscription.[19] The new formula in use in the Church of England is in my opinion a singularly happy one.[20] There is first of all a declaration read by the bishop, followed by a declaration of assent. The bishop says:

> The Church of England is part of the One, Holy, Catholic and Apostolic Church, worshipping the one true God, Father, Son, and Holy Spirit. It professes the faith uniquely revealed in the Holy Scriptures and set forth in the catholic creeds, which faith the Church is called upon to proclaim afresh in each generation. Led by the Holy Spirit, it has borne witness to Christian truth in its historic formularies, the Thirty-nine Articles of Religion, the Book of Common Prayer, and the Ordering of Bishops, Priests, and Deacons. In the declaration you are about to make, will you affirm your loyalty to this inheritance of faith as your inspiration and guidance under God in bringing the grace and truth of Christ to this generation and making him known to those in your care?

To this the response is:

> I, N., do so affirm, and accordingly declare my belief in the faith which is revealed in the Holy Scriptures and set forth in the catholic creeds and to which the historic formularies of

---

19 For an account of this development, see *Subscription and Assent to the Thirty-nine Articles: A Report of the Archbishops' Commission on Christian Doctrine* (London: SPCK, 1968).

20 For a more recent study of the Declaration and its origins, see Podmore, *Aspects of Anglican Identity*, ch. 4: 'The Church of England's Declaration of Assent'.

the Church of England bear witness; and in public prayer and administration of the sacraments, I will use only the forms of service which are authorized or allowed by Canon.[21]

Finally – and this is extremely serious – the position which Professor Sykes had adopted in 1978 led him in 1982 to launch a particularly ferocious attack in *The Modern Churchman* on the *Final Report* of ARCIC. His starting point is the following:

If one compares the present situation with the pre-Oxford movement Church of England, it is patent that within the last 150 years there has taken place the most profound process of de-confessionalization to fall upon any European denomination. Whereas in 1832, at the inception of the University of Durham, which offered to Anglican ordinands the first formally taught and examined course in theology in the country, the basis of the curriculum was the Prayer Book and Articles, in the Church of England of the 1980s the Articles have been decisively demoted and the Book of Common Prayer has an alternative, if not a rival. There is, above all, a quite new declaration and oath of assent, hospitable of a wider variety of theological opinion than any previous clerical oath. This 150-year process is rightly called de-confessionalization. This is a European phenomenon, and it has parallels in the other European Christian denominations. But even the Lutheran and Reformed churches of Europe have retained a stronger hold upon their sources of confessional identity than has the Church of England.[22]

This leads him directly to the climax of his argument:

This process has led, I judge, to a profound crisis of identity, some of the turmoils of which I have analysed elsewhere.

---

21 Canons of the Church of England, Canon C 15.1(1).
22 S. W. Sykes, 'ARCIC and the Papacy: An Examination of the Documents on Authority', *The Modern Churchman*, 25, no. 1 (1982), 9–18 at pp. 9 and 10.

Contemporary evidence of this crisis is the extraordinary volatility of Anglican opinion. It is astonishing to recall that a few years ago the Church of England received a document entitled *Christian Believing*, in which the Apostles' and Nicene Creeds were permitted, after some hesitation, to remain in the life-blood of the Church. All Churches are, by definition, confessing bodies; and Anglicanism seems to be in a strange twilight zone between a confessing past and a future of some unspecified kind. This context poses the question, Does not the whole of the ARCIC movement represent a *re*-confessionalization of Anglicanism?[23]

By re-confessionalization he clearly understands the acceptance by Anglicans of the authority of the dogmatic formularies of the Roman Catholic Church.

We should perhaps conclude by acknowledging that Professor Sykes has done us a service: by giving precise form to the confused and ill-defined fears of many Anglicans he has also given us the possibility of working out a calm and reasoned refutation. For quite obviously there are voices in the Roman Catholic Church too setting off the same kind of alarm signal: would not the acceptance of the *Final Report* of ARCIC inaugurate a process of the 'anglicanization' of the Roman Catholic Church?

By way of conclusion I do not wish to propose solutions but simply to pose four questions which could help to focus our discussion.

1 Is the identity of any church or communion necessarily to be seen as a confessional identity? Could it not equally well be seen as spiritual, liturgical, cultural and even theological? Did not the Greek and Latin Churches have each their own clear identity before the schism? Should we not therefore conclude that a process of de-confessionalization – above all the kind of ecumenical de-confessionalization

---

23 Sykes, 'ARCIC and the Papacy: An Examination of the Documents on Authority', p. 10.

which is the fruit of theological consensus – does not necessarily mean a loss of identity? How should we define the
idea of the *typos* of a church as sketched out by Cardinal
Willebrands[24] in the course of a visit to the Church of
England? What are the elements of positive and permanent
value in our separate traditions that we can each bring at
the moment of the restoration of our unity as the specific
contribution of our own church?

2 Those who have attempted to define a confessional identity in Anglicanism have underlined the fact that all Anglican ecclesiological thinking tends to speak of authority in
the Church as a dispersed authority – that is to say an
authority which cannot be attributed to a single source.
Can one not say then that the two ARCIC statements on
authority exemplify precisely that union of opposites of
which Maurice spoke? Are we not dealing here neither
with a compromise nor with a capitulation of one side to
the other but rather with the reconciliation of two ecclesiologies which we believed – mistakenly – to be in formal
contradiction of each other?[25]

3 In the famous Lambeth Quadrilateral it is a question of
the Bible, the Creeds, the Sacraments and what has come
to be called the 'Historic Episcopate'. In the past certain
Anglicans believed they had to justify their insistence on
episcopacy by appealing to the text of Scripture. The
Preface to the Prayer Book Ordinal, for example, affirms:
'It is evident unto all men diligently reading holy Scripture
and ancient Authors, that from the Apostles' time there
have been these Orders of Ministers in Christ's Church;
Bishops, Priests, and Deacons . . .' Today we are forced
to admit that the matter is no longer 'evident'. So what
should the Anglican Church do? Abandon its insistence

---

24 Cardinal Johannes (Jan) Willebrands (1909–2006) was President of the
Pontifical Council for Promoting Christian Unity from 1969 to 1989.

25 *Cf.* in particular Anglican–Roman Catholic International Commission,
The Final Report (London: CTS/SPCK, 1982), pp. 97–8: 'Authority in the
Church II', para. 33.

on episcopacy – or at least give unequivocal recognition to the ordained ministers of the non-episcopal Churches – or modify the basis of its case – in the way indicated, for example, on the sixth paragraph of the ARCIC statement on ministry?

4 Is not the crisis over the ordination of women to the priesthood, which risks tearing apart the unity of the Anglican Communion, above all and before all else a problem of Anglican ecclesiology? Before the nineteenth century such an evolution would have been unthinkable and the classical Anglican appeal to the Bible and the consensus of the undivided Church allowed no room for the possibility of developments of this nature which would have required the authoritative solution of totally new problems. Does not the admission of the possibility of women priests imply the admission also of the development of Christian doctrine in the sense in which Newman argued? A Church which considers itself a part of the *Una Sancta* – but only a part – can defend and reaffirm what has already been decided by ecumenical authority, but can it resolve alone a totally new question? Ought it not rather to confess its impotence in this field? This debate for us Anglicans is not therefore just a question about our anthropology or about our theology of the ministry, but above all a question about authority in the Church and the limits of purely Anglican authority. It is essentially a question of ecclesiology.

5

Prestige and Patrimony (May 1986)

In this interview, published in the Messenger *of the Catholic League,*[1] *Jeremy Haselock questioned Roger about the importance of the words and actions of Pope Paul VI in relation to the Anglican Communion.*

JMH In the recent history of ecumenical dialogue between Rome and Canterbury, the words and actions of Pope Paul VI in relation to the Anglican Communion remain of particular significance, largely because he was the best informed Pope ever in the area of Anglicanism. As Archbishop of Milan he struck up an important friendship with Bishop George Bell of Chichester, and in 1956 received a delegation of Anglican priests who stayed with him for some ten days and exchanged with him a mass of basic information. He took a great deal of trouble to acquaint himself, not only with the history of Anglicanism, but also with its contemporary outlook. This is the background to the landmark affirmation of October 1970 when, in his homily at the Canonization of the Forty Martyrs of England and Wales, the Pope spoke of the Anglican Church as an 'ever beloved sister'.[2] What do

---

1 *The Messenger of the Catholic League*, 229 (May 1986), 17–21.
2 Paul VI, Homily at the Canonization of Forty Martyrs of England and Wales, 25 October 1970 (www.vatican.va/holy_father/paul_vi/homilies/1970/documents/hf_p-vi_hom_19701025_it.html):

you think Paul VI was trying to say to both churches in this key statement?

RTG First of all, the context is important. The occasion was, as you have said, the Canonization of the Forty Martyrs of England and Wales, and this could have been an embarrassment for Anglican–Roman Catholic relations. Indeed, certain Anglicans expressed their nervousness in anticipating the ceremony. But Pope Paul VI went out of his way to reassure and quieten Anglican fears and to make a very positive statement.

In this statement he was really saying two things. He was getting as close as he could to affirming the full ecclesial status of the Anglican Communion; by using the phrase 'ever beloved sister' he was coming close to the language of 'sister-churches' which was being used at that time in Roman Catholic–Orthodox dialogue. He was also saying something very positive about Roman Catholic expectations of unity with the Anglicans. What was being sought was not unconditional submission or strict uniformity, but the kind of unity in which, I quote, 'the legitimate prestige and the worthy patrimony of piety and usage proper to the

---

May the blood of these Martyrs be able to heal the great wound inflicted upon God's Church by reason of the separation of the Anglican Church from the Catholic Church. Is it not one – these Martyrs say to us – the Church founded by Christ? Is not this their witness? Their devotion to their nation gives us the assurance that on the day when – God willing – the unity of the faith and of Christian life is restored, no offence will be inflicted on the honour and sovereignty of a great country such as England. There will be no seeking to lessen the legitimate prestige and the worthy patrimony of piety and usage proper to the Anglican Church when the Roman Catholic Church – this humble "Servant of the Servants of God" – is able to embrace her ever beloved Sister in the one authentic communion of the family of Christ: a communion of origin and of faith, a communion of priesthood and of rule, a communion of the Saints in the freedom and love of the Spirit of Jesus. Perhaps We shall have to go on, waiting and watching in prayer, in order to deserve that blessed day. But already We are strengthened in this hope by the heavenly friendship of the Forty Martyrs of England and Wales who are canonized today. Amen.

Anglican Church', would be respected, and in which the Anglicans would, in a sense, be contributing something from their own heritage to the riches of a reunited Christendom.

JMH Do you think, then, that Pope Paul VI's 1970 affirmation marked a new attitude on the part of Rome towards the Church of England?

RTG Not so much a new attitude; the new attitude began with Vatican II and its Decree on Ecumenism, but certainly an irreversible and important turning point in that new attitude, and I think I can say irreversible with confidence because it has not proved to be an isolated saying but one that has been picked up, confirmed and followed on in subsequent dialogue.

First of all, Cardinal Hume, on the very same day that he received episcopal ordination and was enthroned in his Cathedral as Archbishop of Westminster (NB), went on to Westminster Abbey to sing vespers with his monastic brethren, and in his reply to the address of welcome from the Dean he spoke these words:

> There are many tombs in this Abbey, but there is one which speaks, if we would listen, with a poignant, indeed tragic eloquence. It is the tomb which contains the remains of two sisters, Elizabeth and Mary. Read there the inscription: 'Consorts both in throne and grave, here we rest; two sisters, Elizabeth and Mary, in the hope of one resurrection.' Think of them as you will, judge them as you will, but pass on in your mind to the last phrase: 'In the hope of one resurrection.' New life springs up out of death. The sister churches can now look back on a past that is dead and buried. We can look forward to new life and new hope and, in God's time, to the goal of Christian unity.

In this statement, Cardinal Hume, as it were, dots the 'I's and crosses the 'T's in Pope Paul's remarks at the Canonization of the Forty Martyrs, and it is all the more significant in that it comes from the lips of someone who is the successor of Cardinal Vaughan and of Cardinal Bourne, two Cardinal Archbishops who were notorious for their hostility to any kind of recognition of the Church of England by Rome.

Then there is the language of gesture, which can often speak more eloquently than mere words. In 1966 Paul VI, well before the Canonization of the Forty Martyrs, after signing the Common Declaration with Archbishop Michael Ramsey, slipped his own episcopal ring onto the finger of the Archbishop of Canterbury and invited him to join him in blessing the crowd.[3] Indeed, this was not an isolated gesture, for all Anglican bishops are now invited to join in giving the blessing at the end of a General Audience with the Pope and the Roman Catholic bishops who are present. A French bishop, whom I have known for many years and who was a great friend of Paul VI, told me that Paul VI was incapable of spontaneous gestures. Those symbolic gestures which he loved to make were all carefully thought out in advance. The Pope knew very much what he was doing when he gave Michael Ramsey his ring. Pope John Paul II is a very different kind of person, but he too knows the importance of gesture. The fact that he presided jointly over a Celebration of Faith in Canterbury Cathedral on the eve of Pentecost in 1982 was certainly an implicit recognition of some sort of ecclesial reality to the Anglican Communion, and of the Archbishop of Canterbury as in some sense the successor of S. Augustine.

JMH   In the light of these statements and eloquent gestures on the part of Rome, how can Catholics in the Church of England best respond and further the cause of reunion? What do you think Paul VI meant by our 'worthy patrimony of piety and usage'? Do we as Anglicans value that heritage sufficiently?

RTG   I think catholic-minded Anglicans are in something of a dilemma. Most of them wish strongly to disavow and repudiate

---

3 See the photograph on the cover of this book, which was taken at the Basilica of St Paul without-the-Walls on 24 March 1966.

the Reformation breach with Rome, and in doing so, they are tempted sometimes to behave as if it had never happened and to act as if they were part of the Latin Church under the Roman Rite, to react to the breach with a deliberate policy of carrying on as if it had never happened. And here we have a Pope, as it were, pleading with Catholic Anglicans, asking them to re-evaluate their own specifically Anglican heritage much more positively.

When it comes to having a look at the content and value of this specifically Anglican patrimony, I think there are a number of separate points we need to make. First of all, I think that Catholic Anglicans need to make the most of existing Anglican liturgical forms; they need to exploit them to the utmost, in spite of their imperfections, in spite of the fact that they do need to be supplemented and interpreted. I think they need to do this for pastoral reasons, because I think we shall not really do our pastoral and missionary work in this country if we do not make use of this heritage, and I think we need to do this for reasons of honesty and integrity. English Roman Catholics and Roman Catholics generally find it very difficult to understand how we can treat the solemn declarations and promises we have to make on so many occasions as if they had no value or binding force whatever. Most Roman Catholics, if they show some real interest in unity with us, do so because they see something positive in our heritage. They are not interested in uniting with a body which is just a pale carbon copy of themselves. Indeed, some of our borrowings can be rather insensitive. If we sing the full version of 'Faith of our Fathers' at a big gathering at which there are Roman Catholics present, can we not understand that they are likely to react by saying, 'Are they trying to steal our Forty Martyrs too?'

But there are more important factors at stake; one of the weaknesses of the Uniate Churches is that that kind of diversity has been seen as something skin deep, something merely at the level of liturgy and spirituality – there has been no deeper consistency, merely a difference of rites, and in the Anglican heritage there is something more than just a liturgical variant.

However much we deeply and bitterly regret the Reformation breach, at that time not only were they many and serious losses in our own Church but there were also some gains. Vatican II set up as an ideal for the Roman Catholic Church the idea of a reformed Catholicism – *ecclesia semper reformanda*. At its best, the Anglican experiment has been trying to embody precisely that vision; trying to hold together the positive insights of the Reformation – and there were some – with the permanent truths of the catholic tradition. The tree of catholic theology, catholic spirituality, catholic custom was cut down to the very roots in the sixteenth century, yet those roots remained and within comparatively few decades they were sending up new shoots of great vitality once more. We have the great heritage of the divines and spiritual teachers of the seventeenth century (some of them used in the English edition of the Roman Divine Office, for example the poems of George Herbert) and we have the astonishing phenomenon of the Catholic Revival in the Church of England and the astonishing achievement of the theological contribution of Newman to Anglican–Roman Catholic *rapprochement*. The fact was that in his own person he took so much of the Anglican heritage, the Anglican tradition, into the Roman Catholic Church, and was in some sense the 'unseen hero' of Vatican II. Particularly is this true of his contribution to modern perception of the role of the laity in the reception and the interpretation of Christian doctrine.

This is where we come to one of the most important statements in the *Final Report* of ARCIC which is to be found in the Co-Chairmen's Preface to the First Authority Statement:

The consensus we have reached, if it is to be accepted by our two communities, would have, we insist, important consequences. Common recognition of Roman primacy would bring changes not only to the Anglican Communion but also to the Roman Catholic Church . . . Roman Catholics, on their side, would be enriched by the presence of a particular tradition of spirituality and scholarship, the lack of which has deprived the Roman Catholic Church of a precious element in the Christian heritage. The Roman Catholic Church has much to learn from the Anglican synodical tradition of involving the laity in the life and mission of the Church.[4]

Moreover, towards the end of the Second Authority Statement we find this statement:

> We have already been able to agree that conciliarity and primacy are complementary . . . We can now together affirm that the Church needs both a multiple, dispersed authority, with which all God's people are actively involved, and also a universal primate as servant and focus of visible unity in truth and love.[5]

We in the Church of England are perhaps all too aware of the inconveniences which occur as a result of the abuses of the synodical process, but here we have a good example of something positive which has developed within our own tradition and which we can contribute from our heritage to the good of the universal Church.

---

4 Anglican–Roman Catholic International Commission, *The Final Report* (London: CTS/SPCK, 1982), p. 50.

5 *The Final Report*, pp. 97–8: 'Authority in the Church II', para. 33.

6

The Bishop as Icon of Christ
(December 1986)

Roger served on the Archbishops' Group on the Episcopate, which was originally appointed in 1985 by the Archbishops of Canterbury and York to identify and examine the theological issues bearing upon the ordination of women to the episcopate. At its first meeting in January 1986 it formed the view that it should examine those issues in the context of, and as part of, a general study of the nature and function of episcopal ministry. The Archbishops agreed to such an extension of its terms of reference that July. The Group's report, Episcopal Ministry, *was published in 1990.[1] This paper, published here for the first time, was written by Roger as a contribution to the group's work.*

It is unique in this collection in that it addresses issues of principle as to whether women could be ordained, rather than the ecclesiological issues posed by the actions of the Church of England and the Anglican Communion in undertaking such ordinations in the absence of a consensus in the wider Church on the issues of principle. As Roger's introduction indicates, the subject was not one that he had chosen.

---

1 *Episcopal Ministry: The Report of the Archbishops' Group on the Episcopate* (London: Church House Publishing, 1990).

Introduction

At the meeting of the Archbishop's Group on the Episcopate held in London on 18 July the Bishop of Wakefield[2] said that he 'felt it was important to look at the whole image of the bishop as icon of Christ' and the Secretary was instructed to ask me to prepare a paper on this subject. I was unfortunately unable to be present either at that meeting or at the following one held in September. I do have to say at the outset that neither the choice of subject and title nor the choice of author have more than my most reluctant assent, and also that I have the additional handicap of having missed the Group's discussions at the last two meetings.

Women and Holy Orders

With regard to the specific question of the admission of women to Holy Orders, I am one of those who believe that a clear distinction can be made between the diaconate on the one hand and the priestly ministries of bishop and presbyter on the other. I do not believe that one can find any strictly theological argument to justify opening the presbyterate to women while barring access to the episcopate to them. Some of those who favour ordaining women to the presbyterate may find other kinds of reasons for saying 'not yet' to women bishops. Most of those who oppose ordaining women to the presbyterate will have reasons for opposing even more strongly their ordination to the episcopate – but these reasons will be found to flow more from a theology of communion (and the essential role of the bishop in the maintenance of communion between local churches) than from a theology of priesthood.

---

2 The Rt Revd Dr David Hope (b. 1940) was Principal of St Stephen's House, Oxford (1974–82), Vicar of All Saints', Margaret Street, London (1982–85) and Bishop of Wakefield (1985–91). He was later Bishop of London (1991–95) and Archbishop of York (1995–2005).

Theological Considerations

The iconic argument cannot be used to drive a wedge between bishop and presbyter, since it derives principally from the shared priesthood of bishop and presbyter, particularly as it is reflected in their presidential role at the Eucharist. With this in mind, I append the following considerations, not as the statement of a theological position but as a possible starting point for reflection and discussion.

'God created man in his own image, in the image of God he created him; male and female he created them' (Gen. 1.27). The primary icon of God is therefore the human race in its God-willed complementarity of man and woman.

Having said this, however, some will want to trace back a theology of images to an even more fundamental level – to set it within a theology of the Trinity. In Philo and the Wisdom literature both *Logos* and *Sophia* were seen as icons of the Almighty; more developed Christian theology has seen the act of creation as essentially Trinitarian, so that it can be said both that mankind is created in the image of the Word (the true Image) and that mankind is created in the image of the Trinity.

Jesus Christ is described explicitly in the Pauline letters as the icon of God (2 Cor. 4.4; Col. 1.15); he is the first-born of all creation, the Second Adam. The idea of Christ as icon of the Father is not absent from other New Testament writings – e.g. the Letter to the Hebrews and the Fourth Gospel.

Jesus our Redeemer came to restore the image of God, defaced by sin, in mankind (*cf.* 1 Cor. 15.49; 2 Cor. 3.18; Col. 3.10). So all the baptized without distinction are sharers in the new life, *filii in Filio*, icons in the Icon. In this baptismal unity 'there is neither male nor female' (Gal. 3.28). But how are we to reconcile this with what Paul writes elsewhere: 'For a man ought not to cover his head, since he is the image of God; but woman is the glory of man' (1 Cor. 11.7)?

The fact that all Christians are icons of Christ (or, perhaps more exactly, icons of God in Christ) need not exclude particular aspects of the icon of Christ being manifested in particular callings, for example, gifts of healing and prophecy, of martyrdom and suffering. In particular, the union in Christian marriage of man and woman has been seen as an icon of the union of Christ and his Church.

All ministry derives from the ministry of Christ the Servant, but different types, models or images have tended to cluster round different ministries. The Dombes statement on 'The Episcopal Ministry' has this to say:

> According to the varied witness of the New Testament, the ministry of episcope is exercised on the model of Christ 'the *episcopos* of our souls' (1 Peter 2.25) and of the Apostles, in so far as their charge was capable of being handed on.[3]

In a later passage it goes on to say:

> The *theology of types* looks at the Church as the image of those whom Jesus grouped round himself to keep them in unity. It sees in the presbyters the image of the Apostles, and in the *episcopos* the image of Christ or of the Father. In other words, not even Ignatius concentrates all the ministry in the episcopos alone: 'Hold the deacons in as great respect as Jesus Christ; just as you should also look on the episcopos as a type of the Father, and the clergy as the apostolic circle forming his council' (*To the Trallians*, 3).[4]

---

3 'Le ministère episcopal: Réflexions et propositions sur le ministère de vigilance et d'unité dans l'Église particulière' (1976), in *Pour la communion des Églises: L'apport du Groupe des Dombes, 1937–1987* (Paris: Le Centurion, 1988), pp. 81–114; Eng. trans: Group of Les Dombes, 'The Episcopal Ministry: Reflection and proposals concerning the ministry of vigilance and unity in the particular church', *One in Christ*, 14 (1978), 267–88 at p. 275: para. 16.

4 'The Episcopal Ministry', p. 278, para. 28.

The Dombes text speaks of the *episcopos* as 'the image of Christ or of the Father',[5] for in the preceding paragraph of his Letter to the Trallians Ignatius writes of 'your obedience to your bishop, as though he were Jesus Christ' and in speaking of the Eucharist in his Letter to the Smyrnians he writes: 'Where the bishop is to be seen, there let all the people be; just as wherever Jesus Christ is present, we have the worldwide Church.' It is on such a basis that the eucharistic ecclesiology propounded by Orthodox theologians is constructed.

A theology of types would need to concentrate on certain roles seen (for example, in the ordination rites) as specifically episcopal and as derived from Christ's own ministry. The Bishop is Teacher, Ruler, Pastor and Priest; his ministry is therefore prophetic, royal and priestly in character. When Vatican II's Constitution on the Church asserts that 'bishops, in a resplendent and visible manner, take the place of Christ himself, teacher, shepherd and priest, and act as his representative [*in eius persona agunt*]',[6] a footnote claims the authority of St Cyprian, St John Chrysostom, St Ambrose, Ambrosiaster, Theodore of Mopsuestia and Hesychius of Jerusalem for this affirmation and gives references to their writings.

If only the Bishop in his paternal role as Father in God or Father in Christ is usually portrayed as Icon of the Father, the description of the Bishop as Icon of Christ is frequently linked to his role as celebrant of the Eucharist, and in this case it is not confined to bishops but is extended to embrace presbyters who share in their priestly, liturgical and sacramental ministry. The

---

5 *Cf.* the model homily addressed by the principal consecrator to the bishop-elect in the new Roman rite: 'Attend to the whole flock in which the Holy Spirit appoints you an overseer of the Church of God – in the name of the Father, whose image you personify in the Church – and in the name of his Son, Jesus Christ, whose role of Teacher, Priest and Shepherd you undertake – and in the name of the Holy Spirit, who gives life to the Church of Christ and supports our weakness with his strength.'

6 Dogmatic Constitution on the Church (*Lumen Gentium*), 21: W. M. Abbott (ed.), *The Documents of Vatican II* (London: Geoffrey Chapman, 1967), p. 42.

Final Report of ARCIC argues in its Canterbury Statement on Ministry and Ordination:

> Because the Eucharist is the memorial of the sacrifice of Christ, the action of the presiding minister in reciting again the words of Christ at the last supper and distributing to the assembly the holy gifts is seen to stand in a sacramental relation to what Christ himself did in offering his own sacrifice.[7]

The Elucidation of 1979 defends and amplifies this argument:

> The Statement . . . explains that the ordained ministry is called priestly principally because it has a particular sacramental relationship with Christ as High Priest. At the Eucharist Christ's people do what he commanded in memory of himself in his self-offering. But in this action it is only the ordained minister who presides at the Eucharist, in which, in the name of Christ and on behalf of his Church, he recites the narrative of the institution of the Last Supper, and invokes the Holy Spirit upon the gifts.[8]

The ARCIC line of argument is taken much further by Cardinal Willebrands in his reply of 17 June 1986 to the Archbishop of Canterbury. He writes:

> Christ took on human nature to accomplish the redemption of all humanity. But as *Inter Insigniores* says, 'we can never ignore the fact that Christ is a man'. His male identity is an inherent feature of the economy of salvation, revealed in the Scriptures and pondered in the Church. The ordination only of men to the priesthood has to be understood in terms of the intimate relationship between Christ the redeemer and those

---

7 Anglican–Roman Catholic International Commission, *The Final Report* (London: CTS/SPCK, 1982), p. 35: 'Ministry and Ordination', para. 13
8 *The Final Report*, p. 41: 'Ministry and Ordination: Elucidation', para. 2.

who, in a unique way, cooperate in Christ's redemptive work. The priest represents Christ in His saving relationship with His Body the Church. He does not primarily represent the priesthood of the whole People of God. However unworthy, the priest stands *in persona Christi*. Christ's saving sacrifice is made present in the world as a sacramental reality in and through the ministry of priests. And the sacramental ordination of men takes on force and significance precisely within this context of the Church's experience of its own identity, of the power and significance of the person of Jesus Christ, and of the symbolic and iconic role of those who represent him in the Eucharist.[9]

There will be those who accept the legitimacy of 'symbolic and iconic' language about priesthood, those who deny it, and those who find it unclear and fraught with ambiguity. Will the further exploration of the theology of the Icon, which we hope will be stimulated by the celebration of the twelfth centenary of the Second Council of Nicaea this year, be able to take on board this particular aspect? But positions taken up on this issue will not necessarily coincide with positions taken up with regard to women in the presbyterate and episcopate. Indeed, a passage in the Archbishop of Canterbury's letter of 18 December 1985 to Cardinal Willebrands makes this abundantly clear:

Some Anglicans . . . would argue that priestly character lies precisely in the fact that the priest is commissioned by the Church in ordination to represent the priestly nature of the whole body and also – especially in the presidency of the Eucharist – to stand in a special sacramental relationship with Christ as High Priest in whom complete humanity is redeemed and who ever lives to make intercession for us at the right hand of the Father. Because the humanity of

9 Cardinal Willebrands to Archbishop Runcie, 17 June 1986, in *The Church of England's Response to BEM and ARCIC: Supplementary Report* (GS 747) (London: Board for Mission and Unity, 1986), pp. 39–42 at p. 42.

Christ our High Priest includes male and female, it is thus urged that the ministerial priesthood should now be opened to women in order the more perfectly to represent Christ's inclusive High Priesthood.[10]

In so far as for many (for example, Cardinal Willebrands) the 'symbolic and iconic role' of the president of the Eucharist is understood to require an exclusively male priesthood, the argument is pushed back to the underlying question of the theological and Christological significance of the maleness of Jesus. Is this to be seen as strictly essential ('an inherent feature of the economy of salvation', to quote again the Cardinal's letter), as merely appropriate (and if so, how?), or as in itself of no real significance (not a 'constitutive factor in the meaning of "God-with-us"', as R. A. Norris argues in *Feminine in the Church*?[11] And what light (if any) is shed on this question by the titles and images attributed to Jesus in the New Testament – for example, that of Second Adam?

Roger Greenacre
8: xii: 86

---

10 Archbishop Runcie to Cardinal Willebrands, 18 Dec. 1985, in *The Church of England's Response to BEM and ARCIC: Supplementary Report*, pp. 33–7 at pp. 34–5.

11 R. A. Norris, Jr, 'The Ordination of Women and the "Maleness" of Christ' (reprinted, with minor revisions, from *The Anglican Theological Review*, June 1976) in M. Furlong (ed.), *Feminine in the Church* (London: SPCK, 1984), pp. 71–85 at p. 80.

7

Lost in the Fog:
An Open Letter to Fr Jean Tillard
(April 1989)

Introduction (2013)

In an article in the Belgian ecumenical journal *Irénikon* the leading Roman Catholic theologian and ecumenist Fr Jean Tillard
OP reviewed the outcome of the 1988 Lambeth Conference
from an ecumenical point of view.[1] As a member of both the first
and the second Anglican–Roman Catholic International Commissions (ARCIC I and ARCIC II), he was particularly committed to Anglican–Roman Catholic dialogue. The article was
republished, in an English translation by Margot Mayne and
Roger, together with this Open Letter by Roger to Fr Tillard, by
the Church Union Theological Committee (of which Roger was
the Chairman) as the third of a series of occasional papers.[2]

In his article, Tillard acknowledged the importance of the
Conference's reception of ARCIC I's Agreed Statements on
Authority in the Church, but pointed to 'the tension between
the price to pay for unity on the one hand and, on the other, the
ardent attachment to provincial independence (that is to say, in
the Anglican vocabulary, to national independence)' as 'one of

---

1 J.-M. R. Tillard, 'La Leçon oecuménique de Lambeth 1988', *Irénikon*, 61
(1988), pp. 530–6.
2 J.-M. R. Tillard and R. T. Greenacre, *Lost in the Fog?: The Lesson for
Ecumenism of Lambeth 1988* (Church Union Theological Committee Occasional
Paper No. 3: London: CLA, 1983).

the problems underlying the Conference'. The Conference had 'shown how provincialism . . . matters more from now on, to many people, than the primacy of the common good of unity, which up to now the Anglican tradition has venerated':

> The massive vote in favour of Resolution 88-001[3] showed unequivocal approval for the principle of local autonomy. Even if this was voted 'to avoid the worst', Lambeth 88 took an ecclesiological option. Without having the time or the means to discuss in depth and to measure the consequences, the priority of the provincial (i.e. the national) over the universal was accepted.[4]

This placed in question how the massive vote in favour of the *Final Report* of ARCIC I, with its stress on the communion of the episcopate and the role of primacy, should be interpreted.
Tillard commented:

> The question of the ordination of women to the episcopate is more serious than that of their ordination to the presbyterate. For in the Church the bishop is both the person who assures the link with the apostolic community and also the one who manifests unity with the universal body of those who exercise authority in the churches. In him, communion is formally brought into play.[5]

By the Conference's acquiescence in the ordination of women to the episcopate, he noted, 'fidelity to the great Tradition – so dear to the Anglican soul – was being abandoned'. His conclusion was that, whereas the ARCIC agreements had the potential

---

3 'This Conference resolves: 1. That each Province respect the decision and attitudes of other Provinces in the ordination or consecration of women to the episcopate, without such respect necessarily indicating acceptance of the principles involved . . .': *The Truth Shall Make You Free: The Lambeth Conference 1988* (London: Church House Publishing, 1988), p. 201.

4 *Lost in the Fog?*, p. 2.

5 *Lost in the Fog?*, pp. 3–4.

to resolve for the future the issue of Leo XIII's judgement in his encyclical *Apostolicae curae* that Anglican ordinations were rendered invalid by a defect of intention, 'The Lambeth 88 dossier will be more difficult than that of *Apostolicae curae*.'[6]

Despite this, Tillard set out four reasons why Anglican–Roman Catholic dialogue 'must continue, and there is no reason why everything should stop'. The first reason he explained as follows:

> The dialogue must continue, so that the progress already made should be durable, even if it does not reach the organic unity desired by the Malta agreement and which ARCIC I thought it was seeing completed. Poor members of ARCIC I! We burned up our energies in it. Now, the goal is hidden in the fog of Lambeth (and Lambeth is in England!). But we have made possible a sort of indissoluble and valid marriage, *ratum* if not yet *consummatum*. We do not have the right before God to break the links that have been thus created.[7]

Tillard identified as problematic for the Anglican Communion and Anglican ecclesiology the 1988 Lambeth Conference's acceptance (or at least acknowledgement) of provincial autonomy in a matter as fundamental for the communion of the churches as ordination to the episcopate. The problem was to be compounded ten years later by the failure of the 1998 Conference to grapple with the Virginia Report of the Inter-Anglican Theological and Doctrinal Commission, which examined the Anglican Communion's structures in the light of the meaning and nature of communion.[8] It is difficult not to see these failures as leaving the Communion open to – and unprepared for – the ecclesiological crisis into which it was plunged in 2003 by another act of provincial autonomy in relation to ordination to

---

6 *Lost in the Fog?*, p. 4.

7 *Lost in the Fog?*, pp. 4–5.

8 'The Virginia Report: The Report of the Inter-Anglican Theological and Doctrinal Commission', in *The Official Report of the Lambeth Conference 1998* (Harrisburg, PA: Morehouse Publising, 1998), pp. 15–68.

the episcopate – the consecration of Gene Robinson as Bishop of New Hampshire despite a warning by the Primates of the Communion that his consecration would 'tear the fabric of our Communion at its deepest level'.⁹ Those developments could not, of course, be foreseen in 1988, but they proved Tillard right in his identification of the problem.

An Open Letter from Roger Greenacre

My dear Jean,

As soon as I read your splendid article in *Irénikon*, I was convinced that it ought to be translated into English and made available to Anglican readers, not least in Great Britain. I am grateful to you and the editor of *Irénikon* for making this possible. You are writing as a Roman Catholic for your fellow Catholics; I would like, as an Anglican, to add a brief commentary, mainly for the benefit of my fellow Anglicans.

Lambeth 1988

Many of us feel that there has been a great deal of rather unrealistic euphoria about Lambeth 1988. There were certainly very positive aspects to it, not only the encouraging response to ARCIC, of which you speak, but notably the outstanding quality of the personal leadership of the Archbishop of Canterbury, a factor singled out for particular mention by most commentators. Yet even here there is perhaps a paradox of an ironic, indeed of a tragic, quality. Dr Runcie made a strong appeal in his masterly opening address on 'The Nature of the Unity We Seek' for a move from independence to interdependence, and it is significant that one of the reasons he adduced for 'looking critically

---

9 'A Statement by the Primates of the Anglican Communion, meeting in Lambeth Palace, 16 October 2003', in The Lambeth Commission on Communion, *The Windsor Report 2004* (London: Anglican Communion Office, 2004), pp. 98–101 at p. 100.

at the notion of the absolute independence of Provinces' was the nature of our ecumenical dialogues with worldwide communions which 'require decision and action at more than provincial level'.[10] Yet one cannot avoid asking whether this appeal came too late, whether it should not have been made and debated as a matter of urgency at the Lambeth Conference of 1978, a conference whose failure to grasp nettles landed its successor last year with an impossible task. It is, to put it mildly, ecclesiologically odd that the Anglican Communion can feel empowered to give a verdict as a communion on the *Final Report* of ARCIC but unable as a communion to give a verdict on the legitimacy of the ordination of women as priests and bishops.

Weakness in Decision-Making Structures

You refer in your article to the question of the nature and status of episcopal conferences in the Roman Catholic Church, the theme of an important colloquium at Salamanca which we both attended in January 1988. In the course of the response requested of me as the Anglican observer, I said:

> I have the impression that we are dealing here with two communions which have trajectories going in reverse directions. Both believe in unity in diversity. It seems to me that the Roman Catholic Church is at this moment aware of the need to put great stress on diversity and to find more adequate structures for this; the Anglican Communion finds – at least I hope it does – that it needs at this moment to put a greater stress on unity and to find more adequate structures for it. In this situation we need above all to listen to each other, to try to benefit from each other's experience (from the failures

---

10 *The Truth Shall Make You Free. The Lambeth Conference 1988* (London: Church House Publishing, 1988), p. 15.

as well as the successes), and to avoid whatever might make this mutual enrichment impossible.[11]

Earlier in my response I had registered a warning that 'any judgement from within the Roman Catholic Church [about the ARCIC statements on Authority in the Church] which gives the impression of minimizing the value and authority of episcopal conferences and of marking a retreat from the positions gained at Vatican II' would have a negative effect on Anglican–Roman Catholic dialogue.[12] I had then acknowledged the crucial weakness in the structures of decision-making within Anglicanism which was leading many Anglicans (not to mention others) to pose the following question:

> What credibility can be given to a communion of churches which possesses no structure of authority strong enough to maintain it in unity and which in the last resort seems impotent in the face of the threat of its own disintegration?[13]

That question, posed in January 1988, is even more acute now in the aftermath of Lambeth 1988 and of the consecration in Boston of a woman bishop in February 1989.

Some Reservations

I turn now to the very few points in your article which lead me to express some reservations. You speak of three 'cements' which up until recently had ensured the coherence of the Anglican Communion. Certainly the Book of Common Prayer was one of these, but its unifying force was not without ambiguity. The variations were surely not quite as secondary as you

---

11 R. T. Greenacre: 'Causa Nostra Agitur? An Anglican Response', in H. Legrand, J. Manzanares and A. García y García (eds), The Nature and Future of Episcopal Conferences: The Jurist, 48 (Washington D.C.: Catholic University of America, 1988), pp. 384–96 at p. 396.

12 Greenacre: 'Causa Nostra Agitur? An Anglican Response', p. 390.

13 Greenacre: 'Causa Nostra Agitur? An Anglican Response', p. 394.

suggest: the existence of two 'families' of eucharistic liturgies, one ultimately deriving from the first Prayer Book of 1549 and the other from the second Prayer Book of 1552, pointed to serious and unresolved theological differences. If it had not been for other factors, I am far from convinced that the introduction of a far wider liturgical pluralism would have led in itself to the crisis in Anglicanism which undoubtedly exists today.

You then speak of the moral authority of the Archbishop of Canterbury as another of the three 'cements'. Many Anglicans, and not only on this side of the Atlantic, will see in the latest Boston Tea Party an anti-imperialist gesture of defiance and rebellion on the part of former 'colonials', which, however understandable at the level of group psychology, is, at the ecclesial level, an act of grave irresponsibility. They will equally regret the inability or unwillingness of the Archbishop of Canterbury, who still in the last analysis defines who is and who is not in communion with the See of St Augustine, to take a sharper line against those whose actions are disrupting communion.

To be fair, however, they must also recognize that there is another side to the question. Historically, as you well know, it was in England itself that the sharpest challenge to the authority of the Lambeth Conference and therefore to the wider primacy of the Archbishop of Canterbury was first expressed in 1867 and it was, in fact, the particular relationship of the Established Church of England with the Crown that was largely responsible for preventing an earlier movement from independence to interdependence.[14] I think that it is in the light of this history that one must interpret the massive majority in favour of Resolution 88-001. I do not believe it necessarily proved 'unequivocal approval' for the principle of local autonomy; could it not have been rather a 'reluctant admission' on the part of many that such local authority is a fact of life for

14 For this, see C. J. Podmore, 'Two Streams Mingling: The American Episcopal Church in the Anglican Communion', *Journal of Anglican Studies*, 9 (2011), pp. 12–37.

the Anglican Communion which in present circumstances can hardly be reversed? In 1988 it was either too late for that or too early.

The Future

It is risky to say anything at all about the future. At the present moment – April 1989 – we await the report of the Eames Commission,[15] set up by the Archbishop of Canterbury as requested by Resolution 88-001; we await the formal evaluation of the *Final Report* of ARCIC I by the Roman Catholic Church, which will presumably appear in the course of the next few months; we await too the outcome of the visit of the Archbishop of Canterbury to Rome in September of this year. However, a singularly well-placed observer, Canon Howard Root, Director of the Anglican Centre in Rome, has written: 'Since the Lambeth Conference of 1988 the ecumenical map has changed. That part of it which covers Anglican–Roman Catholic relations has been stamped with a question mark.'[16] It is important for us to realize why this is the case. It is not just the fact of the consecration of a woman bishop but, even more to the point, the fact that the body with which the Roman Catholic Church entered into dialogue does not have the ecclesial consistency which it was first judged to possess. In what sense, the question must now run, is the Anglican Communion a 'communion' at all, and what is gained from a dialogue with it?

You call upon Catholics not only to be sympathetic to Anglicans in the crisis through which they are passing but to do their best to see that Anglicanism does not disintegrate further and that the Anglican–Roman Catholic dialogue continues. I would

---

15 *The Report of The Archbishop of Canterbury's Commission on Communion and Women in the Episcopate 1989* was published between the writing of this Open Letter and its publication. See *Women in the Anglican Episcopate: Theology, Guidelines and Practice. The Eames Commission and the Monitoring Group Reports* (Toronto: Anglican Book Centre, 1998), pp. 13–44.

16 *The Newsletter of the Friends of the Anglican Centre in Rome*, 8 (Spring 1989), p. 1.

hope that at some time fairly soon someone closely involved in this dialogue on the Roman Catholic side (and preferably you yourself) would feel able to undertake the delicate but very necessary task of spelling out for an Anglican audience – and particularly perhaps for those catholic-minded Anglicans whom recent events have tempted to despair – in what specific ways Catholics can help us and work with us in the present crisis. For those of us on the Anglican side who have shared your hope and belief in what we came to call the ARCIC process now share in your disappointment and in your anxiety about the future. I pray that we can also share in your unshakeable conviction that the dialogue must continue and that the God of hope points us to the certain fulfilment of his purpose and of the prayer of his Son our Lord. In the even darker days of 1896, immediately after Leo XIII's condemnation of Anglican Orders, Lord Halifax wrote to his friend the Abbé Portal: 'Ce n'est pas un rêve. La chose est aussi certaine que jamais': 'It is no dream. The matter is as certain as ever.' For his part the Abbé could repeat again the proverb which gave him so much comfort: God writes straight with crooked lines.

Yours ever, in our common hope,
Roger
Chichester: 10 April 1989

8

Diversity in Unity: A Problem for Anglicans (May 1990)

This paper was given at the Centro Pro Unione in Rome on 2 May 1990, and was published in 1991.[1]

Diversity in unity (or, more strictly perhaps, the reconciliation of the need for diversity with the need for unity) has become in the last two decades an acute and critical problem for Anglicans – and particularly for the Anglican Communion. But I must emphasize from the beginning that, in the first place, it is not a problem uniquely peculiar to Anglicans (for all the Churches are wrestling with it in their own theologies and their own structures, and it is one of the major themes of ecumenical dialogue); in the second place, it must also be said that for Anglicans it is not a new problem but one they have had to confront from the beginning. So what I shall now attempt to describe falls into two parts: a first section of an historical and theological character and a second section which concentrates on the recent and present crisis.

I

Historians will of course differ in their analysis of the sixteenth-century Reformation in England, but they will find it difficult to deny that it was to a very great extent something imposed upon the Church by the State (i.e., the Crown) and that the

---

1 *Bulletin of the Centro Pro Unione*, 39 (Spring 1991), pp. 4–10.

political considerations of national independence (resentment against what was perceived as interference from Rome) and of national unity (the will to comprehend all the subjects of the Crown in one church) were predominant. That is not to deny that theologians like Cranmer and Jewel (to name but two) had a profound influence, but one has only to compare the English Reformation with the Reformation on the Continent (even the Reformation in Scotland) to be struck by the profound difference. The Church of England had no Luther, no Zwingli, no Calvin, no John Knox, and the very words 'Anglican' and 'Anglicanism' (from the pre-Reformation Latin *'ecclesia anglicana'*) afford an historical and geographical description but no hint of any distinctive or exclusive confessional feature – though the title Episcopal Church used by some Provinces of the Anglican Communion outside England does indeed suggest a structure, but not an exclusive structure.

From the reign of Henry VIII there existed what some, politely, might call a theological pluralism and what others might call a power struggle. In the reign of Henry VIII one group of bishops, led by Cranmer (Archbishop of Canterbury) was favourable to the Reformation; another group led by Gardiner (Bishop of Winchester) was profoundly hostile. The triumph of the Reforming party under Edward VI spelt the doom of what might be called 'Henrician Catholicism' (a fully mediaeval, traditional conservatism but without the Pope), but it did not mean the end of pluralism under Elizabeth, although most of her earlier bishops were disciples of the Swiss Protestant theologian Bullinger. There was no more determined advocate of diversity in unity than Elizabeth herself. She was determined to have a national church which, although it embraced the main features of the Reformation, could still contain those whose theological, liturgical and devotional temper of mind was basically catholic. She is reputed to have declared that she did not intend 'to make windows into men's souls' (that is to say, to pin people down to exact doctrinal standards or to particular stances on the controversial issues of the day): she tried to impose, however, conformity to the Church of England; to its

liturgy, to its episcopal structure, to its appeal to the Scriptures
as interpreted by the Creeds and the teaching of the primitive
Church as the supreme rule of faith, and to the Thirty-nine
Articles of Religion – a carefully and deliberately revised form
of a set of Articles originally very sharply Protestant.

Much has been written and said about the Anglican ideal of
the *via media* – what a smugly triumphalist Anglican bishop
of the late seventeenth-century could describe (quaintly but
unecumenically) as 'that golden mediocrity which our Church
observes between the meretricious gaudiness of the Church of
Rome and the squalid sluttery of fanatical conventicles'.[2] Two
things need to be said about it today.[3]

First, there does seem to be very general agreement among
Anglicans (though not total unanimity) that the distinctiveness
of the Anglican *via media* lies not in content but in method.
According to the late Archbishop Michael Ramsey, Anglican
theology is 'neither a system nor a confession (the idea of an
Anglican "confessionalism" suggests something that never has
been and never can be) but a method, a use and a direction'.[4]
More recently this conviction has been given clear and concise
expression by Dr Henry McAdoo, the former Anglican Archbishop of Dublin and Co-Chairman of ARCIC I. In one book
he wrote:

To return then to what is distinctive in the Anglican tradition: the distinctiveness lies not in the content of the faith but
in the *method* by which the Churches of the Anglican Communion make sure that what is being taught and proclaimed
at any stage of history is authentic Christianity, 'the faith once

2 Simon Patrick, Bishop of Chichester (1689–91) and of Ely (1691–1707),
quoted by P. E. More and F. L. Cross, *Anglicanism: The Thought and Practice
of the Church of England, Illustrated from the Religious Literature of the Seventeenth Century* (London, 1951), p. 12.

3 This section of the lecture reprised material that had already appeared in the
article which forms Chapter 4 of this book.

4 A. M. Ramsey, 'What is Anglican Theology?', *Theology*, 48 (1945), pp. 2–6
at p. 6.

for all delivered' . . . The method applies a three-fold criterion by appealing to Scripture, to tradition and to reason.[5]

And in a second book he wrote:

Anglicanism is not a theological system and there is no writer whose work is an essential part of it either in respect of content or with regard to the form of its self-expression. Richard Hooker has some claim to be the greatest Anglican writer, but his work was to state a method in theology rather than to outline a system . . . The absence of an official theology in Anglicanism is something deliberate which belongs to its essential nature, for it has always regarded the teaching and practice of the undivided Church of the first five centuries as a criterion . . . The distinctiveness of Anglicanism proceeds not from a systematic theology but from the spirit in which theological questions are handled.[6]

Secondly, although some Anglican theologians have tried to pin down this *via media* to a very clear middle road between Rome and Geneva, what F. D. Maurice in the nineteenth century attacked as the idea of 'an invisible equatorial line between Romanism and Protestantism',[7] and to do so in the interests of either a rather narrow and static anti-Roman high-church theology or in the interests of a more Protestant theology, this argument fails to do justice to the facts of Anglican history and to the continuing reality of Anglican theological pluralism.

Roman Catholics often find Anglicanism a baffling phenomenon; often their greatest problem is to understand how those who are clearly so close to themselves in their theological ideas, liturgical practices and devotional habits can bear to remain

---

5 H. McAdoo, *Being an Anglican* (Dublin: APCK and London: SPCK, 1977), p. 13.

6 H. McAdoo, *The Spirit of Anglicanism: A Survey of Anglican Theological Method in the Seventeenth Century* (London: A. & C. Black, 1965); p. v.

7 F. D. Maurice: *The Kingdom of Christ* (Everyman Edition, London: J. M. Dent & Co. [1906]), vol. 2, p. 311.

members of a church which contains so many who share none of these. Some catholic-minded Anglicans have indeed never been happy with Anglican 'comprehensiveness'; they have obstinately been holding out in a church which in their own view has suffered from centuries of hostile occupation, ignoring other Anglicans and longing and working for the day when their own cause will prevail. Others, however, have tried to hold on to a more positive and more ecumenical vision. They have seen the continued co-existence within Anglicanism of three major traditions – the Catholic or 'high church', the Evangelical or 'low church' and (the hardest of all to define) the liberal-Erasmian or critical and radical 'broad church' – neither as an unlimited blessing nor as a simple disaster but as a *challenge* and a *burden*.

The challenge was expressed by F. D. Maurice. In refusing the idea that the *via media* represented 'an invisible equatorial line' between Rome and Protestantism he substituted for it the model of a *union of opposites,* that is to say the holding together of apparent contradictions in the hope and with the intention of working for their resolution and reconciliation. In this understanding, the *via media* is not a claim that Rome is wrong or that the Reformation is wrong; nor is it a claim that Anglicanism has successfully achieved a solution to the problems that divided Western European Christendom in the sixteenth century. It is more like an act of hope (maybe a rather blind act of hope), a fairly desperate effort to hold together elements which (at least until the fairly recent past) Christians have separated and set in opposition against each other. The Anglican Church is very much a pilgrim church, a seeking church (*ecclesia quaerens*), a church trying to work through internal divisions to a better unity which at the moment still eludes it. The French Catholic philosopher, Etienne Gilson, once wrote of the opposition within the Roman Catholic Church between Thomism and Augustinianism as follows:

> Adversaries whose conclusions are in conflict must be allowed time to understand each other better, and to be reunited with

each other again at a point still undetermined but certainly situated beyond their present positions.[8]

He could have been describing the tensions within Anglicanism!

In this vision the *via media*, the union of opposites, is certainly a *challenge*: it is also a *burden,* a cross willingly accepted for a wider ecumenical good, the reconciliation of the Catholic and Evangelical traditions, the healing of the sixteenth-century divisions. This, in my view, has never been expressed better than by Archbishop Michael Ramsey in his classic work *The Gospel and the Catholic Church*:

> While the Anglican Church is vindicated by its place in history, with a strikingly balanced witness to Gospel and Church and sound learning, its greater vindication lies in its pointing through its own history to something of which it is a fragment. Its credentials are its incompleteness, with the tension and the travail in its soul. It is clumsy and untidy, it baffles neatness and logic. For it is sent not to commend itself as 'the best type of Christianity', but by its very brokenness to point to the universal Church wherein all have died.[9]

The vision, I believe, has received considerable justification in the work of ARCIC. The aim behind both the *Final Report* of ARCIC I and the continuing work of ARCIC II – the aim which has inspired their method – has been neither compromise ('the invisible equatorial line') nor the capitulation of one side to the other but the reconciliation of two theologies of which it had been believed – mistakenly and too hastily – that they were in formal contradiction the one of the other. Let me briefly give two examples.

---

8 As quoted by Yves Congar in *Chrétiens en dialogue* (Paris, 1964), p. 102. *Cf.* Y. M.-J. Congar, *Dialogue between Christians: Catholic Contributions to Ecumenism,* tr. P. Loretz (London: Geoffrey Chapman, 1966), p. 128.

9 A. M. Ramsey, *The Gospel and the Catholic Church* (London: Longmans, 1936), p. 220.

In its work on Eucharistic Doctrine ARCIC I saw the traditional Catholic doctrine of the objectivity of the real presence
of Christ and the Protestant insistence on the necessity of faith
and of reception in faith not as contradictory but as complementary. The presence of Christ in the Eucharist is both *for* the
believer and *with* him.

In its work on Authority in the Church ARCIC I saw the
need to hold together in the future the Catholic conviction of
the necessary role of a primatial ministry of unity and communion in the universal Church, exercised by the Bishop of
Rome, and the Anglican vision of a *dispersed* authority, i.e., of
an authority that cannot be attributed to a single source. 'We
have already been able to agree', states the *Final Report* in the
last paragraph of its last statement, 'that conciliarity and primacy are complementary. We can now together affirm that the
Church needs both a multiple, dispersed authority, with which
all God's people are actively involved, and also a universal primate
as servant and focus of visible unity in truth and love.'[10]

II

I move on now to the present critical situation for Anglicans in
the hope that what I have said so far will furnish a background
for understanding the nature of the crisis. Everybody knows that
Anglicanism is in crisis and that this crisis has arisen over the ordination of women first to the priesthood and, more recently, to the
episcopate. Not everybody, however, finds it easy to understand
why this particular crisis more than others – for example, the radical questioning by some of the virginal conception of Our Lord
and of his bodily resurrection – should threaten (or, indeed, be
beginning already to operate) the disintegration of Anglicanism.

It is not enough to say that the issue is highly emotive, nor that
it involves fundamental questions about *Creation* (the complementarity of man and woman in the purposes of God), about
Redemption (the significance of the maleness of the incarnate

---

10 Anglican–Roman Catholic International Commission, *The Final Report*
(London: CTS/SPCK, 1982), pp. 97–8: 'Authority in the Church II', para. 33.

Lord) and about the *Priesthood*. It is not enough even to say that it has introduced new divisions within the ranks both of Evangelical and Catholic Anglicans. It has also to be recognized that because differences of theology in the past have been largely contained within the unity of a common structure, a fundamental change of practice can be more threatening to unity than changes in theology. A male bishop or priest may be judged to hold heretical beliefs but this has not affected recognition of the validity of his sacramental acts. Above all – and this is a point I would want to underline with particular emphasis – this controversy has revealed a weakness in Anglican ecclesiology, long latent but now at last uncovered and laid bare. The Common Declaration of the Pope and the Archbishop of Canterbury of 2nd October 1989 acknowledged the vital importance of ecclesiology when it affirmed that the 'differences of faith' on this issue 'reflect important ecclesiological differences'. This weakness is a dual one; a weakness in ecclesiological *thinking* and a weakness in ecclesiological *structure*.

Weakness in Ecclesiological Thinking

The weakness in ecclesiological thinking relates to the doctrine of development. At a great ecumenical service held in Westminster Cathedral in January this year to mark the twenty-fifth anniversary of the Second Vatican Council's Decree on Ecumenism, Robert Runcie, Archbishop of Canterbury, paid tribute in this centenary year of his death to John Henry Newman:

> Many have dubbed Vatican II 'Newman's Council'. If that is the case, much must be linked with his pioneering work on the development of doctrine. I am clear that our own Church and most other communions have not yet begun to think seriously about this. Apostolic faith is our gift. But how is it appropriately expressed?[11]

---

11 R. A. K. Runcie, Address at an Ecumenical Service to mark the 25th anniversary of the Second Vatican Council's Decree on Ecumenism at Westminster Cathedral on 22 January 1990, *Living Stones*, 4, no. 1 (March 1990), 9–12, at p. 11.

I find this a very significant admission. But if our own church, as our Archbishop has said, has not yet begun to *think* seriously about the doctrine of development (and I totally agree with this analysis), has it not already begun to act upon it? For one thing surely is indisputable; if there is any theological justification for the ordination of women, it can only be found through some theology of the development of doctrine.

The classical Anglican appeal, we have seen, is to the threefold criterion of Scripture, Tradition and Reason – not to three independent and equal sources but to Scripture as primary source, and to Tradition and Reason (the continuous life of the Church and our attempt to understand it and to see how the total sum of human knowledge helps us to interpret it) as ways of making Scripture contemporary with us. Though the classical Anglican divines would appeal to 'the Scriptures interpreted by the perpetual practice of God's Church'[12] – to quote one of them (Herbert Thorndike) – in fact their appeal to Tradition gave a privileged place only to the first four centuries. In case of doubt as to the legitimacy of some doctrine or practice, if it could be found neither in Scripture nor in the period of the first four Councils and if it seemed that scriptural and patristic testimony was not merely silent but hostile, then the question was settled. The classical Anglicans used the same word 'novelists'[13] to describe, not the writers of fiction, but those whom they accused of innovating, whether these innovations came from Papist or Puritan, from Rome or Geneva. Though they hoped for the future possibility of General Councils of the Church there was no real urgency about it. The Church of England as a pure reformed part of the One Catholic Church of Christ

12 H. Thorndike, *Just Weights and Measures* (1662), in *The Theological Works of Herbert Thorndike*, vol. 5 (Oxford, John Henry Parker, 1854), pp. 69–298 at p. 248.

13 E.g. James I, *A Premonition to All Most Mighty Monarchs, Kings, Free Princes, and States of Christendom* (1609), quoted by P. E. More and F. L. Cross, *Anglicanism: The Thought and Practice of the Church of England, Illustrated from the Religious Literature of the Seventeenth Century* (London: SPCK, 1951), pp. 3–8 at p. 4.

had all that was necessary to defend, teach and reaffirm with solid authority what had already been decided by ecumenical authority.

The emergence of a doctrine of development and its gradual reception throughout the Christian world give ground for allowing that new questions may arise which must be answered not simply by an appeal to the past for an answer already given, but by an attempt to discern how from what is already given a new answer to a new problem can still be faithfully rooted in Scripture and Tradition. But a doctrine of development also necessarily brings into play an enlarged role for the Church's *magisterium*, that is to say for a way in which the Church can discern between true and false developments. It also presents a new problem for a church or a communion of churches which does not claim, and never has claimed, that she is the Catholic Church or that the Catholic Church *subsists* in her alone. Defending and reaffirming what is already defined poses no problem but discerning new developments does. If some matters can be authoritatively settled by each province and others ideally need to be referred to the whole Communion, there must in principle be some, more fundamental, which cannot even be resolved by the whole Communion acting together.

Weakness in Ecclesiological Structure

It is here that we come to our second problem for Anglicans, a weakness in ecclesiological structure.

It is an undeniable fact of history that the twenty-seven provinces of the Anglican Communion are strictly autonomous. Lambeth Conferences of all the bishops of the Communion have met more or less every ten years since 1867 but the Conference is neither a synod nor a Council and its resolutions neither decrees nor canons; they have no force of law until or unless they are given legislative shape and force by the synods of the constituent churches. In 1867 many bishops (especially in Canada and South Africa) hoped that the Conference would acquire synodical authority, but there were others so hostile that, like the Archbishop of York of the time, they refused to attend or, like the Dean of Westminster of the time, they closed the doors of the Abbey against the visitors. In fact the particular relationship of the Established Church of England with the Crown would have frustrated any attempt to give the Conference any real legislative authority. Nevertheless the fact that between the 1968 and 1978 conferences some churches of the Anglican Communion proceeded to ordain women as priests – as they were legally entitled to do – and that for the first time in the history of the Anglican Communion some of its ordained ministers were not recognized or accorded the right to minister as priests in some of the other provinces provoked a real crisis, increased when it became clear before the 1988 Conference that some churches were determined to advance to the ordination of women to the episcopate. The agonized question began to be asked: 'What credibility can be given to a communion of churches which possesses no structure of authority strong enough to maintain it in unity and which in the last resort seems impotent in the face of the threat of its own disintegration?'[14]

Lambeth 1988 was in many ways a paradox. In a masterly opening address on 'The Nature of the Unity We Seek' the Archbishop of Canterbury, Dr Robert Runcie, made a strong appeal for a move from independence to interdependence; it is significant that one of the reasons he adduced for 'looking critically at the notion of the absolute independence of Provinces' was the nature of our ecumenical dialogues with worldwide communions which 'require decision and action at more than provincial level'.[15] But that appeal came too early or too late.

14 R. T. Greenacre: 'Causa Nostra Agitur? An Anglican Response', in H. Legrand, J. Manzanares and A. García y García (eds), The Nature and Future of Episcopal Conferences: The Jurist, 48 (Washington D.C.: Catholic University of America, 1988), pp. 384–96 at p. 394.

15 The Truth Shall Make You Free: The Lambeth Conference 1988 (London: Church House Publishing, 1988), p. 15.

Resolution 001, concerned with the Ordination of Women to the Episcopate, confirmed and underlined the principle of provincial autonomy. The Anglican Communion itself, though it had massively approved the ARCIC dialogue, was powerless to act as a communion to decide the issue of the ordination of women. This led one of Anglicanism's greatest, most loyal and most experienced friends, Fr Jean Tillard OP (a member of both ARCIC I and ARCIC II) in a powerful article in the Belgian review *Irénikon* (republished in English in the booklet *Lost in the Fog?*) to conclude with great sadness:

> At the moment when it seemed that the dossier of *Apostolicae curae* could be settled we have to open the dossier of Lambeth 88. Can I be allowed to say, on the basis of a certain experience of ecumenical questions, that the Lambeth 88 dossier will be more difficult than that of *Apostolicae curae*?[16]

It has to be admitted that what distressed so many friendly observers, especially from the Roman Catholic, Eastern Orthodox and Oriental Orthodox Churches, was not just the fact that the ordination of women to the episcopate was now clearly going to take place but the fact that the Anglican Communion could not act as an ecclesial body with any real supranational authority; it was this second revelation that seemed to put a serious question mark against all dialogues at the international level between Anglicans and other Christians. The question other churches can no longer avoid asking is precisely what kind of ecclesial consistency the Anglican Communion has and what authority it has to implement any apparent agreement at the international level.

In this situation what options are open to the Anglican Communion? Will it try – even at this late stage – to go into reverse and move from independence to interdependence? Will its own

---

16 J.-M. R. Tillard and R. T. Greenacre, *Lost in the Fog?: The Lesson for Ecumenism of Lambeth 1988* (Church Union Theological Committee Occasional Paper No. 3, London: CLA, 1983), p. 4. *Cf.* p. 64 above.

clearly perceived lack of any effective ministry of unity and communion able to prevent communion within and between its member churches from being impaired or destroyed lead Anglicans to re-evaluate more positively the role of the Petrine ministry? Or will each province go its own way and therefore its own way ecumenically, with some provinces entering into union with churches of the Reformation and others examining the possibility of some kind of union with Rome?

A few weeks ago my secretary had a problem with a manuscript of mine: there was a word there she did not recognize and could not find in the dictionary; the word was 'subsidiarity'. By a curious coincidence I came across it on Monday on my way out to Rome in the political pages of *The Independent*: British politicians were arguing about it in the context of the relationship between national autonomy and supranational authority in the European Economic Community. In fact the concept seems to have developed between the two world wars in a social and political context, largely as a protest against the increasing encroachment of the totalitarian state upon the rights of the individual, the family, local and regional communities. It asserts that decisions ought to be taken at the appropriate level, that is to say as low down as possible. From the time of Pius XII, and with increased momentum from the Second Vatican Council, it became clear that the Roman Catholic Church could not preach the principle of subsidiarity to civil society without also applying it to her own life. Here too the rights of the individual, of the family, of the local community, of the diocese and (more recently and more controversially) of the national Episcopal Conference cannot simply be subsumed into the centralized authority of the See of Rome.[17]

More recently, in 1988, the Bishop of Birmingham, Mark Santer,[18] Anglican Co-Chairman of ARCIC II, has reminded

---

17 *Cf.* J. A. Komonchak: 'Subsidiarity in the Church: The State of the Question' in Legrand, Manzanares and García y García (eds), *The Nature and Future of Episcopal Conferences*, pp. 298–349.

18 Mark Santer was Principal of Westcott House, Cambridge (1973–81), Bishop of Kensington (1981–87) and Bishop of Birmingham (1987–2002).

Anglicans of the complementary lesson of the principle of sub-sidiarity; that questions which concern the maintenance of unity at a supranational level should not be decided at a lower level:

> Communion between churches, at whatever level, requires more than instruments of consultation. Guidance is at times required, and also decision. Organs of authority must be present, recognized in common as able to speak for and to the churches. In good times, things will be easy – but when there is severe dispute within or between churches, the test of an authority's acceptance as an instrument of communion is whether its judgements and decisions are accepted even when unwelcome.

As Anglicans we are accustomed (even if some of the machinery is rusty) to such organs of authoritative deci-sion-making at diocesan and provincial level, and have (to my mind) uttered a lot of pious hot air to justify this fact. Before we too readily accept the notion that it is *ipso facto* not Anglican to have organs of authority between national churches, let us not forget that the Thirty-nine Articles do not repudiate the notion of general councils, and that in point of fact the Jacobean Church of England sent delegates to an inter-church council, namely, the Synod of Dort. The modern doctrine of provincial autonomy is rather a child of the nineteenth century – the fruit of a strange union between English bishops and lawyers who were scared stiff of any-thing which might appear to impugn the Royal Supremacy over the Church of England and the gut reaction of ex-colonials who did not wish to submit to a religious form of a colonialism which their grandfathers had repudiated at a political level.

'In thinking of the exercise of authority, it is always important to remember the principle of *subsidiarity*. If we are concerned with communion in a diocese, only diocesan authority is involved; if with communion at a provincial level, only provincial authority. But if we are talking about those elements in the life of the churches whereby they are able to recognize one another as sharing one communion of faith and life, then some joint organs of authority, recognized by all, are required.[19]

At the beginning of 1988 I was privileged to attend as the Anglican observer (nominated, in fact, by the Bishop of Birmingham) a colloquium at Salamanca organized by a number of Catholic universities on 'The Nature and Future of Episcopal Conferences'. Diversity in unity, it was clear, is not only a problem for Anglicans; it poses many crucial questions to the Roman Catholic Church also. I hope you will forgive me if I draw this lecture to a conclusion by quoting the concluding paragraph of my own intervention at that colloquium:

> I have the impression that we are dealing here with two communions which have trajectories going in reverse directions. Both believe in unity in diversity. It seems to me that the Roman Catholic Church is at this moment aware of the need to put greater stress on diversity and to find more adequate structures for this; the Anglican Communion finds – at least I hope it does – that it needs at this moment to put a greater stress on unity and to find more adequate structures for it. In this situation we need above all to listen to each other, to try to benefit from each other's experience (from the failures as well as the successes), and to avoid whatever might make this mutual enrichment impossible.[20]

The final word, however, should surely point to a more positive conception of the relationship between diversity and unity, expressed not so much in terms of a problem to be resolved

---

19 M. Santer, 'The Way Forward', in J. Draper (ed.), *Communion and Episcopacy: Essays to Mark the Centenary of the Chicago-Lambeth Quadrilateral* (Oxford: Ripon College Cuddesdon, 1988), pp. 107–14 at p. 109.

20 Greenacre, *'Causa Nostra Agitur? An Anglican Response'*, in Legrand, Manzanares and García y García (eds), *The Nature and Future of Episcopal Conferences*, p. 396.

as in terms of a vision to be realized. In the address which he gave during Vespers at San Gregorio Magno in Rome on 30 September 1989 the Archbishop of Canterbury quoted words spoken by Pope John Paul II during his visit to Sweden: 'Unity not only embraces diversity but is verified in diversity.'[21]

---

21 John Paul II, Homily in Stockholm, 8 June 1989: http://www.vatican.va/ holy_father/john_paul_ii/homilies/1989/documents/hf_jp-ii_hom_19890608_ stockholm_en.html: '"The miracle of Pentecost" shows the Church in her unity: a unity that embraces diversity and that is verified in diversity'; Robert Runcie, 'Our Commitment to the Search for Unity' (address during Vespers in Rome, 30 September 1989), in *One in Hope: Documents of the Visit of the Most Reverend Robert Runcie, Archbishop of Canterbury, to His Holiness John Paul II, Bishop of Rome, 29 September 1989 to 2 October 1989* (London: CHP/CTS, 1989), pp. 16–21 at p. 20.

9

Hope for Catholic Anglicans:
An Unpublished Letter to *The Times*
(23 February 1991)

Introduction (2013)

On 23 February 1991 the Roman Catholic journalist Clifford Longley wrote an article in *The Times*,[1] occasioned by the appointment of the leading Anglo-Catholic Dr David Hope as Bishop of London, in which he argued that 'Anglo-Catholicism in the Church of England, at least as a distinct movement, is sick, even dying'. Paradoxically, he suggested, it had become 'a sect for Anglicans who believe (or whose forefathers believed) that Anglicanism must not become a sect'.

He criticized its attitude to ecclesiology and its response to the movement for women's ordination as follows:

> To most Anglicans, the continuity of the Church of England with the medieval English Church is a matter of historical fact. And it is symbolic of this attitude that to the Church of England, 'ecclesiology' meant the study of old church buildings. Only in the present generation has the Roman Catholic use of the term for study of the theology of the church as a supernatural institution been adopted by Anglicans, who traditionally preferred bricks and mortar to metaphysics.

---

1 C. Longley, 'The Greatest of These is Hope', *The Times*, 23 February 1991.

Even so, Anglo-Catholics have yet to take spiritual ecclesiology seriously.

As well as offering veiled threats and mysterious totems to resist women's ordination, the Anglo-Catholic party has relied on the inertia of tradition, on the residual misogyny of many conservative churchmen (sometimes allied to concealed homosexuality), on block votes in the General Synod, and on the threat to the prospect of unity with the Roman Catholic Church. None of these arguments or prejudices amounts to a serious case against ordaining women. Nor do they amount to a coherent strategy for an Anglo-Catholic future. If they lose the battle, they will be down or out, if they win they will be unbearable, and with nothing further to contribute.

In response, Roger Greenacre wrote the following letter to the Editor, but it was not published.

Hope for Catholic Anglicans

From the Chancellor of Chichester Cathedral

Sir,
The Catholic Movement in the Church of England is quite evidently going through a very difficult patch at the moment, but Clifford Longley's obituary notice (23 February) is not only premature; it suffers from internal contradiction.

There are, among both proponents and opponents of the present legislation for the ordination of women to the priesthood in the Church of England, many whose reactions are instinctive, unreflective and visceral. In the present climate it is not easy for a more nuanced position to be heard, let alone understood.

Yet the more theologically reflective among the Catholic Anglican opponents of the legislation perceive – and always have perceived – the heart and core of their case to lie in the ecclesiological argument (and, incidentally, only a minority of present-day Anglicans familiar with the rare word 'ecclesiology' associate it with church buildings). They are saying, in effect, that even if the theological case for the admission of women to the priesthood is seen to be convincing, a radical change in the essential structures of Catholic Order is not something that any or all of the provinces of the Anglican Communion can legitimately make alone. This is not quite the same argument as that which points to 'the threat to the prospect of unity with the Roman Catholic Church'; it is basically about what kind of church we are, about the identity and authority of Anglicanism, about what Anglicans can do on their own (and often supremely well) and what, on the other hand, they have no right to do on their own.

Catholic Anglicans may be perceived by others as 'sectarian'; Christians of every tradition must not be surprised to see their convictions misunderstood and caricatured. But, as Clifford Longley himself recognizes, the Catholic Movement in the Church of England grew out of a conviction that was the precise opposite of sectarianism, 'the conviction that the Church of England was part of Catholic Christendom' and needed to realize this more consciously and to act upon it more consistently.

It is that very same conviction which still animates the mainstream of the Catholic Movement in the Church of England. It has forced the movement into the position of a threatened minority, and under that pressure some of its reactions may indeed appear negative and sectarian. Nevertheless, to claim the name Catholic at all is to affirm that, however deep are our loyalty to and our love for the Church of England, we owe a prior loyalty to something even greater and more universal. If there are sectarians in the Church of England, Clifford Longley must look elsewhere for them.

Yours faithfully,
ROGER GREENACRE

10

Subsidiarity (February 1992)

The General Synod's debate in February 1992 on the Standing Committee's report on the reference of the draft women priests legislation to the dioceses marked the beginning of a period in which campaigning on both sides intensified. Roger's contribution to the campaign against the legislation was this article, which was published that month in the Newsletter of the Association for Apostolic Ministry.[1]

The history of language is fascinating. There are words that are so new that it is difficult to find them even in the best dictionaries, but which – almost overnight – seem to acquire so much importance that one is driven to wonder how we managed so long without them. Such a word is *subsidiarity*, a word of growing importance in both the political and ecclesiastical worlds but still unknown perhaps to most people.

The word and the concept which it defines were first articulated in Germany between the two world wars and were given expression for the first time in a formal and authoritative document by Pope Pius XI in his encyclical of 1931 on social questions, *Quadragesimo anno*. It is held to be a principle of natural law and was first called into service to defend the rights of the human person, the family and other smaller and local communities in the face of the absolute claims of Fascist and Marxist totalitarian states. It presupposes some kind of

---

1 *AAMBIT* (Newsletter of the Association for Apostolic Ministry), 9 (February 1992). A lightly revised text was published as 'Subsidiarity in Church and State', in *Contemporary Review*, 260, issue 1517 (June 1992), 287–90.

hierarchical ordering of society, but, in order to counter the natural tendency of the larger unit to centralize all author-ity and power and so to deprive the smaller unit of any real autonomy, it posits the principle that just as smaller units exist to provide help (*subsidium*) to the human person in his search for self-realization, so the higher levels of authority exist to provide help and support for the smaller in their search for self-realization. The 'distribution of competencies' within the social and political reality must therefore begin with a 'presumption of competency' accorded to the smaller unit; it is intervention at a higher level that has always to justify itself. It requires *posi-tively* that all communities encourage individuals to exercise their own self-responsibility and that larger communities do the same for smaller ones; it requires *negatively* that commu-nities must not deprive individuals or smaller communities of their right to self-responsibility.[2]

It is easy to see how important this principle is as the key to the distribution of competencies between individuals and com-munities and between smaller and larger communities in the political sphere and how it is increasingly being used by people like Jacques Delors[3] (himself a practising Roman Catholic, deeply influenced by Catholic social teaching) as the ideological tool for the regulation of the European Community. It has important – increasingly important – implications for the work-ing out of relationships within federal states and within new Commonwealths, for example in Yugoslavia and in the former Soviet Union.

In the Roman Catholic Church the principle of subsidiar-ity first enunciated by Pius XI was further championed as a key principle of civil society by his successors; the first indi-cation that it also applies *within* the Church was given by

---

2 J. A. Komonchak, 'Subsidiarity in the Church: The State of the Question', in H. Legrand, J. Manzanares and A. García y García (eds), *The Nature and Future of Episcopal Conferences: The Jurist*, 48 (Washington D.C.: Catholic University of America, 1988), pp. 298–349 at p. 302.

3 Jacques Delors (b. 1925) was President of the European Commission from 1985–94.

Pius XII in 1946. It was more widely invoked at the time of the Second Vatican Council, both with regard to the rights of the laity and with regard to the role of bishops in the government of their dioceses and in the newly emerging episcopal conferences. At this time it began to be realized more clearly that the Church would face a severe credibility problem if it failed to apply to its own structures a principle it was so insistently urging upon civil society. It is still very much a live issue in the Roman Catholic Church with regard to the continuing controversy about the authority of episcopal conferences (under attack both from the Curia and from some individual bishops) and about the rights of particular dioceses, particularly those which had managed to hold on to the right of capitular election.

It could be argued that in the Church of England the principle of subsidiarity, although nowhere formally acknowledged, is implicitly assumed in the ordering of synodical government, with the guaranteed rights of parochial church councils and deanery and diocesan synods acting as a restraint on the authority of General Synod, and with the authority of the bishop in his diocese subject also to similar restraints. It might also be concluded after a rather superficial acquaintance with the concept that Anglicans have an exemplary record in honouring the principle – whether they know that they are doing so or (as is more likely) not!

It must be remembered, however, that the principle of subsidiarity works in two directions. Historically speaking, both in the political and ecclesial spheres, it has been called into service as a necessary amber light to warn centralized autocracies not to intervene in matters which can properly be resolved at a lower rung of the hierarchical ladder. But it can and should sometimes be called into service as a no less necessary amber light to warn local communities not to make authoritative decisions which affect the well-being of the wider community and could threaten the ability of such local communities to continue to live together harmoniously in a wider community. Catholic

Anglicans in England should welcome the growing authority of the European Community and its courts, if for no other reason than that it effectively gives the lie to the Erastian myth and heresy of absolute national sovereignty claimed by Henry VIII in the triumphalist language of the Act in Restraint of Appeals of 1533. If a supranational authority now begins to make itself felt in secular affairs, should it not also do so in the affairs of the Church? If the Queen's 'supreme governorship' of the State is no longer exempt 'from the intermeddling of any exterior person or persons', what about her 'supreme governorship' of the Church?

It needs perhaps to be added that the crucial failure of the 1988 Lambeth Conference lay not in its refusal to give an authoritative ruling on the question of the ordination of women to the priesthood and the episcopate, but in the reason given for that refusal. It could (and should) have appealed to the need for consensus among the churches and, more particularly, within the universal episcopate of the Church Catholic (not the same thing as the episcopate of the Anglican Communion); instead it left each autonomous province to resolve the question for itself.

The doctrine of absolute and sovereign 'provincial autonomy' formally accepted for the Anglican Communion at the Lambeth Conference of 1988 is in its way as much a threat to the principle of subsidiarity as Vatican 'interference' in the life of local churches in the Roman Catholic Church seems to be. The carefully graded relationship worked out for synodical government in the Church of England comes to an abrupt summit in the General Synod (and in the Parliament of the United Kingdom); there is no provision for any supranational authority with any binding force whether within the Anglican Communion or beyond it. To the question 'What matters of faith and order must the Church of England declare itself incompetent to resolve unilaterally?' there is no authoritative answer, and so the further question as to where and by whom such matters can be resolved barely arises. The challenging question put so sharply a little while before Lambeth 1988 by the late Canon

G. V. Bennett in his *Crockford's* Preface[4] as to what credibility can be accorded to a communion of churches which possesses no structure of authority strong enough to maintain it in unity and to preserve it from the threat of its own disintegration has still received no answer; the failure of the Anglican Communion to act credibly as an ecclesial reality no doubt goes a long way in explaining the cool reception given by Rome to the *Final Report* of ARCIC.[5]

The *Final Report* of ARCIC I does not invoke the principle of subsidiarity by name, but in its treatment of the need for both conciliar and primatial authority in the Church at every level – including the universal – and in its vision of the ministry of the Bishop of Rome in maintaining and safeguarding unity and communion between the local churches at the universal level it is surely acknowledging the principle's validity. It is, moreover, difficult to deny that a question such as the ordination of women to the priesthood and the episcopate is a matter which affects vitally the ability of local churches to recognize one another and to recognize one another's sacraments and ordained ministries, and so affects unity and communion at the universal level.

Among the bishops of the Church of England no one has shewn a more perceptive awareness of this issue than Mark Santer, Bishop of Birmingham and Co-Chairman of ARCIC II. He is personally in favour of the ordination of women to the priesthood, but it is difficult to see how he (and any who share his thinking) can vote for Final Approval of the present legislation in General Synod when he can write:

<hr />

4 G. V. Bennett, 'Preface to Crockford's Clerical Directory 1987/88', in G. V. Bennett, *To the Church of England*, ed. G. Rowell (Worthing: Churchman Publishing, 1988), pp. 189–228. Dr Bennett (1929–87) was a Fellow of New College, Oxford (1959–87) and represented the clergy of the University of Oxford on the General Synod of the Church of England (1975–87).

5 The Official Roman Catholic Response to the *Final Report* of ARCIC I (1991), in C. Hill and E. J. Yarnold (eds), *Anglicans and Roman Catholics: The Search for Unity* (London: SPCK/CTS, 1994), pp. 156–66.

Communion between churches, at whatever level, requires more than instruments of consultation. Guidance is at times required, and also decision. Organs of authority must be present, recognized in common as able to speak for and to the churches. In good times, things will be easy – but when there is severe dispute within or between churches, the test of an authority's acceptance as an instrument of communion is whether its judgements and decisions are accepted even when unwelcome.

As Anglicans we are accustomed (even if some of the machinery is rusty) to such organs of authoritative decision-making at diocesan and provincial level, and have (to my mind) uttered a lot of pious hot air to justify this fact. Before we too readily accept the notion that it is *ipso facto* not Anglican to have organs of authority between national churches, let us not forget that the Thirty-nine Articles do not repudiate the notion of general councils, and that in point of fact the Jacobean Church of England sent delegates to an inter-church council, namely, the Synod of Dort. The modern doctrine of provincial autonomy is rather a child of the nineteenth century – the fruit of a strange union between English bishops and lawyers who were scared stiff of anything which might appear to impugn the Royal Supremacy over the Church of England and the gut reaction of ex-colonials who did not wish to submit to a religious form of a colonialism which their grandfathers had repudiated at a political level.

In thinking of the exercise of authority, it is always important to remember the principle of *subsidiarity*. If we are concerned with communion in a diocese, only diocesan authority is involved; if with communion at a provincial level, only provincial authority. But if we are talking about those elements in the life of the churches whereby they are able to recognize one another as sharing one communion of faith and life, then some joint organs of authority, recognized by all, are required.[6]

---

6 M. Santer, 'The Way Forward', in J. Draper (ed.), *Communion and Episcopacy: Essays to Mark the Centenary of the Chicago-Lambeth Quadrilateral* (Oxford: Ripon College Cuddesdon, 1988), pp. 107–14 at p. 109.

Many of us are accused of lack of candour when we consistently argue that though agnostic or even marginally in favour of the proponents on the strictly theological question as to whether women can become priests, we cannot recognize that any province of the Anglican Communion (let alone – as it is now a distinct possibility in Australia – any diocese) or indeed even the Anglican Communion as a whole (if it had the will and the authority so to decide) possesses the necessary authority to resolve this question. In fact we are only guilty of holding firmly to a clear and coherent ecclesiological principle, the principle of subsidiarity. Incidentally, it is by reference to that same principle that we have to reject some of the compromise plans now being put forward by certain members of the House of Bishops of the Church of England. The credibility of the appeal of our church to be a part of the Catholic Church depends upon the recognition of the necessary deference of the part to the whole, as well as the necessary respect of the whole for the part. If for the Church of England 'provincial autonomy' means not according full, final, universal and ecumenical authority to any organ of the Anglican Communion, well and good. If it means not recognizing any authority at all outside 'this realm of England', then in all honesty we should relinquish the claim to catholicity.

11

An Amber Light:
Speech in the Convocation of
Canterbury (July 1992)

On 11 July 1992 the Convocations of Canterbury and York and the House of Laity met in York to consider motions approving the legislation for the ordination of women to the priesthood. Roger spoke as follows in the debate in the Lower House of the Convocation of Canterbury.[1]

Some of you on holiday in France may have stopped at a small level crossing and seen a notice saying 'Attention, un train peut cacher un autre' – 'Look out, one train can hide another'. We need that warning today, for it is too often assumed that the issue before us is a single, simple and straightforward question – should women be admitted to the priesthood? – requiring a single, simple and straightforward answer.

My plea this morning is more particularly addressed to those like the last speaker, those who have been convinced by the theological arguments that women ought to be admitted to the priesthood and perhaps even to the episcopate. There may be many whose initial red light of categorical 'No' turned to amber and then, without further pause, turned to green. I would

---

1 *The Chronicle of Convocation, Being a Record of the Proceedings of the Convocation of Canterbury: Nova Convocatio Elizabetha Secunda Regnante*, Session II: Saturday, 11 July 1992, Lower House, pp. 33–6. The speech was also published in the *The Messenger of the Catholic League*, 248 (October 1992), pp. 2–5.

argue that there is a strong case for remaining with amber, with an amber light that may stay that way for some time before, eventually – I do not know which way it will turn – it will either go back to red or on to green. For the second train, partly hidden by the first and therefore some of us have not really noticed it, is the perhaps even more radical and fundamental question: what kind of a church is the Church of England? What, if any, are the limits of its internal authority? Even this question is not single, simple or straightforward. It is rather a cluster of questions, ranging round the whole ecumenical and ecclesiological area of the relationship of the Church of England, indeed the churches of the Anglican Communion, to the Church universal.

The so-called 'ecumenical argument', the appeal for an ecumenical consensus of the Christian world and, more particularly on this issue, of those churches with whom we claim to share the historic threefold ministry, has seemed to many to have been killed stone dead by the official response of the Roman Catholic Church at the end of last year to the *Final Report* of ARCIC. To many people the whole ARCIC process seems to have come to an end. For some, this is a matter of rejoicing, or at least for relief, for others, a cause of profound sorrow. Rome, so they say, has said 'No' to the whole process, in particular any hope for the near future of a formal mutual recognition and reconciliation of ordained ministries has been extinguished, both by Rome's rather negative judgement of the Statement on Ministry and Ordination and by the fact that many provinces of the Anglican Communion have already gone ahead and ordained women as priest and bishop. Rome's dialogue is with the Anglican Communion, they will remind us, not with the Church of England. So what can be gained at this stage by the Church of England saying 'No'? Those who still hope it might have a dramatic effect on this dialogue are trying to close the stable door after the horse has already bolted.

This is a serious argument and calls for a serious reply. In the time at our disposal this morning I can only begin to sketch an outline of a reply, in four points.

Firstly, on this issue we do not look to Rome alone but also to the ancient churches of the East. The solemn appeals we have received in the last few years, and appeals directed more particularly to the Church of England, from the Ecumenical Patriarch, from the Patriarch of Moscow, and Pope Shenouda of Alexandria have been at least as forceful as any made by the Bishop of Rome.

Secondly, it needs to be said very loudly, very clearly, that the Roman response to ARCIC is not totally negative. It is notoriously a mixed document and it does not need very great skill in order to detect which passages in it come from which source. But it does include a strong commitment to the continuation of this dialogue; a commitment repeated and reaffirmed at the time of our Archbishop's visit to Rome in May. Our own response to the Response needs to be robustly critical, but at least we do finally have a text on which to build an agenda for future work and at least we can take heart from the fact that some of the most devastating critiques of that Response have come from Roman Catholic theologians – even from fairly conservative theologians, professors at the Gregorian University for example.

Thirdly, those of us who are committed supporters of this process – seen from both sides until recently as the most hopeful of all the bilateral dialogues in which we were engaged because it seemed to go the furthest and to have the most chance of success – are not expecting quick results. We admit that *Apostolicae Curae* will probably still be unrepealed in 1996, 100 years after its promulgation. Progress was being made. Some years ago (in 1985) a letter from Cardinal Willebrands suggested a way through, and a small working party of the English Anglican–Roman Catholic Committee, on which I had the honour to serve with the then Principal of Trinity College, Bristol[2] – not now a member of this House – reported that

---

2 Dr George Carey (b. 1935), now Lord Carey of Clifton, was Principal of Trinity College, Bristol (1982–88), Bishop of Bath and Wells (1988–91) and Archbishop of Canterbury (1991–2002).

the way was now open for a mutual recognition of the ordination rites of the two churches. That report and those conclusions have been put on hold by recent developments, but only on hold, I believe; they are not now simply to be sent to the shredder.[3]

Lastly, there is a longer-term objective to the dialogue and to all our dialogues. Anglicans need to say more than that ecumenical consensus is desirable. They need to say that on some issues it is a necessary precondition for change; they need to say it in the name of ecclesiological principle and in obedience to a strong and ancient strand in Anglican self-understanding which has tried to make us sharply aware that we do *not* constitute the whole Church but only a fragment of the *Una Sancta*, and that a fragment of a divided church does not have the right to act as if it were the whole. If that imposes limits on our freedom of action – yes, there is an Anglican freedom, a proper Anglican freedom, but there are also limits to that freedom – those limits we can experience sometimes as intensely painful and frustrating, then at least that could serve to convert our search for visible unity from a low priority aspiration into a matter of the most intense urgency.

In this continuing dialogue there are three areas of ecclesiology that need urgently to be explored. We need to remember that both Archbishop Runcie and Archbishop Carey, in the joint statements or communiqués that followed their visits to Rome, agreed to a continuing dialogue on the question of the ordination of women in the context of ecclesiology.

Of these three issues, the first is the whole vast field of the nature of the development of doctrine and the way in which the Church comes to a common mind in discerning between true and false development. I will not say any more on that except to commend to you a paper which you will all have received, by Canon John Halliburton, *Can the Church Change?*[4]

---

3 For further details, see pp. 121–3 below.

4 J. Halliburton, *Can the Church Change? The Ordination of Women to the Priesthood and the Development of Doctrine: A New Enquiry* (London: Church Literature Association, 1992).

Secondly, there is the question of the role, if any, of a universal primacy. The case for such a primacy and a vision of what in the future it might look like were set before us in the *Final Report* of ARCIC, in the texts on Authority. If there is a place for it and if it has a role – and non-Roman Catholics are by no means the only ones to find the present exercise of that primacy totally unacceptable – then, *at the very least*, it will be a ministry of vigilance at the service of the maintenance of unity and *koinonia* at the universal level. Surely that which so vitally affects the ability of local churches to recognize each other's ministry and each other's sacraments (or, rather, to recognize in each other the one universal ministry and the universal sacraments of the Church – for both are of their very nature universal and not the possession of particular churches[5]) does require a decision, a consensus, at the universal level? To decide otherwise is tantamount to formal rejection of the *Final Report* of ARCIC on the part of the Church of England.

Lastly there is the question of subsidiarity, which has now become a fashionable concept but not necessarily one that is correctly understood – misunderstood even in the letter pages of yesterday's *Independent* by Bishop Patrick Rodger.[6] It is about taking decisions at the appropriate level, a lower one if at all possible but, where more than local considerations are involved, then a higher one. If this legislation fails to get through the General Synod in November, then perhaps the Synod needs to give serious attention to the proper limits of its own authority; not just the legal limits, where it has to defer to Parliament and to the Crown, but to the theological and ecclesiological limits, particularly in the area of the Lambeth Quadrilateral, in the areas of Scripture, the Creeds, the sacraments and the ministry. Before we legislate for change we need to answer the question and the challenge: by what authority do we do these things?

---

5 Roger added this phrase when he published the text in the *Messenger of the Catholic League*.

6 Patrick Rodger (1920–2002) was Bishop of Manchester (1970–78) and Bishop of Oxford (1978–86).

PART 3

After

12

The Advent Hope:
A Sermon on the First Sunday of Advent
(November 1992)

Roger's response to the Synod's approval of the women priests legislation was to begin work on his 'Epistola ad Romanos', which was published in March 1993 and forms Chapter 13 of this book. As a residentiary canon, he did not preach every Sunday, so it was on 29 November that he preached his first sermon after the General Synod vote. Preaching to his regular cathedral congregation rather than in an Anglo-Catholic church, Roger could only allude in half a sentence to 'the near certainty of profound breaches of communion within the Church of England', not even naming the reason. But his theme – the light of the Christian hope burning in the darkness – gave a strong indication of his feelings.

✠ Soli Deo Gloria: Advent I (29.xi.92): Chichester Cathedral at 11.00

One of the best-known and best-loved passages in the New Testament (and for that reason I had better quote it in the Authorized Version) is St Paul's hymn to charity in the thirteenth chapter of his First Letter to the Corinthians. It ends like this: 'And now abideth faith, hope, charity, these three: but the greatest of these is charity.' These are the three great virtues, the three Theological Virtues as they are sometimes called.

I think we could agree to call hope the Cinderella of the three – provided, of course, that we do not think of faith and charity as ugly sisters! Is it not the case that for every ten sermons on faith or love, we would be lucky to hear one on hope? Yet if Advent is about anything at all, it is about hope. The mood of its liturgy, its hymns, its prayers and its Scripture readings is one of yearning, expectation, vigilance and hope. Now the one thing we can say straightaway about hope is that if we already possessed in fullness everything we long for, there would be no more place for hope. So in Bishop Christopher Wordsworth's hymn, inspired by 1 Corinthians 13, we sing:

Faith will vanish into sight;
Hope be emptied in delight;
Love in heaven will shine more bright;
Therefore give us love.[1]

One saying of last week that we are in no danger of forgetting is one made by the Queen: '1992 is not a year on which I shall look back with undiluted pleasure . . . it has turned out to be an *Annus Horribilis*.'[2] And I think that struck an echo in so many hearts not just because of sympathy for her plight, but because it mirrored the experience of so many of us.

The first paragraph of the Editorial in yesterday's *Independent* had this to say:

It is difficult to recall a time when so many British institutions were challenged as fundamentally as they are at present. The monarchy, the Church of England, the BBC, the Bank of England, the City, the judiciary, schools, local government, Parliament . . . the list can be extended. Many of these institutions are being required not merely to adapt to new conditions or adopt new procedures, but also to answer

---

1 From 'Gracious Spirit, Holy Ghost' (*New English Hymnal*, no. 367).
2 Speaking at the Guildhall, London, on 24 November 1992, the fortieth anniversary of her Accession to the Throne.

basic questions about the purposes they serve and, in some cases, the reasons for their existence. It is as if some tremor were running through British life, rocking its oldest structures to their foundations and threatening to bring some of them down unless they are rapidly altered.

The crisis is not confined to institutions, even less to British institutions. It is difficult to think of a time when one has known so many people (close friends and members of our own families among them) who are out of work or desperately worried by the imminent threat of redundancy and financial ruin. And then, for one like myself who has a deep love of France and knows a number of French farmers (you will be less surprised to know I have French friends than to know I have friends who are farmers), it has been almost as painful to watch on TV the spectacle of French farmers burning the Union Flag as to contemplate the near certainty of profound breaches of communion within the Church of England. The European Community is in crisis, the world community too – as the euphoria over the collapse of the Soviet-dominated communist empire gives way to sober awareness of the deadly potency of racial, religious and nationalist bitterness in Germany and Eastern Europe and of the frustrated impotence of the United Nations both in the former republics of Yugoslavia and in Somalia.

Against so sombre a background – but one of which Our Lord warns us in today's Gospel[3] ('on earth nations will stand helpless, not knowing which way to turn from the roar and surge of the sea; men will faint in terror at the thought of all that is coming upon the world') – how can we make sense of the promise which Our Lord also gives to us in the same passage: 'Hold your heads high, because your liberation is nigh'; and how can we, with the Prophet, 'break forth together in shouts of triumph'?[4]

---

3 Luke 21.25–33.
4 Isaiah 52.9.

Hope must not be confused with optimism: optimism is simply the cheerful conviction (congenial to certain temperaments and impervious to the weight of evidence to the contrary) that everything is going to get progressively better, that everything is going to be all right for us. Hope is in the first place something very fundamental not only to specifically Christian or even religious existence, but to all human existence; it is the presupposition behind the will to live, the refusal of despair and suicide, the determination to go on because somehow, despite all the evidence to the contrary, we need to gamble on finding purpose and meaning in living, and we need to struggle to be faithful to our ideals and our convictions. This is hope of an unfocused kind – though often lived with a kind of desperate courage which puts Christians to shame. As Christians, we have a clear focus for our hope in the Coming of Christ – the one 'who comes in the Name of the Lord' – and in his death and resurrection, which spell out for us the ultimate triumph of good and the present availability of that victory to us here and now in our continuing combat with the powers of evil, sin, darkness and alienation. It is the hope of a victory which is ultimately *beyond* history, but which it is still our duty to try to realize *in* history. History is not a graph of smooth and gradual progress (the word 'progress' is not part of the vocabulary of the Gospel), but in every age, through the faithful witness of men and women inspired by the Spirit, some irreversible victories are won, although they are also accompanied by terrible retreats and defeats. Nothing of the work of grace is ever in vain, ever wasted.

What is true of human history as a whole must also be true of our own personal histories. They are full of falls from grace, of defeats and humiliations and failures; but they are also marked by grace and by the power of hope – seen not only, not primarily even, as a looking *forward* to the future, but as a looking *up* to God, a self-emptying openness and receptiveness to God's will for us today and tomorrow and his power to achieve it.

The Advent Hope does not invite us to take refuge in illusion, in naive optimism or in flight from reality. It invites us to look to God with confidence, to the God who raised Jesus from the dead and whose same power of bringing new life out of death is at work in our lives. We must realize soberly that things may have to get worse for us before they get definitively better, but there is no doubt about the final outcome. Perhaps the Candle of Hope burns brightest when the darkness is at its most pervasive.

A great English mystic of the fourteenth century, the author of *The Cloud of Unknowing*, had these words of comfort for those whose prayer seemed only an experience of darkness:

> Cease not, therefore, but travail therein till thou feel list. For at the first time when thou dost it, thou findest but a darkness, and as it were a cloud of unknowing, thou knowest not what, saving that thou feelest in thy will a naked intent unto God. This darkness and this cloud . . . is betwixt thee and thy God, and hindereth thee so that thou mayest neither see him clearly by light of understanding in thy reason nor feel him in sweetness of love in thine affection. And therefore shape thee to bide in this darkness as long as thou mayest . . . For if ever thou shalt see him or feel him . . . it must always be in this cloud and in this darkness. And if thou wilt busily travail as I bid thee, I trust in his mercy that thou shalt come thereto.[5]

And surely something of this same experience and in this same teaching shines through that famous hymn which John Henry Newman penned in a moment of darkness and doubt:

> Lead, kindly light, amid the encircling gloom,
>   Lead thou me on;
> The night is dark, and I am far from home,
>   Lead thou me on.
> Keep thou my feet; I do not ask to see
> The distant scene; one step enough for me.

---

5 *The Cloud of Unknowing*, ch. 3.

13

Epistola ad Romanos: An Open Letter to some Roman Catholic Friends (March 1993)

This Open Letter was published in the Jesuit periodical The Month,[1] *which introduced it as follows:*

> *Last November's decision of the General Synod to ordain women to the priesthood has raised critical questions for Anglo-Catholics in the Church of England. In this open letter, Canon Roger Greenacre expresses the dilemma: 'to stay in the Church of England and to leave the Church of England both seem almost equally painful and equally impossible choices at the moment'.*

As I sit down to begin this letter in the week after the vote in the General Synod of the Church of England to enable women to be ordained to the priesthood, I have no clear idea as to what conclusions, if any, I shall reach. One of my reasons for writing, therefore, is the need to clarify my own thinking; another is gratitude for the affection, sympathy, understanding and discretion you have shown me; yet another the realization that so many of your fellow Roman Catholics have little understanding of, and consequently little sympathy with, the

---

1 *The Month*, 254, no. 1503 (second new series, vol. 26, no. 3): March 1993, pp. 88–96.

painful dilemma in which so many catholic-minded Anglicans now find themselves.

The particular course of my own ministry over the last thirty years at least has given me the feeling of living in real and growing, although, of course, imperfect, communion with the Roman Catholic Church. In 1961 I went to the Catholic University of Louvain for a year on an Anglican scholarship to study in the *schola maior* of theology. It was an exciting year, for it was the one immediately preceding the opening of the Second Vatican Council and some of our professors – men like Moeller, Thils, Aubert and Philips – were directly involved in work on the preparatory *schemata*, while at the monastery of Chevetogne I was able to meet many of the pioneers of Roman Catholic ecumenism both among the monks and among the visitors and the participants in the annual Ecumenical Weeks. On my return to England I found myself working with the Archbishop of Canterbury's staff at Lambeth in following closely, particularly in the French language press, reports from the Council. I also found myself in contact with English Roman Catholic ecumenists and writing for journals like *Old Palace* and *The Clergy Review* (to which I contributed a regular 'Letter from an Anglican').

I was also at the time involved in a number of conferences, including one in Holland hosted by Mgr Willebrands,[2] at which Hans Küng read a paper and which led to a number of meetings (at Mirfield and at Chevetogne) between members of the Catholic Conference on Ecumenical questions, of which Willebrands was then chairman, and a group of catholic-minded members of the Orthodox, Anglican, Old Catholic and Protestant Churches associated together in an organization called ILAFO (The International League for Apostolic Faith and Order).

In 1965 I was appointed Chaplain of St George's, Paris, and was privileged to exercise a pastoral and ecumenical ministry

---

2 Cardinal Johannes (Jan) Willebrands went on to serve as President of the Pontifical Council for Promoting Christian Unity from 1969 to 1989.

there for ten years. It fell to me, for example, to accompany Michael Ramsey, Archbishop of Canterbury, during part of three separate visits he paid to France; to give lectures and lead seminars at the newly founded Institut Superieur d'Etudes Oecumeniques of the Institut Catholique de Paris, and to act as Anglican Co-Chairman of the Anglican–Roman Catholic Joint Working Group in France, created in 1969.[3] I also found a spiritual home at the Abbey of Notre Dame du Bec, a link which has grown stronger since I left France – especially when I was admitted as an oblate in 1982.

Since my move to Chichester in 1975 I have been deeply involved in Anglican–Roman Catholic relations not only in this country but in continental Europe. It would be tedious to make a list of all these activities; they have included a lot of work contracted through my membership (since 1980) of the English Anglican–Roman Catholic Committee – such as my joint authorship of the Study Guide to the *Final Report* of ARCIC (1982) and papers read at Chevetogne and at the Catholic Universities of Milan, Salamanca and Lyon.

Convergence and Reconciliation

One conviction has dominated my involvement in all this activity, a conviction which was encouraged and confirmed by the work of ARCIC and the publication of its successive statements. It was that our two communions, after centuries of estrangement and bitter hostility, were now clearly set on a course of convergence and reconciliation which could surmount the remaining obstacles to full visible unity, and that both communions needed each other's insights, having so much to offer each other and so much to receive from each other. As the two Co-Chairmen of ARCIC I put it in their preface to the first statement on Authority in the Church:

---

3 The Joint Working Group later became known as the French Anglican–Roman Catholic Committee (French ARC).

The consensus we have reached, if it is to be accepted by our two communities, would have, we insist, important consequences. Common recognition of Roman primacy would bring changes not only to the Anglican Communion but also to the Roman Catholic Church. On both sides the readiness to learn, necessary to the achievement of such a wider *koinonia*, would demand humility and charity. The prospect should be met with faith, not fear. Communion with the see of Rome would bring to the churches of the Anglican Communion not only a wider *koinonia* but also a strengthening of the power to realize its traditional ideal of diversity in unity. Roman Catholics, on their side, would be enriched by the presence of a particular tradition of spirituality and scholarship, the lack of which has deprived the Roman Catholic Church of a precious element in the Christian heritage. The Roman Catholic Church has much to learn from the Anglican synodical tradition of involving the laity in the life and mission of the Church. We are convinced, therefore, that our degree of agreement, which argues for greater communion between our churches, can make a profound contribution to the witness of Christianity in our contemporary society.[4]

Between them, the Second Vatican Council and the ARCIC dialogue (one of its fruits) profoundly changed the attitude to Rome of a majority (surely) of catholic-minded Anglicans. Before the Council, a clear majority of Anglo-Catholics rejected Vatican I's definition of papal infallibility and universal primacy; only a tiny minority (the so-called 'Papalists') accepted it. After the Council and, more particularly, after the publication of *The Final Report* there has been a much larger group of what – for convenience – we could call 'ARCIC Anglicans' – people who have come to accept 'that

---

4 Anglican–Roman Catholic International Commission, *The Final Report* (London: CTS/SPCK, 1982), p. 50.

the maintenance of visible unity at the universal level includes the *episcope* of a universal primate' and that 'the primacy of the Bishop of Rome can be affirmed as part of God's design for the universal *koinonia*'.[5]

Catholic-minded Anglicans in this group have not felt under any individual obligation to come to terms with the claims of the Roman primacy, since they saw the two churches on a convergence course on this issue, with only a narrow gap of remaining disagreement spelt out in the second statement on Authority in the Church, and one which the Commission itself saw reasonable hope of bridging. Even the Lambeth Conference of 1988, in many ways so disastrous, was able in its response to the *Final Report* to welcome

> *Authority in the Church (I & II)* together with the *Elucidation*, as a firm basis for the direction and agenda of the continuing dialogue on authority and . . . to encourage ARCIC II to continue to explore the basis in Scripture and Tradition of the concept of a universal primacy, in conjunction with collegiality, as an instrument of unity, the character of such a primacy in practice, and to draw upon the experience of other Christian Churches in exercising primacy, collegiality and conciliarity.[6]

Anglican Betrayal

But what has happened now? Since the 1970s the movement for the ordination of women to the priesthood and the episcopate in the Anglican Communion has gathered momentum and encountered almost overwhelming success. Until this year one could speak of a real division among the member churches on this issue and also of the real possibility that this advance

---

5 *Final Report*, p. 76.
6 *The Truth Shall Make You Free: The Lambeth Conference 1988* (London: Church House Publishing, 1988), p. 211: Resolution 8, para. 3.

could be halted (at least for a time) in the Provinces of Canterbury and York. This is no longer the case, and very soon the Archbishop of Canterbury, the senior primate of the Anglican Communion and president of the Lambeth Conference, will be ordaining women to the priesthood. It is doubtful whether many other member churches will be able to resist this trend, and we can foresee a situation in which it will have become a distinguishing mark of Anglicanism that women are admitted to the priesthood and the episcopate. The Roman Catholic, Eastern Orthodox and Oriental Orthodox Churches would thus find themselves in dialogue no longer with a communion divided on this issue but with a communion that appears to be moving towards an almost unanimous and therefore, surely, official mind on the subject.

Will not the divisions have hardened to a point which, from a human point of view, is a point of no return? It is difficult to see therefore what is the future of the ARCIC process now. It is either dead or has been quietly relegated to the back burner. In terms of the original purpose as defined by Pope Paul VI and Archbishop Michael Ramsey in 1966, that is to say 'restoration of complete communion of faith and sacramental life' between our two churches,[7] it does indeed appear to be dead (for a long sleep in the tomb before resurrection); only if the original aims are watered down or rolled back to an indefinite future can the process be said to have much life in it still.

With regard to the ordination of women to the priesthood and the episcopate, it needs to be made abundantly clear that very few Catholic Anglicans are absolute 'impossibilists'. Our protest at unilateral action from our side will not be rendered invalid (though most people will have difficulty seizing this point) if at some future date the Roman Catholic and Eastern Churches come to accept the principle of women priests and women bishops and to act upon it. Our principal ground for opposition has always been located in our understanding of

---

7 Common Declaration by Pope Paul VI and the Archbishop of Canterbury, Rome, 24 March 1966: *Final Report*, pp. 116–17 at p. 117.

the nature of doctrinal authority in the Church. The Anglican claim to catholicity (fidelity to the whole and not just to a part) has thus been weakened or even forfeited by this innovation in two distinct ways.

A Departure

First, it has involved a radical departure from the classical Anglican appeal to Scripture and the Primitive Church – a departure which looks like an act of Anglican self-betrayal. To illustrate this, let me simply quote from a sermon preached by Dr Geoffrey Rowell, Fellow and Chaplain of Keble College, Oxford, at All Saints', Margaret Street, on 22 November:

> At the heart of Keble's concern was ecclesiology, the doctrine of the Church, its order, ministry and sacraments. His protest was not in favour of a novel doctrine but was grounded in the theological principles of the English Reformation, and in particular of its greatest theologian, Richard Hooker, whose works he was to edit. The Church of England was grounded on Scripture. It took as its guide to the interpretation of Scripture the ancient common traditions of the Church of the early centuries, from which it had received the pattern of Christian worship and the continuity of Christian ministry: bishops, priests and deacons. Anglicans had a liberty: they were required to receive nothing as of faith save what was required by Holy Scripture and the ancient common traditions.
>
> It has been one of the most major planks of Anglican apologetic against the Church of Rome that Rome has required acceptance, as being matters of faith, of doctrines and practices which have no sure grounding in Scripture or Tradition. The vote of the General Synod to permit the ordination of women to the priesthood was therefore historic. By implication the Church of England, through its constitutional organs of government, agreed to enact legislation

which can only be justified ecclesiologically as a development of doctrine. That in turn immediately raises the question of the authority of the Church of England so to act. We are told that this is a development of the tradition. No one reasonably doubts that this is a new thing nor that it is a disputed question. It may well be true that the changes in the position of women in society press particularly on the Church, but opinion polls have never been a sufficient ground for doctrinal change and development. If the Church of England claims authority to develop the tradition in this way we should be clear that it is claiming for the first time an authority to discern what is such a development of doctrine, where Scripture or tradition are either silent or may be cited against it. Anglican arguments against Roman developments are made null and void. And we might also add that there is rather more scriptural support for a Petrine office in the Church than there is for the ordination of women to the priesthood and episcopate.

Secondly, this innovation has involved a betrayal of the ecclesiology which was moving us on from the rather static position of classical Anglicanism and which was set out in the ARCIC Agreed Statements. For the *Final Report* saw clearly the need to hold in balance a respect for legitimate diversity and a degree of autonomy at the level of particular or local churches with a recognition of the necessity for authority at the universal level, both conciliar and primatial, in order to maintain and protect the unity and communion of such local churches with each other in the One, Holy, Catholic and Apostolic Church of Christ.

It must be abundantly clear that the ordination of women to the priesthood and, *a fortiori*, to the episcopate is a radical obstacle to the maintenance – let alone the restoration – of such unity and that, if it is nothing more, the universal ministry of the See of Rome must at least be able to act as a ministry of vigilance guarding against breaches in communion and able therefore to restrain particular local churches from action that would lead to such breaches. 'To decide otherwise', as

I argued in a speech on this subject to the Lower House of the Convocation of Canterbury in July, 'is tantamount to formal rejection of the *Final Report* of ARCIC by the Church of England.'[8] Can it be denied that the vote of General Synod in November constitutes precisely such a formal – even though implicit – rejection?

Roman Betrayal

Of course, if I am to be fair and honest, I have to say that the ARCIC process has been betrayed by both sides and that holding up before our fellow Anglicans the ARCIC vision has not been made easy by recent developments in the Roman Catholic Church. In 1559 Nicholas Heath, the last Archbishop of York to be in communion with the Holy See, pleaded desperately in the House of Lords against a second breach with Rome, acknowledging with a kind of bitter honesty that his case had not been made easier by the then reigning Pope, Paul IV, who had proved himself, as he acknowledged, 'a very austere stern father unto us'. It is neither my desire nor my intention to indulge in any personal criticism of the present Pope,[9] whose courage and integrity I – in company with many fellow-Anglicans – greatly admire: I admit too that many of us began to discern a certain reaction to what we had welcomed as Vatican II's vision of collegiality and greater openness in the Church beginning to set in even during the pontificate of Paul VI, the Pope who with Archbishop Michael Ramsey had given such admirable stimulus and encouragement to the ARCIC process.

At that time there were clear signs from Rome of a determination to put the brake on moves towards giving practical application to the Council's teaching on the collegiality of the episcopate by limiting the effective authority both of the Synod of Bishops and of episcopal conferences; these signs have become even clearer during the present pontificate. For it

---

8 For the full speech, see Chapter 11 of this volume.
9 Pope John Paul II.

must not be imagined that what has given concern to sympathetic Anglican observers of recent developments in the Roman Catholic Church is confined to the narrow sphere of Anglican–Roman Catholic dialogue; the concern (the deep anxiety even) has found its focus in Rome's return to curial centralization, characterized by a distrust of local initiatives, a disregard for the voice of the local church in the choice of its bishop, and a severe curtailment of the limits of theological pluralism. It is in this wider context that one must set the long and frustrating wait for the official Roman Response to the *Final Report* of ARCIC I and what we perceived as the discouraging and negative tone of that Response when it was finally published in December 1991.

A Lengthy Process

Let us remind ourselves briefly of the process of response, evaluation and reception to which both communions committed themselves after the publication of the *Final Report* in 1982, set out notably in the Joint Declaration of Pope John Paul II and Archbishop Robert Runcie signed in Canterbury later in the same year.

The Declaration paid tribute to the work of ARCIC I and announced that the next stage would involve the evaluation of its *Final Report* by authoritative procedures in each Communion and the setting up of a new Commission, ARCIC II, with a triple brief. Firstly it had to examine, 'especially in the light of our respective judgements on The Final Report' the outstanding doctrinal differences between the two communions; secondly, it had to 'study all that hinders the mutual recognition of the ministries of our Communions'; thirdly, it had to recommend what practical steps would be necessary for 'the restoration of full communion'.[10] The work of evaluating

---

10 Common Declaration of Pope John Paul II and the Archbishop of Canterbury: www.vatican.va/roman_curia/pontifical_councils/chrstuni/angl-comm-docs/rc_pc_chrstuni_doc_19820529_jp-ii-runcie_en.html

the *Final Report* began soon after, but it was impossible for ARCIC II to tackle properly its first objective until the repeatedly delayed official response of the Roman Catholic Church was finally published in 1991, nine and a half years after the Canterbury Declaration.

In the meantime all the churches of the Anglican Communion and all the episcopal conferences of the Roman Catholic Church had been asked to respond to the *Final Report* and to answer the same fundamental question, as to whether they judged the teaching of its Agreed Statements to be 'consonant in substance' with the faith of Anglicans or with 'the faith of the Catholic Church'. The response of the various churches of the Anglican Communion was available to the Lambeth Conference of 1988; after scrutinizing the exhaustive series of consultations – often, as in England, held at deanery, diocesan and national or provincial level, the Conference was able to affirm quite categorically that the statements on Eucharistic Doctrine and Ministry and Ordination, together with their Elucidations, were indeed 'consonant in substance with the faith of Anglicans'. Its more guarded welcome to the Authority statements (in which, of course, ARCIC had not claimed to have reached substantial agreement) I have already quoted.[11]

At the same time the episcopal conferences of the Roman Catholic Church were studying and evaluating the *Final Report*, and three of their responses were published in English or in English translation: that from England and Wales[12] and those from the United States and France.[13] A subsequent directive from the Holy See laid down that no further responses were to be released to the press! All these responses, though pressing for further clarification on some issues, were entirely positive in tone, notably that from the bishops in England and Wales. It is important to emphasize this and to try to destroy

---

11 See p. 114 above.

12 *One in Christ*, 21 (1985), 167–80; C. Hill and E. J. Yarnold (eds), *Anglicans and Roman Catholics: The Search for Unity* (London: SPCK/CTS, 1994), pp. 94–110.

13 *One in Christ*, 21 (1985), pp. 320–48.

EPISTOLA AD ROMANOS

the dangerous falsehood that all 'Continental' Catholics are pro-Anglican while all those in this country are anti-Anglican.

One of the more astonishing features of Rome's 'definitive response' of 1991, so devastatingly analysed and criticized by such responsible and respected Roman Catholic theologians as Fr Francis Sullivan SJ of the Gregorian University, was its failure even to mention, let alone quote, any of the responses received from episcopal conferences. Its most distinguishing feature, however, was its inability (or refusal) to allow any difference between the concepts of 'consonance' and 'identity'. For in its penultimate paragraph it remarked:

It must, however, be remembered that the Roman Catholic Church was asked to give a clear answer to the question: are the agreements contained in this Report *consonant* with the faith of the Catholic Church? What was asked for was not a simple evaluation of an ecumenical study, but an official response as to the *identity* of the various statements with the faith of the Church.[14]

So Fr Sullivan can conclude that for the Vatican it cannot be said of any Agreed Statement that substantial agreement has been reached unless it fully corresponds to Catholic doctrine and indeed to the official language in which it has been formulated.[15]

Recognition of Ministries

This conclusion is of crucial importance when we turn to the second objective set out by Pope and Archbishop in their Canterbury Declaration. On this issue – the recognition of ministries – Cardinal Willebrands addressed an important letter to the Co-Chairmen of ARCIC II in 1985, in which he outlined a

14 Hill and Yarnold (eds), *Anglicans and Roman Catholics: The Search for Unity*, pp. 156–66 at p. 166 (italics mine).

15 F. A. Sullivan: 'The Vatican Response to ARCIC I, *One in Christ*', 28 (1992), pp. 223–31; Hill and Yarnold (eds), *Anglicans and Roman Catholics: The Search for Unity*, pp. 298–308 at p. 305.

possible new way forward through the *impasse* created by Leo XIII's Bull of 1896, *Apostolicae Curae*, condemning Anglican Orders as null and void. It is important to note that at that date a number of churches of the Anglican Communion were already ordaining women to the priesthood, though not yet to the episcopate; nevertheless, the Cardinal evidently did not consider this as inhibiting a new approach to the reconciliation of ministries and to a re-evaluation by Rome of the question of Anglican Orders.

He began by emphasizing that this re-examination could not take place in isolation or as a purely historical study but only as an integral part of the whole process of reconciliation between the two communions. He then identified Leo XIII's fundamental objection to the Ordinal as being located in the total theological context of the Anglican Reformation and in particular in its defective teaching on Eucharist and priesthood. The theological context within Anglicanism could be judged to have changed, he argued, in the light of the *Final Report*'s Agreed Statements on the Eucharist and on Ministry and Ordination and the judgement, then hopefully awaited, of both communions that they professed on these two questions 'the same faith concerning essential matters where doctrine admits no difference'. In that case the texts of the ordination rites of the Anglican Communion (both the 1662 Ordinal and the more modern rites) could now be read in a new context and with a new basis for interpretation. In calling for a new consideration of these ordination rites, the Cardinal made it clear that 'such a study would be concerned with the rites in themselves, prescinding at this stage from the question of the continuity of the apostolic succession of the ordaining bishop'.[16]

As a result of this letter and the enthusiastic reply of the Co-Chairmen of ARCIC II, the English Anglican Roman-Catholic Committee (English ARC) was asked to set up a small sub-group

---

16 For the text of the Cardinal's letter and the Co-Chairmen's reply see *One in Christ*, 22 (1986), pp. 199–204 and *Anglican Orders: A New Context* (London: CTS Do 574, 1986).

to study the ordination rites of both communions, limiting its examination of Anglican rites to those in use in England: the Ordinals of 1662 and of *The Alternative Service Book 1980*. That group consisted of Fr Edward Yarnold SJ and Sister Cecily Boulding OP from the Roman Catholic side and Canon Hugh Wybrew (later replaced by Dr George Carey) and myself from the Anglican side; it produced a Short Answer in 1986 and a Full Assessment in February 1987. With some reservation occasioned by the lack of any explicit prayer for the conferring of the Holy Spirit in the ordination of deacons in the 1662 rite and with the clear proviso that the Agreed Statements in the *Final Report* would first need to be positively endorsed, it was agreed both that the Roman Catholic Church should find no difficulty in judging the Anglican ordination rites to be perfectly adequate and also that both communions could recognize in each other's ordination rites the same fundamental faith as to the nature of ordination. The report was accepted by English ARC and thereafter transmitted to ARCIC II; it then encountered nothing but the most profound silence.

The reason for this silence became unambiguously clear only in 1991, with the publication of Rome's Response to the *Final Report*. In denying that substantial agreement had been reached on Eucharistic Doctrine and on Ministry and Ordination it effectively denied the existence of the new context necessary for any re-evaluation of Anglican Orders. To be fair, it must be added that after the Lambeth Conference of 1988 the Anglican churches in the USA and New Zealand proceeded to consecrate women to the episcopate, a course which Rome could not but regard as making a grave situation even graver. One of you warned us of this at the time and wrote:

The question of the ordination of women to the episcopate is more serious than that of their ordination to the presbyterate. For in the Church the bishop is both the person who assures the link with the apostolic community, and also the one who manifests unity with the universal body of those who exercise oversight in the Churches. In him, communion is formally brought into play.[17]

So, in my speech to the Canterbury Convocation in July I referred to 'recent developments on both sides which had put the dossier on the re-evaluation of Anglican Orders 'on hold'. I argued then that it had 'not been sent to the shredder', but I could not now repeat that assertion with any confidence.

Many Roman Catholics feel that Anglicans have what can only be described as an obsession with the question of the validity of our Orders. However, it was Cardinal Willebrands in his letter of July 1985 who said that of the many issues involved in the study of the mutual recognition of ordained ministries, 'the most fundamental and deeply felt issue relates to the judgment of the Roman Catholic Church upon the validity of Anglican ordinations'.[18] All I want to say about the question at this point is to express the difficulty we have been confronting in recent months and years when faced with the challenge – put sometimes as a serious question and sometimes as a taunt: 'Why worry about Rome's refusal to recognize women priests when it refuses even to recognize our *male* priests?' You and I know that there is an answer to that challenge; that there was a possible way out of the *impasse* over *Apostolicae Curae*, but that the recognition of women priests and of priests, male and female, ordained by women bishops posed problems of a quite different and more fundamental nature. It has not, however, been an easy answer to make.

I have said earlier that holding up before our fellow Anglicans the ARCIC vision has not been made easy by recent developments in the Roman Catholic Church. I have written at some length of the hardening of what might be called the official line, but alongside that there has been an increasingly

---

17 J.-M. R. Tillard, 'The Lesson for Ecumenism of Lambeth 1988', in J.-M. R. Tillard and R. T. Greenacre (eds), *Lost in the Fog?: The Lesson for Ecumenism of Lambeth 1988* (Church Union Theological Committee Occasional Paper No. 3, London: CLA, 1983), pp. 1–6 at pp. 3–4.

18 *Anglican Orders: A New Context*, p. 4.

vociferous lobby within the Roman Catholic Church, especially in English-speaking countries, for the ordination of women to the priesthood. This, of course, has taken place in a different ecclesiological context (with the expectation of a decision at the universal level), but the proponents of women priests in the Church of England have been able in debate to draw attention to this fact and to quote from the Roman Catholic theologians and other writers who argue in favour of women priests. Some of these latter have indeed been urging Anglicans to 'pioneer' the ordination of women to the priesthood on the grounds that this will make it easier for their own church to follow suit, a course of reasoning which I find neither very convincing nor very responsible. But meanwhile the Catholic Anglican plea for ecumenical consensus and moral unanimity on this issue, rather than a series of unilateral decisions at local level made despite strong minority opposition, has been ground out of existence between the upper millstone of the hardliners in Rome and the lower millstone of the Roman Catholic radicals.

Discerning the Way Forward

Those of us for whom the ARCIC process has provided a basis for our ecclesiology, together with a *raison d'être* for the positive vocation of Anglicanism in the working out of a renewed and reunited catholicism and a set of priorities for ecumenical work, now face the destruction of that vision and the urgent need to find a *terra firma* on which to stand. The nightmare image that has most haunted me since 11 November is that of standing with one foot on one raft and the other on another as those two rafts seemed to be moving forward together and realizing with a shock that they were now moving apart and that unless I jumped firmly and decisively on to one of the two rafts I was going to fall into the water and be drowned. Even so one hesitates, for to *stay* in the Church of England and to *leave* the Church of England both seem almost equally painful and equally impossible choices at the moment.

To decide to stay in the Church of England once the Canons have been promulged and women begin to be ordained to the priesthood would itself involve a further choice. To accept the legislation (with whatever private reservations) and to agree to live and work with it would require us to adopt a radically new ecclesiology from that on which we have operated up till now. I do not think that those within the Church of England who support the legislation while affirming that they remain within the catholic tradition have as yet seriously addressed this challenge and, although I do not anticipate being able to accept their answer, I do look forward to seeing it articulated.

The other option is to organize resistance from within. 'It is not at all desirable', as one of you has written in a private letter, 'that Anglicans hostile to this decision should come over to the Roman Catholic Church; it is necessary that they stay within their church as an element of resistance and as a powerful ferment of rapprochement with the Roman Catholic Church.' The various proposed models of Alternative Episcopal Oversight represent a possible way forward, but they raise almost as many problems as they solve. At the ecclesiological level they raise the following question. If the Church of England has now seriously compromised its claim to catholicity by the action of its General Synod in November, is it possible with any real integrity to stay within that Church of England even if provided with a degree of structural separation?

A clean break and the formation of some kind of 'nonjuring' or 'continuing' Anglican Church might be logically more coherent, but for me – and, I think, for nearly all those who think as I do – it is not one we can bear to contemplate. Apart from the responsibility of creating further schisms, we would face the prospect of dying of claustrophobia in a single-issue church. I am personally in a fortunate position for the immediate future, since I share the theological and ecclesiological vision of my bishop, the Bishop of Chichester [Bishop Eric Kemp], and I know that in this he has the support of a clear majority of his clergy and a sizeable number of his lay people. He set out his position starkly and frankly in his statement to the Diocese after the General Synod's vote:

> The decision will raise for a number of people the question whether they can regard the Church of England as any longer a true part of the One, Holy, Catholic and Apostolic Church. They will have to consider carefully whether they can any longer remain in it. I feel this question deeply myself but I hope that all who are disturbed by the vote will take time to reflect before making any serious decision about their future.

For the time being therefore, until or unless I am persuaded to the contrary, it seems to be my clear and imperative duty to stay with my bishop and give him my fullest support. The study of church history, moreover, clearly demonstrates that synodical or conciliar decisions are rarely the final word in doctrinal controversy; they have often proved to be the beginning, rather than the end, of a long and painful period of conflict and debate.

The 'Roman Option'

To decide to leave the Church of England would mean, for me at least, to seek to become a Roman Catholic. Despite my very close sympathy with much in the theological tradition of Eastern Orthodoxy and my agreement with the ecclesiological thinking of a theologian like John (Zizioulas), Metropolitan of Pergamum, Orthodoxy (even in the form of some kind of Western Rite), does not seem to be for me a realistic option. The real challenge comes from Rome.

One of the difficulties in the so-called 'Roman Option' is the re-evaluation of the Anglican past (and of one's own Anglican past) which would be the inescapable consequence of such a step. I hope it would still be possible to affirm that, in the context of the sixteenth-century break-up of Western Christianity,

God had a particular and providential role for Anglicanism, in maintaining a certain necessary witness to a wholeness which was in danger of being lost in the extreme and bitter polarization of Reformation and Counter-Reformation, but that the time had now come for that witness to be made no longer in separation but within a renewed post-conciliar Roman Catholicism, within a Church now able to describe itself as ecclesia *semper reformanda*.

On this view Rome would need to value, and to find some permanent place for, this witness, not only where it corroborates its existing position but even – in some cases – where it challenges it. Of course, such a positive appreciation of the Anglican experience would not rule out the acknowledgement that the present crisis in Anglicanism (and it *could* so easily have been one of a number of other issues that brought it into the open) has revealed the Achilles' heel of Anglican ecclesiology – the inability of national or provincial churches to cope with issues of doctrinal development which require resolution at the universal level.

The question of a rite in the narrow sense of a particular liturgical tradition is secondary. I speak as one who has always valued and lived fully within the Anglican tradition and would miss it terribly, if separated from it. The Anglican rites cannot be seen simply as variants of the Roman rite in the same sense as the Ambrosian and Mozarabic rites. Of Anglicans it can be said with particular force that there can be no division between liturgy – *lex orandi* – and doctrine – *lex credendi*. In Anglicanism there has been a mutual interaction between theology and liturgy and the formation of a spirituality, *pietas anglicana*, which has been both profoundly theological and profoundly liturgical. As a certain kind of 'Uniatism' has shown only too clearly, it is no use preserving artificially an Eastern rite unless there is a genuinely Eastern character to the theology and spirituality which accompany it. If nothing of Anglicanism is to survive within the Roman Communion but some elements of its liturgy, then some of the most tragic and divisive features of 'Uniatism' will be perpetuated and the lessons of history ignored.

In a paper I gave at Chevetogne in September (and at that time I was reasonably confident that the measure would fail to get the necessary majority in General Synod) I was asked to reflect on the difficult problem of the Eastern Catholic Churches (the theme of the Colloquium) from the perspective of Dom Lambert Beauduin's famous Malines thesis of 1925, 'L'Eglise anglicane unie non absorbée', remembering that that formula, if not the details of the thesis, had been taken up and appropriated by Pope Paul VI in his address of welcome to Archbishop Donald Coggan in 1977. I argued that if Anglicanism represented what Cardinal Willebrands in an important sermon in Cambridge in 1970 could call a *typos*, a concrete realization of Christianity that was properly *sui generis*, such a *typos* 'could not be reduced to a tradition of liturgy, spirituality and practical organization without theological content' and that 'concessions limited to the domain of liturgy and discipline would constitute an absorption scarcely concealed by a skin deep make-up'.[19] But, of course, I was then discussing the union of Rome and Canterbury and not the situation of a small minority within the Church of England, even if joined by Anglicans from other parts of the Communion. If, therefore, like the Prophet Ezekiel, we are going to be called to prepare for ourselves 'an exile's baggage' and to go into exile (or, perhaps rather, as some of you would prefer me to say, to 'return home'), we need to ask ourselves and to ask you how much baggage we are to bring with us and what it should contain.

Mistaken Faith?

Some of you – and, indeed, many of my fellow-Anglicans – will perhaps tell me that I have been mistaken in putting so much faith in, and pinning so many hopes on, the ARCIC process. ARCIC is but one of the dialogues in which the Roman Catholic

---

19 R. T. Greenacre, 'La signification des Églises orientales catholiques au sein de la communion romaine dans la perspective de "l'Église anglicane unie non absorbée"', *Irénikon*, 65 (1992), pp. 339–51 at p. 350.

Church has been involved, even if it was seen at one time by so many on both sides and by many outside observers as the most promising of all the bilateral dialogues. Is it not faintly absurd – I can hear my critics saying – to conjure up an ideal, call it rather pompously 'the ARCIC ecclesiology' and make of it a *locus stantis aut cadentis ecclesiae*, a criterion of the authenticity of a church's claim to catholicity? Without capitulating altogether to my critics, I do have to admit the force of the argument that one does have to belong to a real, not an ideal, church and that there is no church in existence at the moment which exactly corresponds to the ARCIC ideal.

Many of us lost any remaining belief in the Anglican Communion (as such) when Lambeth 1988 surrendered to the theologically dubious notion of unfettered 'provincial autonomy' and accepted as part of the price to be paid the sad new reality of 'impaired communion' between the member churches. What we even then perceived as Rome's weakening commitment to ARCIC was clearly attributable in large measure to the evident inability of the Anglican Communion to act with any credibility as a communion of churches and so to be a real partner in an international dialogue. Now, since 11 November, we find ourselves hanging on by the skin of our teeth to the Church of England, a Church we have loved and tried to serve with loyalty and devotion; asking whether the decision taken on that day has not destroyed its 'immune system' and turned it into a liberal protestant sect unable any longer to fight off further attacks on what remains of its catholic faith and order. We have now to live with a faith like Abraham's, setting out in pilgrimage from the comfort of our exploded securities not knowing where we are to go.

Need for a Universal Primacy

For if Rome is the answer, Rome must be embraced because she is right and not simply because Canterbury is wrong. Before the 1960s, as I have already said, most Anglicans and not least those in the high-church tradition, were non-papalists, even anti-papalists. I would describe myself now as a semi-papalist, more conscious than ever of the need in the Church for a universal primacy – and, paradoxically perhaps, precisely because the question of women in the priesthood has made so much clearer to us both the inescapable reality of development in doctrine and the need for discernment at the universal level of such developments. For, as the Roman Catholic Bishops of England and Wales pointed out in their *Response to the Final Report of ARCIC I*, there is present in any doctrinal decision demanding our acceptance both the inner authority of the truth proclaimed (*id quod docetur*) and the authority of the person or persons who proclaim it (*a quo docetur*). With regard to the question of the ordination of women to the priesthood and the episcopate some of us cannot accept *id quod docetur* because we cannot accept the authority of the General Synod of a national church (*a quo docetur*) to resolve it.

At the same time, I am no less conscious that I still have real difficulties about accepting the dogmas of 1854, 1870 and 1950. These difficulties are not confined to Anglicans, though they were articulated by the Anglican members of ARCIC I in the second statement on Authority in the Church; they represent crucial and delicate items on the agendas of all the ecumenical dialogues in which the Roman Catholic Church is involved, and not least those with the Eastern and Oriental Orthodox Churches. I also have difficulties about a number of important but relatively secondary questions of current teaching and discipline, some of which many of you may share.

There has been a continuity of witness to the vital importance of the question of the Roman primacy and to the need of a positive response to it in the Anglican tradition (even if it has been at times the stillest of small voices) at least since Herbert Thorndike, one of the most learned and eirenic of the seventeenth-century Caroline Divines, whose prophetic words might have been written for our own time: 'I insist upon such a principle as may serve to reunite us with the Church of Rome: being well assured, that we never can be well reunited with ourselves otherwise; [and] that not only the Reformation but the common Christianity must needs be lost, in the divisions, which will never have an end otherwise.'[20] This witness became stronger with the Tractarians, particularly with Dr Pusey and his disciple, Lord Halifax, and stronger still since the publication of the *Final Report*; it was faithfully upheld by the previous Archbishop of Canterbury, Dr Runcie, who, in replying to a letter from the Pope in 1985, could read it 'as an expression of that responsibility in pastoral care for the unity of all God's people which is part of the office of the Bishop of Rome'[21] and who could use similar language at the 1988 Lambeth Conference and during his visit to Rome in September 1989. In the present crisis therefore I feel that I have seriously to address the challenge of the papal claims and to try to come to some kind of answer to it within the next year or two.

That is a challenge which each one of us has to face and to resolve individually. It does not inevitably follow, however, that any consequent action must be taken immediately and individually. For, together with the demands of personal integrity and personal conscience, we have also to take into consideration our solidarity with those who are caught up in the same dilemma as ourselves and those who look to us for theological, spiritual and pastoral guidance. This is particularly true for those of us who are ordained and serve in pastoral ministry. Catholic-minded Anglicans have quite properly a strong sense of corporate loyalty to the Tractarian Movement, which, they will hold, deserves to end not in piecemeal desertion, discord and disintegration but in a clear resolution that will give meaning to what was surely a noble and heroic venture of faith. 'In my end is my beginning.'

---

20 H. Thorndike, *A Discourse of the Forbearance or Penalties, which a Due Reformation Requires* (1670), in *The Theological Works of Herbert Thorndike*, vol. 5 (Oxford: J. H. Parker, 1854), pp. 381–488 at p. 404.

21 Letter of Robert Runcie, Archbishop of Canterbury, to Pope John Paul II, 11 December 1985, in *Women Priests: Obstacle to Unity? Documents and Correspondence, 1975–1986* (London: CTS Do 576, 1986), pp. 53–4 at p. 53.

Response by Fr Edward Yarnold (May 1993)

Fr Edward Yarnold SJ, one of the Roman Catholic friends to whom the Open Letter was addressed, responded with a Letter to the Editor in the May 1993 issue of The Month.[22] *He commented:*

It would be a tragedy if an Anglican 'Uniate' church in communion with Rome became an institutional ghetto which was cut off from its Anglican past without being integrated into the Roman Catholic life of the country. Not only would this be a sad fate for the ex-Anglicans themselves; it would also be a sad loss for the wider Roman Catholic community, which has lessons it could well learn from ex-Anglicans. One of these lessons, if you will allow me to say so, would be the very integrity and distinction of thought and expression which your own letter shows.

Fr Yarnold sought to respond to Roger's suggestion of 'betrayal' of the ARCIC process on the Roman Catholic side – first, by a 'return to curial centralization, characterized by a distrust of local initiatives, a disregard for the voice of the local Church in the choice of its bishop, and a severe curtailment of the limits of theological pluralism', and second by the 'discouraging and negative tone' of the Vatican's response to the Final Report. He summarized his comments thus:

I would not care to defend the brief that Rome has not contributed to the general discouragement. My point is simply that, paradoxically, what Rome has done is to attempt, over-cautiously perhaps, to put into practice two ARCIC principles: (1) the need for a universal authority to protect the unity of the Church; (2) the need for the two churches to satisfy themselves that the *Final Report* was in accordance

---

22 *The Month*, 254, no. 1505 (second new series, vol. 26, no. 5): May 1993, pp. 172–3.

with the faith of each. Perhaps in ecumenism excessive caution can be as harmful as excessive liberalism.

As to the effect of the ordination of women on the future of the dialogue, he concluded:

Although the ordination of women to the priesthood will clearly impede the search for unity between our two churches, it will not put an end to that search . . . Even if we cannot see how to get over or through the brick wall that we have come up against, at least we must make sure that we reach the wall, and explore it all along. There are plenty of opportunities for growing together in faith, worship and life, both locally and at the worldwide level, even though, for the moment at least, that great problem seems insoluble.

The ARCIC dialogue was now a very different enterprise from that on which the two churches had embarked a quarter of a century earlier.

Postscript (May 1993)

*Among Roger's papers are notes about his 'present position' that he made in preparation for a meeting with Fr Jean Tillard in Paris on 7 May 1993. He felt himself to be in a 'no man's land', but had concluded that he '**must** stay until or unless **must** move'. The outlook was 'no clearer'. He regarded the 'prospect for the Church of England' as 'ecclesiologically unbearable', but was conscious of the danger – pressed upon him by a French Roman Catholic bishop among others, of 'reinforcing Rome's centralism'. The choice before him could be summarized thus:*

Either change theology (ecclesiology) to stay in [the] same church or change church in order to remain faithful to certain theological/ecclesiological convictions.

With a different pen he added as an afterthought:

When I look at the present state of the CofE I think I have to become a Roman Catholic; when I look at the present state of the Roman Catholic Church I think I have to remain an Anglican!

14

The Place of Reception:
An Open Letter to the
Archbishop of York
(October 1993)

Introduction (2013)

In June 1993 the House of Bishops published a report containing its proposals for 'pastoral arrangements' for those opposed to the ordination of women to the priesthood. This contained a document entitled 'Bonds of Peace', which detailed the proposals,[1] and a draft Episcopal Ministry Act of Synod. The group which drafted the House's report had been chaired by the Archbishop of York, Dr John Habgood.[2]

In July the General Synod debated the report on a 'take note' motion, which enabled members of the Synod to comment on the proposals without a substantive vote being taken. Moving the motion, the Archbishop drew attention to a paper entitled

---

1 '"Bonds of Peace": Arrangements for Pastoral Care following the Ordination of Women to the Priesthood in the Church of England', in *Ordination of Women to the Priesthood: Pastoral Arrangements. Report by the House of Bishops* (GS 1074) (London: General Synod, 1993), pp. 5–15.

2 The Most Revd Dr John Habgood (b. 1927) was Bishop of Durham (1973–83) and then Archbishop of York (1983–95).

'Being in Communion',[3] which provided the theological background to the proposals. He explained:

> It was written by the working party that produced the report but has been published separately because the House of Bishops did not have the time to give it the detailed attention that a theological paper from the House normally requires. There was no dissent, though, from its general thrust. It is an examination of how the Church has understood the notion of communion and how communion in a restricted sense can still be possible even where there are fundamental disagreements.[4]

In August Roger sent Archbishop Habgood the draft of an Open Letter to him which he planned to offer to the *Church Times* for publication (since it referred to an article by the Archbishop about the proposals, which had appeared in the *Church Times* in July). The Archbishop replied that he found it 'a clear, charitable and helpful letter' and 'would endorse your interpretation of the process of reception as set out in its second half'. He added, 'I am sure your letter could spark off some useful discussion.'[5]

Roger accordingly sent the text to the editor of the *Church Times*, mentioning Archbishop Habgood's support for its publication. He received an enthusiastic response from the paper's senior reporter Betty Saunders, whose obituary by Andrew Brown characterized her as 'a convinced Anglo-Catholic, of the sort whose world was smashed when the General Synod decided to ordain women'.[6] However, the *Church Times*, founded in 1863 as an Anglo-Catholic newspaper, was now edited by a liberal protestant, John Whale.[7] Despite the fact

---

3 *Being in Communion* (GS Misc 418) (London: General Synod, 1993).

4 General Synod, *Report of Proceedings*, 13 July 1993, pp. 672–3.

5 J. Habgood to R. Greenacre, 7 September 1993.

6 R. Greenacre to J. Martin, 22 September 1993; obituary: Betty Saunders (1928–97), *Independent*, 9 April 1997.

7 John Whale (1931–2008) edited the *Church Times* from 1989–1995. He had previously been head of religious programmes at the BBC (1984–89).

that the article was about the House of Bishops' recently proposed Act of Synod, rather than the ordination of women as
such, Whale replied:

> Dear Canon Greenacre –
> It was good of you to let me see your open letter. It's not
> a journalistic form I care for, and on women priests as a
> theoretical question there is very little new left to say. For
> those reasons I have decided not to publish the piece, and
> I have told Bishopthorpe so. I'm sorry to be a source of
> disappointment.[8]

Roger accordingly offered the Open Letter to the *Church
of England Newspaper* – an evangelical publication which,
under its then editor John Martin, was reaching out to Anglo-
Catholics who were disaffected with the liberal establishment
that the *Church Times* had come to represent under John
Whale. The Open Letter was duly published in the *Church of
England Newspaper* on 8 October.[9]

The Place of Reception:
An Open Letter to the Archbishop of York

Your Grace,

There must be many catholic-minded Anglicans opposed to
the decision taken by General Synod in November who, in the
course of the last six months or so, have come to acknowledge
that they owe you a debt of gratitude.

You did not vote with us in November and have never made
any secret of your own conviction that women should be
ordained to the priesthood in the Church of England, but we
have come to respect your understanding of our position and

8 J. Whale to R. Greenacre, 16 September 1993.
9 *Church of England Newspaper*, 8 October 1993, p. 7.

your efforts to try to find a way in which, without compromise to our integrity, we can remain within the Church of England. Now, after the two meetings of the House of Bishops at Manchester this year and the debate in General Synod in July, it may help to move things forward a little if one of us tries to respond to your initiative and to put on record both the way in which things seem to us to have got worse and also the way in which there seems to be a possible fresh glimmer of hope.

The Relationship between Bishop and Diocese

Let me start with the bad news. The principal difficulty with the proposals put forward by the House of Bishops – a difficulty which will be felt on both sides of the debate – is that they seem fatally to undermine any coherent theology of the episcopate. This is a subject which those of us who served on the Archbishops' Group on the Episcopate (whose report, *Episcopal Ministry,* was published in 1990[10]) wrestled with over a number of years as we tried to set the particular issue of women in the episcopate in a wider theological and historical context.

It was clear to us, for example, that in the relationship between the bishop and his diocese – the local or particular church over which he presides – there is, or there should be, an unbreakable unity between his roles as Ruler, Pastor, Teacher and Eucharistic President, since each one of these functions is intimately related to all the others. This unity is nowhere more visibly manifested than when the bishop presides over a great diocesan liturgy; when he first exercises his ministry of leadership and teaching from his *cathedra* or chair and then, surrounded by his college of presbyters and assisted by his deacons, with the full and active participation of all the People of God, exercises his pastoral and sacramental ministry from the altar.

---

10 *Episcopal Ministry: The Report of the Archbishops' Group on the Episcopate* (London: Church House Publishing, 1990).

The painful situation in which the Church of England now finds itself will mean the impairment (some, more brutally, would say the destruction) of the organic and eucharistic unity of every diocese. This would apply both in dioceses where the bishop belongs to the 'majority' and will proceed to ordain women to the priesthood and also in dioceses where the bishop belongs to the 'minority' and will neither ordain women to the priesthood himself nor authorize his suffragans to do so.

In the first case the bishop will find that he has priests and congregations within his diocese who cannot regard him as being any longer their Pastor and Father-in-God and who cannot recognize all the members of his college of presbyters as priests; they will therefore be looking elsewhere, to another bishop, for pastoral care and sacramental ministrations. Provincial Episcopal Visitors are proposed for precisely this contingency.

In the second case, although the bishop will allow neither himself nor his suffragans to ordain or to license women priests, he will be obliged to 'acquiesce' in their being ordained or licensed by a commissary of the Archbishop of his Province.[11] Such women will be in a painfully anomalous situation; they will be in his diocese, but in what sense will they be of it, if they can never stand alongside their diocesan bishop at the same altar?

Since the bishop's ministry of oversight is one, it is unnatural to separate jurisdiction from pastoral and sacramental care. Theologically the two belong together and only make sense when exercised together; to divorce them is to surrender to theological incoherence of the most dubious kind.

---

11 As part of the agreement which resulted in the Episcopal Ministry Act of Synod (under which bishops opposed to the ordination of women to the priesthood would exercise functions in the dioceses of bishops who ordained women), the diocesan bishops who were opposed had indicated that they would not make use of their right under the Priests (Ordination of Women) Measure to prevent women from being ordained to the priesthood in their dioceses. They would not themselves commission bishops to ordain women to the priesthood in their dioceses, but would acquiesce in the Archbishop of the Province issuing such commissions.

In his Presidential Address to the General Synod in York on 10 July the Archbishop of Canterbury spoke of the determination of the House of Bishops 'to maintain the ecclesial integrity of the Church of England as a whole and of each diocese under the pastoral authority of its bishop'.[12] It puzzles many of us profoundly that the House of Bishops can imagine that it has succeeded in doing this. In their zeal to avoid overlapping or non-territorial jurisdictions the bishops have set their face against one anomaly, but have they not escaped from Scylla only to fall victims to Charybdis? The problem is that there is no longer any escape from the fragmentation of the structures of communion which hold us together, from what *The Observer* has called the 'Balkanization' of the Church of England.

The Theology of Reception

Let me now move to the (relatively) good news. This may possibly be found in the area of the theology of reception, which underlies the proposals of the House of Bishops and which has been helpfully spelt out by yourself.

The doctrine of reception has re-emerged as a key issue in contemporary ecumenical dialogue, for example in the ARCIC discussion of Authority in the Church. It clearly calls for deeper exploration and for sharper definition. Yet I take it that we would both understand by reception the idea that any formal ecclesial decision (whether conciliar, synodical or primatial) is only fully integrated into the faith and life of the Church if and when it has clearly been 'received' by a consensus of the whole People of God. In this process of reception, moreover, no fixed time limit can be imposed and no percentage quota can be used to determine that such a consensus has been achieved.

Many of us have argued for some years that it is a questionable novelty to extend this notion of reception to the testing of an innovation in the realm of sacramental praxis and ministerial order. Nevertheless, that is the situation in which the

---

12 General Synod, *Report of Proceedings*, 10 July 1993, p. 392.

Church of England now finds itself: those of us who opposed last November's decision need, therefore, to temper our continuing objection with an appreciation of the generous intention that underlies the present stance of the House of Bishops. The bishops do now seem to be affirming that the Church of England is still seeking to come to a common mind on this issue in an 'ongoing process of the discernment of truth' and that those who cannot accept November's decision 'will continue to hold a legitimate and recognized position within the Church of England'.[13]

The crucial question is surely to determine the criteria for this process of discernment or reception. In his Presidential Address to the General Synod in July the Archbishop of Canterbury argued that if there are from the outset women priests in every diocese 'we shall be able to learn from one another's experience'.[14] I am puzzled as to what this might mean. I hope I am wrong, but it does seem to me to suggest a purely domestic setting and a purely one-way flow for this process of reception: that when the opponents actually come to meet women priests face to face their feeling of being 'threatened' by them and their fear that they will be the aggressive embodiment of a radical challenge to Christian orthodoxy will simply melt away.

But 'Bonds of Peace', the statement of the House of Bishops after their second meeting at Manchester in June, had already made it clear that something more than a sharing of experiences was envisaged. The Church of England made its decision to ordain women to the priestly ministry of the Church of God as one part of the universal Church using its own decision-making structures, in consultation with the wider Anglican Communion and in knowledge of the differing practices of its ecumenical partners. Discernment of the matter is now to be seen within a much broader and longer process of discernment within the whole Church under the Spirit's guidance. You yourself have emphasized first of all the two-way nature of the

---

13 'Bonds of Peace', pp. 6–7, paras 3 and 4.
14 General Synod, *Report of Proceedings*, 10 July 1993, p. 392.

process of reception when you wrote of the November decision: 'At this stage there can be no guarantees. Not all such pioneering actions prove to be of God.'[15] You then went on to identify what gave the decision its provisional character and makes its eventual reception or non-reception more than a 'purely internal matter' for the Church of England. What is at stake is the universal aspect of the historic ministry and the difficult question as to the authority of one part of the universal Church to make a change of this kind in a ministry which Anglicans have claimed to be the historic and universal ministry of the whole Church. The process of reception must therefore of necessity be ecumenical and not merely internal to the Church of England or to the churches of the Anglican Communion. It seems to me to follow inescapably from this premise that the way in which the other churches, and especially those with whom we claim to share the threefold historic ministry, evolve – if they do evolve – in their evaluation of our decision must be a crucial element in the ongoing process of discernment.

The Church of England has not as yet included the teaching that the ministerial priesthood is open to women among its formal doctrines and can only apparently do so if and when the process of discernment indicates that it has received a clear affirmative consensus. If this is so, it may yet be possible for those who saw the November decision as destructive of the catholicity of the Church of England to regard the Church of England as still 'part of the One, Holy, Catholic and Apostolic Church', professing 'the faith uniquely revealed in the Holy Scriptures and set forth in the catholic creeds' and to make the Declaration of Assent without too queasy a conscience. It would also seem to argue for considerable delay before going on to tackle the even more controversial question of women in the episcopate.

Others in the weeks and months ahead will no doubt be arguing the merits of the proposed Act of Synod, which for

---

15 J. Habgood, 'Creating Distance without Separation', *Church Times*, 2 July 1993, p. 10.

some goes too far and for others not far enough. I am deliberately leaving that aside and concentrating on more fundamental issues. A better theologian and more experienced ecumenist than myself, Canon Christopher Hill, has located the 'fault-line' in Anglican ecclesiology in the power, assumed in the sixteenth century, 'to take decisions at a national level which ought properly to be taken in the wider communion of churches'; this therefore makes the ecumenical goal a priority, 'not a luxury or optional extra'.[16] The most recent thinking of the House of Bishops would seem to indicate that this argument is now increasingly the object of their attention and perhaps also an important factor behind the concrete proposals they are making. Does one rejoice at this or does one have to conclude with regret that it comes too late?

Archbishop Habgood's Response

In the following week's edition of the *Church of England Newspaper*, Archbishop Habgood published a response which set out much of the thinking underlying the Act of Synod.[17] In it he explained, 'My concern has been to try to give shape to the strong desires within the Church of England to retain its traditional diversity, while allowing real change in response to what many believe is God's will.'

He acknowledged the seriousness of the impairment of communion between a bishop and some of his clergy, but did not believe that this would weaken the unity of dioceses beyond

16 These quotations were taken from an unpublished address given by Christopher Hill to the London Chapter of the Society of the Holy Cross, at St Paul's Cathedral on 22 January 1993, in which he offered an ecclesiological assessment of all the options facing Anglicans following the Church of England's decision 'unilaterally' to ordain women to a priesthood that is not its 'sole posession' but rather part of 'the ministry . . . of the One, Holy, Catholic and Apostolic Church'. (Roger had sent him a typescript of his *Epistola ad Romanos* in advance of publication and he had sent Roger a copy of his paper in response.)

17 J. Habgood, 'Why Women's Ordination may be Better News than Some Fear', *Church of England Newspaper*, 15 October 1993, p. 7.

repair. The essence of the proposals was that the bishops would 'maintain the diversity of the Church of England by acting together more collegially' – allowing other bishops to 'complement their ministry' by ministering to those in their dioceses to whom they could not offer a complete ministry. Of this he commented:

> What this entails . . . is a self-emptying and an acceptance of interdependence, which undoubtedly softens the hard edges of the traditional concept of monarchical episcopate, but may do so in a way which brings it nearer to the New Testament.

He envisaged collaboration between neighbouring parishes in order to ensure adequate provision for laypeople:

> It is clear also that if we are to make adequate provision for lay people within the diversity of our traditions, this is going to have to be done by a greater degree of conscious planning and interdependence between parishes at deanery level. Far from 'Balkanizing' the Church of England, one effect of any loosening of some bonds of communion may be the strengthening of others.

The 'Open Process of Reception' he explained as follows:

> The Church of England has made its own decisions about women priests, and that decision is both clear and firm. We have made it, however, consciously as part of the One, Holy, Catholic and Apostolic Church, mindful of our history and our ecumenical partnerships, and this is the context in which discernment has to take place. There can be no arbitrary cut-off point, nor should we rely on purely internal criteria. It seems to me that in taking the responsibility for making our own decision – because this is the only way in practice in which such decisions can be made – we have also set ourselves the task of sharing with others in an open process of mutual learning.

While agreeing with Christopher Hill's location of the fault-line in Anglican ecclesiology as the power 'to take decisions at national level which ought properly to be taken in the wider communion of churches', he asked whether there were not 'similar fault-lines, albeit in somewhat different forms, in every other church'.

His response concluded:

If, as you say, our present difficulties can help to sharpen our sense of the urgency of the ecumenical task while at the same time making us more realistic about it, then there may be exciting discoveries ahead.

15

The Episcopal Ministry Act of Synod: Speech in the General Synod (November 1993)

The General Synod considered the draft Episcopal Ministry Act of Synod and possible amendments to it on 9 November 1993. Speaking in the debate, Roger argued that the provision in the Act of Synod 'for the continuing diversity of opinion in the Church of England' was 'not a measure of generosity nor a concession' but rather was a necessary consequence of the Church of England's understanding of itself as merely a part of the One, Holy, Catholic and Apostolic Church – a part which could not act as if it were the whole Church.

Speech by Canon Roger Greenacre[1]

I was hoping to be called early in the debate – and I am grateful that you have seen fit to call me early, Mr Chairman – because I wanted to stand back a little from the detail which will quite properly concern us from now on and to reflect on the funda-mental theological option which lies behind this debate, which has been underlined by both the Archbishop of York and Fr Flatman and which I believe can be expressed in the two fol-lowing questions. First, what kind of church is the Church

---

1 General Synod, *Report of Proceedings*, 9 November 1993, pp. 725–6.

of England? Second, what degree of authority and certainty attaches to last November's synodical decision?

One possible answer is to affirm very strongly that the Church of England is a sovereign and independent church and can decide all issues which affect its life without having to defer to any other Christian body, that when it has made a decision it does so with unfettered authority, without hesitation, doubt, scruple or backward glance, and that it therefore has the right, even the duty, to demand compliance with such a decision from all its members: the Church of England has decided and if you do not like it you must shut up or clear out. This is a simple, clear-cut attitude to take and, if the Church of England, through its Synod, wishes to take it, it will reject this Act of Synod and people like me will have to bow to that decision and leave.

What ecclesiology, however, what understanding of the Church of England and its doctrinal authority, lies behind such an attitude? Surely it is basically, perhaps unconsciously, a Roman Catholic ecclesiology? The Roman Catholic Church can take this line because that is the basis of its own self-understanding: the Church of Christ subsists in the Roman Catholic Communion. But the Church of England only claims to be part of the Catholic Church. Leo XIII, in condemning Anglican Orders, could thunder, 'Wherefore of our own motion and certain knowledge we pronounce and declare that ordinations carried out according to the Anglican rite have been and are absolutely null and utterly void.' Is the General Synod planning to mirror that kind of language and say, 'Wherefore of our own motion and certain knowledge we pronounce and declare that ordinations of women to the priesthood are absolutely valid and utterly sure'?

For there is another possible ecclesiology, one which I see behind this year's statements of the House of Bishops and behind the proposed Act of Synod, and one which I have ventured to explore recently in correspondence with the Archbishop of York in the Church of England's better, fairer newspaper.[2] According to this, the Church of England is acutely aware of the fact that it, and indeed the churches of the Anglican Communion as a whole, only constitute a part of the universal Church. There is, therefore, an inevitable fragility or provisionality about decisions that it may make which affect more than its own domestic life. The courts have ruled against the Church Society that General Synod has full powers 'in matters relating to the Church of England'. 'I find it hard to imagine plainer language,' commented Lord Justice McCowan.[3] Yet the Church of England claims to have continued the historic threefold ministry of the Catholic Church, and a change which radically affects and puts in question that continuity must be more than a matter relating to the Church of England. That is why the House of Bishops has spoken of the necessity of a period of discernment or reception, and argues that this process cannot be merely domestic but must involve a continuing dialogue with the other churches and especially those with whom we claim to share the threefold historic ministry. Perhaps in fifty years' time Pope Paul VIII and Patriarch Bartholomew IV will issue, with other Church leaders, a joint statement, and perhaps – though it is not certain – it will affirm the priesthood of women, in which case that process of reception will have worked and the opposition of many of us will have been overcome.

On the theological understanding that I have just outlined, however, 'to make provision' (to quote the preamble to the Act of Synod) 'for the continuing diversity of opinion in the Church of England' is not a measure of generosity nor a concession but a necessary consequence of this second model of Anglican self-understanding. So what is at stake in this debate is not

---

2 The *Church of England Newspaper* (see Chapter 14, and especially pp. 137–8).

3 Regina v. Ecclesiastical Committee of the Houses of Parliament and another, *ex parte* Church Society: Queen's Bench Divisional Court (Lord Justice McCowan and Mr Justice Tuckey), 28 October 1993.

merely the acceptance or the refusal of the draft Act of Synod but our whole understanding of the place of the Church of England within the One, Holy, Catholic and Apostolic Church of Christ.

Inopportunists, Impossibilists and Ecclesiologists

The Synod went on to debate proposed amendments to the draft Act of Synod. One of these was moved by Canon Philip Crowe, the Principal of Salisbury and Wells Theological College:[4]

> *In clause 1 add at the end the words 'save only that the Church of England will in future neither ordain nor appoint to senior office any person who holds that it is impossible for a woman to be a priest in the Church of God.*

Roger spoke in the debate on this amendment as follows.

The trouble with Canon Crowe's amendment is that it is both too exclusive and not exclusive enough. The vast majority of those opposed do not recognize themselves in either of the two categories that he has mentioned: those who oppose because they doubt the wisdom of the legislation or perhaps its timing, and those who are impossibilists. The vast majority, I believe, of those who voted against fall into neither category. They are not impossibilist; they are simply unable to recognize the authority of this Synod or of a purely national body to define a question which remains for them open. Are people like me – I do not say myself but people younger than me – who might be considered for senior office and who hold this view to be excluded? Canon

---

4 The Revd Canon Philip Crowe (b. 1936) trained for ordination at Ridley Hall, Cambridge and was ordained deacon in June 1962 and priest on 1 January 1963. He was a tutor at Oak Hill Theological College (1962–67) and then Editor of the *Church of England Newspaper* (1967–71). He was Principal of Salisbury and Wells Theological College from 1988 until it was closed in 1995.

Crowe's amendment is not sharp enough, although in another sense it is too sharp.[5]

The amendment was rejected. Two days later, on 11 November 1993 (the anniversary of the Final Approval of the Priests (Ordination of Women) Measure, the Synod approved the draft Act of Synod.

---

5 General Synod, *Report of Proceedings*, 9 November 1993, p. 759.

16

To Move or to Stay?
(August 1994)

This talk was given at New Hall (now Murray Edwards College), Cambridge, on 1 August 1994. Roger spoke from very full notes, from which the text has been reconstructed for this publication.

Catholic Anglicanism

What does it mean to call oneself a 'Catholic Anglican'? This self-designation reflects an understanding that goes back to the Reformation, at which the Church of England retained enough of the essentials to be able to claim continuity. Different views of the legitimacy of the rupture with Rome are possible (and different views of 'co-existence' with other traditions are also possible). The clear appeal to the maintenance of catholic ministry is an essential element in this claim to continuity.

The stance of the post-Reformation catholic tradition in the Church of England was generally anti-Roman. A less anti-Roman view came in with the Tractarians. The need for unity with Rome was realized more keenly, and the nineteenth century saw the first overtures.

Immense hope was kindled by the Second Vatican Council and the ARCIC process. The *Final Report* of the first Anglican–Roman Catholic Commission contained Agreed Statements on three subjects: Eucharist; Ministry and Ordination; and Authority in the Church. The Commission claimed to have

achieved 'substantial agreement' on the first two of those subjects and 'convergence' on the third. In its Agreed Statements
on Authority in the Church, the Commission said that the
Church needs both a multiple, dispersed authority, with which
all God's people are actively involved, and also a universal primate as servant and focus of visible unity in truth and love.
(*Pace* Fr John Coventry, authority was on the agenda from the
beginning as a crucial question.) It was in its 1979 Elucidation
of its 1973 text on Ministry and Ordination that ARCIC made
its first reference to the ordination of women.

Two Possible Ecclesiologies for Catholic Anglicans

In my *Epistola ad Romanos* (published in *The Month* in March
1993)[1] I outlined two possible ecclesiologies for Catholic
Anglicans.

The first is the classic position of the high-church tradition,
especially the Caroline Divines. According to this, Scripture
is interpreted by the universal consent of antiquity and the
perpetual practice of Christ's Church. There is no room for
innovations. 'Papists' and 'Puritans' were both criticized as
'novelists', who sought to introduce novelties into the life of
the Church. The Reformation was understood in this sense – to
quote Herbert Thorndike (1598–1672), 'the restoring of that
Church which hath been not the building of that which hath
not been'.[2] This ecclesiology was basically the same as that of
the French theologian Jacques-Bénigne Bossuet (1627–1704),
though of course with differences as to what antiquity really
teaches.

The second possible ecclesiology for Catholic Anglicans
includes the possibility of development, as adumbrated by John
Henry Newman in his *Essay on the Development of Doctrine*

---

1 Chapter 13 of this volume.
2 H. Thorndike, *The Due Way of Composing the Differences on Foot* (1660),
in *The Theological Works of Herbert Thorndike*, vol. 5 (Oxford: John Henry
Parker, 1854), pp. 25–68 at p. 48.

(1845). Such development takes place under the leadership of the See of Peter (with papal primacy understood in the way proposed by ARCIC), but this is balanced by the need for consensus among the faithful, and the reception by them of the doctrine concerned.

(There is a third ecclesiology to be found among Catholic Anglicans – full-blown Papalism – but I exclude that from this account.)

The Impact of the Ordination of Women

Does the decision of 11 November 1992, as now implemented, undermine both of these positions? Surely, yes.

The difficulty for the first position is that, though the priesting of women can be defended (and like many of those who went into the No lobbies at the General Synod, I am personally agnostic on the question), it can only be defended as a development. The case for women deacons is not the same. The ordination of women to the diaconate is partly a restoration of ancient practice, partly creative adaptation. But only if you have a low view of ordained ministry (whereby any particular church is free to make any changes at will, and basically all the baptized are understood as sharing a common priesthood) can the ordination of women as bishops and priests be regarded as a secondary question. Clerical marriage, for example, is quite different.

If the doctrine and practice of the undivided Church offers no basis for change, the first position is clearly undermined. There is an ironic reversal of positions: Anglicans used to attack Roman Catholics for introducing or imposing 'developments', but now it is the Pope who argues that on this issue the Church is not free to change. The judgement of the Caroline Divines is damning – especially that of Herbert Thorndike, whom Archbishop McAdoo called 'perhaps the most rigorous and systematic of seventeenth-century Anglican theologians' and (Bishop) Kenneth Stevenson 'the most thorough and self-critical exponent of the primitive Church that we have so far seen':

But the unity of all parts being subordinate and of inferior consideration to the unity of the whole, we shall justly be chargeable with the crime of schism, if we seek unity within ourselves by abrogating the laws of the whole, as not obliged to hold communion with it . . . unless a part may give law to the whole; which who so do, are for so doing schismatics.[3]

For, the unity of the Church being a part of the common Christianity, the breach of it will be chargeable upon that side, which makes such a change as the rest have not reason to embrace.[4]

In fine, matter of faith is to the world's end the same, that the whole Church hath always from the beginning professed. If you impose more, the Church of Rome will have a better pretence than you can have; namely, a better claim to the authority of the Church.[5]

Those who take the second position can argue that Anglicans can and should take an innovative and prophetic line on some issues which may anticipate the consensus of Christianity. However, these must not touch the fundamentals of Faith and Order. They may be issues of scholarship and interpretation (as over the question of a critical approach to Scripture, on which Anglican scholars took up a pioneering position); they may be issues which engage the conscience of individuals (ethical questions like contraception and homosexuality); they may be questions of discipline (for example, the admission of remarried divorcees to Holy Communion) – even when it is a question of innovations which go beyond the shared practice of the Latin West and the Greek East (for example, marriage after ordination).

3 H. Thorndike, *The Due Way of Composing the Differences on Foot*, pp. 28 and 42.

4 H. Thorndike, *Just Weights and Measures* (1662), in *The Theological Works of Herbert Thorndike*, vol. 5, pp. 69–298 at p. 113.

5 H. Thorndike, *Just Weights and Measures*, p. 122.

The criterion which must determine where the line must be drawn between acceptable and unacceptable unilateral action surely depends on the answer given to the following question:

> Does the proposed innovation encounter an unclear or negative verdict from the recourse to the judgement of Scripture and Tradition, and would it render impossible the recognition by other churches of the possession of a common Faith and a common Order, either breaking existing communion or rendering its restoration impossible?

The ordination of women to the priesthood (and *a fortiori* to the episcopate) has meant adopting what (at least since Newman) can be called a catholic principle, but without Newman's careful safeguards, and then applying it according to a protestant principle – the full autonomy of national churches. Where will it lead? (To the Diocese of Sydney?[6]) So, curiously, to argue for the ordination of women to the priesthood leads those Catholic Anglicans who do so to argue along lines (of development) which point to Rome . . . only to find that the official voice of Rome says No.

To Move or to Stay?

What then are Catholic Anglicans who cannot accept the rightness of the Synod's decision to do? If they are to consider the Roman 'option' (or 'imperative'), they need both a necessary and a sufficient reason to move.

The necessary reason would be that it is no longer possible to maintain a catholic position in the Church of England with any integrity, or the realization that such a possibility was always a delusion. That would be a necessary reason for leaving the Church of England, but becoming a Roman Catholic is not itself the inevitable consequence.

---

6 The reference is to proposals by the Diocese of Sydney, Australia, to authorize laypeople to preside at the Eucharist.

The sufficient reason for becoming a Roman Catholic would be that one can believe *ex animo* all that the Roman Catholic Church teaches as being part of the Faith and can accept and live with its discipline. In the Church of England there is a small group of full Papalists and a larger group of Semi-Papalists. The position of the latter (my own position) is the most difficult of all. The reason for not accepting the General Synod's decision was the need for any such decision to be taken at the universal level – but where is that level? Is it capable of operating still, and if so, how? Is the following a legitimate interpretation of *Lumen Gentium*'s statement that the Church of Christ 'subsists in' the (Roman) Catholic Church:[7] that though the Roman Catholic Church is not to be identified as the whole Church, it has power to act *as if it were* the whole Church?[8]

The Case for a Move

The case for a move can be outlined in three points.

First, ARCIC's genuine, if qualified, move to acceptance of the Roman primacy has now been undermined by Anglican unilateral action. If the See of Peter *is* the God-given centre of unity, then it is legitimate and even praiseworthy to remain within a church that is separated from that see while accepting this claim, *provided* there is a convergence between the two churches and a reasonable prospect of unity at the end of the horizon, with a hope too that the pressure of the dialogue could help bring about a better articulation of that primacy. But if the primacy of that see is once again either explicitly or implicitly repudiated and fresh obstacles placed from the Anglican side across the road to unity, is not the only way left to Anglicans who accept that claim to dissociate themselves from this action and to seek reconciliation with the See of Rome?

---

7 Dogmatic Constitution on the Church (*Lumen Gentium*), 8: W. M. Abbott (ed.), *The Documents of Vatican II* (London: Geoffrey Chapman, 1967), p. 23.

8 Here Roger made a note to refer to comments by Pope Paul VI on Councils.

Secondly, Catholic Anglicans need an ecclesiology. Can they now find one that is not basically liberal-protestant (with no authority, only probability)?

Thirdly, a pragmatic point: does the ordination of women to the priesthood represent the 'end of Tractarianism'?

The Case for Staying

The case for staying can be outlined in four points.

First, Rome still needs the witness and challenge that Anglicans and Orthodox were applying through the international bilateral dialogues, with their pressure for a reformed papacy. The collapse of Catholic Anglicanism could reinforce more conservative elements in the Roman Catholic Church (not that all 'converts' are conservative – see, for example, Sara Maitland!⁹) If the General Synod's decision revealed a 'fault line' in Anglican ecclesiology (whereby no limitation is placed on decisions at the national level), are there no fault lines in Roman Catholic ecclesiology? Is there not a call for *metanoia* on both sides? Ecumenical dialogue is dialogue between churches (Paul VI referred to the Anglican Church as Rome's 'ever-beloved sister'¹⁰); in this dialogue individual 'conversions' may be necessary (to witness to the seriousness of and absolute priority of the claims of truth), but they solve no long-term problems. There is a complementarity between Rome and Canterbury that speaks for subsidiarity and for the holding together of unity an diversity.

Secondly, to leave would be seen by those who remain as betrayal and abandonment. When a priest leaves the Church of England for Rome, his congregation feels a sense of betrayal.

---

9 Sara Maitland (b. 1950), a feminist writer of novels and short stories, became a Roman Catholic in 1993.

10 See p. 47–8 above.

There is a need to 'hope against hope' – to be, with Lord Halifax, 'le chevalier errant de l'esperance chretienne'.[11]

Thirdly, the Act of Synod of November 1993 has initiated an 'open process of reception and discernment' based on a recognition of the provisionality of the November 1992 decision. To leave before the answer to the process is overwhelmingly clear (or the process is seen to be unreal) would be to anticipate and help bring in one answer rather than the other. It should be noted that the process of reception is a process of reception within the universal Church – it involves reception of the ordination of women to the priesthood not just by the Church of England but also by other churches.[12]

Fourthly, the Act of Synod further weakens Anglican unity. But Michael Ramsey once pointed to the true vocation of Anglicanism being to use its very weakness, brokenness and fragility to say something important to the rest of Christendom.[13] The vocation of Anglicanism is to be a kind of microcosm of the ecumenical movement and to live out in its own life the tensions and divisions that belong to the whole Body.

---

11 Jean Guitton wrote of him, 'Il fut, pendant plus de cinquante ans, le héros et le chevalier errant de l'Espérance chrétienne, le prophète de cette consommation dans l'Unité pour laquelle le Christ s'est offert': J. Guitton, 'Lord Halifax' in A. Gratieux and J. Guitton, *Trois serviteurs de l'unité chrétienne: le P. Portal, lord Halifax, le cardinal Mercier* (Paris: Éditions du Cerf, 1937), pp. 31–72, also available at http://catholicapedia.net/Documents/ACRF/documents/Portal_Halifax_Mercier.pdf (see p. 18).

12 Episcopal Ministry Act of Synod 1993: Preamble, para. 3: 'The General Synod regards it as desirable that (a) all concerned should endeavour to ensure that (i) discernment in the wider Church of the rightness or otherwise of the Church of England's decision to ordain women to the priesthood should be as open a process as possible'. See also '"Bonds of Peace": Arrangements for Pastoral Care following the Ordination of Women to the Priesthood in the Church of England', in *Ordination of Women to the Priesthood: Pastoral Arrangements. Report by the House of Bishops* (GS 1074) (London: General Synod, 1993), pp. 5–15 at p. 5, para. 2.

13 A. M. Ramsey, *The Gospel and the Catholic Church* (London: Longmans, 1936), p. 220: see p. 40 above.

A Personal Conclusion

Many – including one whom I respect and admire as a theologian and love dearly as a close friend – have moved into the wilderness, left the Church of England without knowing where they will go next.[14] This cannot be my way: I cannot live as a Christian without integration into an ecclesial community. So I stay where I am until and unless I have to move. If I do move, the pressure will probably come from both ends – that is, increasing pressure of the Roman claims and increasing disintegration of Catholic Anglicanism.

---

14 This friend eventually became a Roman Catholic.

17

Uncomfortable Truths: A Response to Edward Yarnold's Heenan Memorial Lecture (February 1995)

In his 1994 Cardinal Heenan Memorial Lecture 'Thirty Years On', published in the Jesuit review The Month *for February 1995,[1] the Roman Catholic ecumenist Fr Edward Yarnold SJ, who had been a member of the first Anglican–Roman Catholic Commission (ARCIC I), looked back on the development of Anglican–Roman Catholic relations in the thirty years since the promulgation of the Second Vatican Council's Decree on Ecumenism,* Unitatis Redintegratio, *which included the significant statement that among the churches of the West 'the Anglican communion occupies a special place'.[2] The published text of the lecture was accompanied by two responses – by Roger Greenacre and Christopher Hill.*

The first two sections of the lecture, reproduced here, concerned the ordination of women to the priesthood and the reception of the Final Report of ARCIC I.

---

1 *The Month*, 264, no. 1526 (February 1995), 55–62.

2 Decree on Ecumenism (*Unitatis Redintegratio*), 13: W. M. Abbott and J. Gallagher (eds), *The Documents of Vatican II* (London: Geoffrey Chapman, 1967), p. 356.

Thirty Years On
by Edward Yarnold

The Ordination of Women

I do not intend to say much about the decision of a growing number of the churches of the Anglican Communion to
ordain women to the priesthood, and in some provinces to the
episcopate. As early as 1976 Pope Paul VI wrote to the then
Archbishop of Canterbury, Dr Donald Coggan, that the taking
of such a decision in the United States constituted a new and
grave obstacle to reunion between the two churches.[3] In 1988
the present Pope observed that such ordinations appear to 'pre-
empt' one of the tasks entrusted to ARCIC II at its foundation,[4]
namely the study of 'all that hinders the mutual recognition of
the ministries of our Communions';[5] and this year he tried to
settle the matter by declaring that the Church has no authority
whatsoever to confer priestly ordination on women and that
this judgement is to be definitively held by all the Church's
faithful.[6]

Nevertheless, these Anglican innovations have not made such a
radical difference to relations between the two churches as might
have been expected. After all, the affirmation by Vatican II of the

3 Pope Paul VI to Archbishop Donald Coggan, 23 March 1976: *Women Priests: Obstacle to Unity? Documents and Correspondence, 1975–1986* (London: CTS Do 576, 1986), pp. 49–50 at p. 50.

4 Pope John Paul II to Archbishop Robert Runcie, 8 December 1988 in *Women in the Anglican Episcopate: Theology, Guidelines, and Practice. The Eames Commission and the Monitoring Group Reports* (Toronto: Anglican Book Centre, 1998), pp. 143–4 at p. 144.

5 The aim was formulated in the Common Declaration of Pope John Paul II and Archbishop Robert Runcie at Canterbury on 29 May 1982: *The Pope in Britain: Collected Homilies and Speeches* (Slough: St Paul Publications, 1982), pp. 97–9 at p. 98.

6 Apostolic Letter *Ordinatio Sacerdotalis* to the Bishops of the Catholic Church On Reserving Priestly Ordination to Men Alone, 22 May 1994: http://www.vatican.va/holy_father/john_paul_ii/apost_letters/documents/hf_jp-ii_apl_22051994_ordinatio-sacerdotalis_en.html

Anglican Communion's special place was made at a time when it was already the judgement of the Roman Catholic Church that Anglican Orders were absolutely null and utterly void, and when it was still unable to say of Anglicans, as it said of the Orthodox, that, though separated from Rome, they possess 'true sacraments, above all, by apostolic succession, the priesthood and the Eucharist, whereby they are still linked with us in closest intimacy'.[7]

The Reception of ARCIC I

The solid achievement of the Anglican–Roman Catholic International Commission, in the twenty-four years of its first and second incarnations, substantially consolidated the Anglican special place. This point needs to be made with especial emphasis in view of the widespread conviction that the ARCIC process has come to little. Uppermost in many people's memories is the Vatican's decision of 1991 not to endorse the Commission's claim for 'substantial agreement' regarding the doctrines of the Eucharist and the ordained ministry contained in its *Final Report*.

Nevertheless it appears that the verdict was not intended to be as negative as it was taken to be. Phrases in the *Response* commending 'notable progress toward a consensus' and 'very consoling areas of agreement or convergence' should not be dismissed, as many commentators have dismissed them, as no more than a sugar coating over the bitter pill of rejection. Pope John Paul reminded a group of Roman Catholic bishops a year later of 'the need to place the difficulties encountered along the path to Christian unity within the general context of changed and much improved ecumenical relations'. He took the *Response* as evidence that 'It is possible to go to the heart of the serious divisions between divided Christians and still persevere in a fraternal and friendly dialogue.' He found the value of the *Final Report* not only in the agreements themselves,

---

7 *Unitatis Redintegratio*, 15.

but in the very fact that the two churches were conducting 'a truly ecclesial dialogue'.[8] The point of that remark seems to be that the dialogue has reached a new plane: hitherto carried on by an official commission, it has been taken over by the churches themselves, now that they have each made an official response.

This year has seen a further stage in the process, when ARCIC II issued *Clarifications on Eucharist and Ministry* designed to remove the doubts raised by the Vatican's *Response*. Cardinal Cassidy, the President of the Pontifical Council for the Unity of Christians, in a letter of acknowledgement written in consultation with the Congregation of the Doctrine of the Faith, welcomed the *Clarifications* for the 'new light' which they shed on the *Final Report*, and spoke of the 'remarkable consensus' which the Commission had achieved. 'No further study', he judged, 'would seem to be required at this stage.'[9]

Though the Vatican seems as reluctant to speak of substantial agreement as Sinn Fein is to speak of a permanent ceasefire, the Cardinal comes close to saying that, as far as the Roman Catholic Church is concerned, the two doctrines no longer present an ecumenical problem. However, the last three words, 'at this stage', perhaps take some of the gloss off this favourable verdict, for they seem to give warning that still further study may be required later before the Vatican can recognize that substantial agreement really has been achieved.

Moreover it has been asked in some quarters whether the Commission has hazarded more than it has accomplished by its publication of these clarifications. For anything which they achieve in convincing Rome that the accord on Eucharist and ministry rests on true agreement and not crafty or naive ambiguity, they are likely to disturb the delicate balance of the *Final*

---

8 Extract from Pope John Paul's Address to a Group of English Roman Catholic Bishops (1992), in C. Hill and E. Yarnold (eds), *Anglicans and Roman Catholics: The Search for Unity* (London: SPCK/CTS, 1994), pp. 170–1.

9 Cardinal E. Cassidy to the Co-Chairmen of ARCIC II (1994), in Hill and Yarnold (eds), *Anglicans and Roman Catholics: The Search for Unity*, pp. 206–7 at p. 207.

Report which made it acceptable to many Evangelical as well as Anglo-Catholic judges.

. . .

Response to the Lecture[10]
by Roger Greenacre

Dear Ted,

The Editor has asked both Christopher Hill and myself to respond to your Heenan Memorial Lecture and we are grateful for that invitation. We thought that the best way to share this responsibility would be for Christopher Hill to adopt an optimistic viewpoint and for me to adopt a pessimistic one; this in fact corresponds closely with the positions we actually hold but does involve for both of us giving a more 'univocal' testimony (to coin a phrase!) than either of us would have done if we were giving the sole Anglican response.

If the virtue of hope is high on the list of priorities for anyone involved in the ecumenical task, so is the need for honesty and lucidity. Both of these have characterized your own ministry and both are admirably demonstrated in your lecture; both therefore need to be reflected in any Anglican response, difficult though it is to get the balance right.

I believe very strongly that my primary duty as an ecumenically engaged Anglican in a situation which has seen relations with the Roman Catholic Church seriously deteriorate is to be honest and lucid about the faults of my own Church. This is not disloyalty but rather the proper extension to the ecclesial sphere of the Christian duty of self-examination, repentance and confession: we do not go into the confessional to accuse others but only ourselves.

There are, it seems to me, two fundamental questions to be addressed. Firstly, to what extent has the 'special place' which

---

10 *The Month*, 264, no. 1526 (February 1995), pp. 63–5.

the *Decree on Ecumenism* accorded to the Anglican Commu-nion changed significantly? Secondly, if in fact it *has* changed (and for the worse), what share of responsibility can justly be attributed to the Anglican side of the dialogue?

The Ordination of Women

In one sense I have to agree with you that the ordination of women to the priesthood and the episcopate in a growing num-ber of churches of the Anglican Communion has not 'made such a radical difference to relations between the two Churches as might have been expected'. You rightly point out that Rome's acknowledgement of the Anglican Communion's special place was cautious as well as vague; it never, for example, involved – even by implication – any admission that Leo XIII's judgement on Anglican Orders was considered redundant or even open to question. (It can be argued that the same caution and the same vagueness characterized Paul VI's famous statement in 1970 about the Roman Catholic Church's longing to embrace 'her ever-beloved sister' [the Anglican Church].[11] It certainly gave rise to very different interpretations from Roman Catholic commentators.)

Yet surely there were hints (more than hints in fact) that, given the right progress and the right climate, *Apostolicae Curae* would not prove an insuperable obstacle. I think in par-ticular of Pope Paul VI's prophetic gesture in slipping his ring onto the finger of Archbishop Michael Ramsey and of what was said in the ARCIC *Final Report*[12] and in the *Common Dec-laration* signed by Pope John Paul II and Archbishop Robert Runcie in 1982; enough to encourage Cardinal Willebrands to take an initiative in search of a way through the *impasse* in 1985, an initiative that has quite clearly run out of steam.[13]

11 See pp. 47–8 above.

12 Anglican–Roman Catholic International Commission, *The Final Report* (London: CTS/SPCK, 1982), pp. 38–9, 44–5: 'Ministry and Ordination', para. 17, and Elucidation, para. 6.

13 See pp. 121–3 above.

The relegation of that particular dossier to limbo is one clear sign (though not the only one) of a significant change in the Roman Catholic Church's assessment of Anglicanism's special place. The ordination of women to the priesthood and the episcopate has therefore *at the very least* delayed the prospect of any mutual recognition of ministries. It has also had, indirectly rather than directly, a negative effect on the dialogue between our two churches in two other respects.

The Nature of the Anglican Communion

The first of these has been Rome's changed perception of the *nature* of the Anglican Communion. When the dialogue began, the way in which the Communion as a whole, under the leadership of the Archbishop of Canterbury, was able to assume responsibility for its initiation and its continuation, and the fact that it did appear to have more ecclesial consistency than some of the world federations of the protestant confessions and more of an ability to get its member churches to work together than the Eastern Orthodox churches, made a favourable impression in Rome. More recent developments however – and the acceptance (reluctant or enthusiastic) of the principle of 'provincial autonomy' – have given the Roman Catholic Church understandable reasons for doubting whether the Anglican Communion really is a credible partner in dialogue, capable of committing its member churches to a coherent and united position on fundamental questions of faith and order. The crisis was occasioned (if not caused) by the question of women priests and women bishops, but it has now embraced other issues such as that of lay presidency of the Eucharist.

Roman Primacy

The second of these is the apparent 'U-turn' taken by the churches of the Anglican Communion on the issue of Roman primacy. This history of a major step forward followed by a major step backward – or, strictly speaking, of a step backward which partially overlapped with a step forward – explains not only the present crisis in relations between the two churches but the fact that a large number of Anglicans (particularly in the Church of England) are feeling impelled to ask to be admitted to full communion with the Roman See. Do I perhaps exaggerate? Though ARCIC believed it had reached 'substantial agreement' (a phrase which many in Rome seem to dislike but which, as Professor Henry Chadwick has shown, goes back to St Anselm[14]) on the Eucharist and on ministry and ordination, it had not quite resolved all the problems which stood in the way of a similar agreement on Authority in the Church. Moreover, although the Commission was agreed that there was a necessary place for a universal primacy in the Church and that such a primacy belongs 'as part of God's design for the universal *koinonia*' to the Bishop of Rome, it had neither discussed nor agreed the precise scope of the authority and jurisdiction properly to be attributed to the universal primate.

But for Anglican churches to ignore the warnings and pleadings of the Bishop of Rome on an issue which so vitally affects the ability of local churches to live together in communion of faith and order is surely tantamount to rejecting the need for a universal primacy or, at the very least, to reducing its role to an almost meaningless primacy of honour. I am not accusing the Anglican Communion of deliberate bad faith; I do have to accuse it of a failure of 'reception'; of not listening seriously enough to the verdict of a dialogue which it had itself authorized and to which it had pledged its serious commitment. We have perhaps to set against this the fact that a 1993 Act of Synod of the Church of England (not so far paralleled in any other church of the Anglican Communion) does accord to its decision of the previous year to admit women to the priesthood a degree of provisionality occasioned by the non-reception of this decision not only within the Church of England but also

---

14 H. Chadwick, *Tradition and Exploration* (Norwich: Canterbury Press, 1994), pp. 18 and 144.

within the universal Church. It remains to be seen how long this delicate tightrope act can or will be maintained.

Clarifications on Eucharist and Ministry

In view of Rome's understandable and, in my view, not entirely unjustified loss of confidence in the degree of Anglican commitment to the ARCIC dialogue, it is not surprising that many friendly observers, after an initial reaction of delight and relief, now register a degree of unease or puzzlement (even in some cases a sense of unreality) with regard to the *Clarifications on Eucharist and Ministry* published by ARCIC last year.[15] You have raised some of the delicate issues raised by their publication in your own lecture.

I would want to raise another, by asking what status and authority they have and whether they in their turn will need to be 'owned' or ratified by our two Communions. Will the Anglican Diocese of Sydney, for example, take to heart what is so strongly affirmed about the reservation to the episcopally ordained priest of the presidency of the Eucharist? And will Anglicans and Roman Catholics be able to agree that there is no contradiction between what the *Clarifications* have to say about episcopal succession and the understanding of this succession embodied in the Porvoo Declaration? And finally, if unconditional ordination is still required of most Anglican priests wishing to exercise their priestly ministry in the Roman Catholic Church because 'the clarifications achieved through the work of ARCIC on Eucharist and Ministry have not . . . yet proved to be sufficient grounds for verifying such a change in the *nativa indoles ac spiritus* of the Anglican ordinal' (to repeat your quotation from Mgr Michael Jackson[16]), have the

---

15 ARCIC II, 'Requested Clarifications on Eucharist and Ministry' (1993) in Hill and Yarnold (eds), *Anglicans and Roman Catholics: The Search for Unity*, pp. 197–206.

16 M. Jackson, 'The Case of Dr Leonard', *The Tablet*, 30 April 1994, pp. 541–2.

Clarifications, published some months after this statement, achieved the required 'clarifications' – and if not, why not?

November 1992

It is of course absolutely correct to say that if the Roman claims were unacceptable to Anglicans before 11 November 1992 then it is difficult to see that what happened since then has now made them acceptable. But, long before 1992 and thanks largely to the work of ARCIC, many Anglicans had moved from a rejection of those claims to a position where they had real grounds for hope that the gap between the Roman and Anglican positions could be closed. And for them what happened in November 1992 sharpened the question painfully.

Already one of the greatest of the seventeenth-century Anglican divines, Herbert Thorndike, had written:

> But the unity of all parts being subordinate and of inferior consideration to the unity of the whole, we shall justly be chargeable with the crime of schism, if we seek unity within ourselves by abrogating the laws of the whole, as not obliged to hold communion with it . . . unless a part may give law to the whole; which who so do, are for so doing schismatics.[17]

And, if that were not serious enough, he had gone on to say:

> *In fine*, matter of faith is to the world's end the same, that the whole Church hath always from the beginning professed. If you impose more, the Church of Rome will have a better pretence than you can have; namely, a better claim to the authority of the Church.[18]

---

17 H. Thorndike, *The Due Way of Composing the Differences on Foot* (1660), in *The Theological Works of Herbert Thorndike*, vol. 5 (Oxford: John Henry Parker, 1854), pp. 25–68 at pp. 28 and 42.

18 H. Thorndike, *Just Weights and Measures* (1662), in *The Theological Works of Herbert Thorndike*, vol. 5, pp. 69–298 at p. 122.

Some of us feel that it is our duty to recall our fellow Anglicans to these uncomfortable truths. We do it in the desperate hope – hoping against hope – that we may yet be heard, for we still believe that Rome and Canterbury have so much to learn from each other and to give each other in a continuing dialogue. So we try to make our own the conviction which in 1903 led Lord Halifax to write: 'There are defeats which are the necessary steps to victories; present failures which spell future success.'[19]

Yours ever,
Roger.

Roger's response was followed by a response by Christopher Hill.[20]

---

19 *Cf.* J. G. Lockhart: *Charles Lindley, Viscount Halifax*, part 2 (London, 1936), p. 389.

20 *The Month*, 264, no. 1526 (February 1995), 65–7.

18

The Communion Between and Within Our Churches: The Anglican Experience of its Fragility (July 1995)

This article was published in the French ecumenical periodical Unité des Chrétiens in July 1995.[1]

Not being a theologian in the strict sense of the term, I prefer to tell you a story, punctuating my account from time to time with some reflections which one could, just about, characterize as theological. This account concerns events in the history of the Church of England which have had, and still have, ecumenical repercussions. I will limit myself to a period beginning in 1991 and continuing up to the present. It is dominated by the vicissitudes of relations between the churches of the Anglican Communion and the Roman Catholic Church, but this dominant theme does not permit us to forget the other dialogues in which Anglicans are engaged. My account will concentrate on the history of the Church of England, but it will not exclude the other member churches of the Anglican Communion.

---

1 R. T. Greenacre, 'La communion entre nos Églises et à l'intérieur de nos Églises: l'expérience anglicane de sa fragilité', in *Unité des Chrétiens*, 99 (July 1995), pp. 11–17. The article has been translated into English for inclusion in this volume, with the original explanatory endnotes integrated into the main text.

The Meissen Declaration (January 1991)

In January 1991 the Meissen Declaration (the central text of a common statement signed in Meissen, Saxony, by official delegations of the churches in question) was formally approved by an act of synod of the Church of England. Having also been approved by the Evangelical Church in Germany (EKD), it came into force immediately. I will attempt to summarize the characteristics of this agreement and at the same time to define its achievements and its limits.

This was not an 'international dialogue' (in the sense of a dialogue at the world level) nor, strictly speaking, a dialogue between two confessions; an international dialogue between Anglicans and Lutherans exists and is being pursued. Nor is it a case of full communion between two churches being achieved: the common statement signed at Meissen in 1988 is entitled 'On the Way to Visible Unity'. It is rather a question of a highly significant stage on the way to such unity between two churches: the Church of England on the one hand and the Evangelical Church in Germany on the other (although in 1988 there were three churches involved, the Protestant churches of West and East Germany still being separate from each other).

The Meissen Declaration begins with a commitment:

On the basis of our sharing the common apostolic faith and in the light of what we have re-discovered of our common history and heritage . . . [we] commit ourselves to strive together for full, visible unity.[2]

The Declaration continues by citing points of mutual acknowledgement: the fact that the churches belong to one and the same *Una Sancta*; faithfulness to Christ in the ministry of the

---

2 'The Meissen Common Statement: On the Way to Visible Unity', para. 17, in *The Meissen Agreement: Texts* (London: Council for Christian Unity, 1992), pp. 3–30 at p. 20.

word, the sacraments and ordained ministries. This latter affirmation is very carefully worded, and I will quote it in full:

> We acknowledge one another's ordained ministries as given by God and instruments of his grace, and look forward to the time when the reconciliation of our churches makes possible the full interchangeability of ministers.[3]

After this first part, the Declaration includes a second part which lists practical steps that are to be taken towards a common life and mission (set out in more detail in a further document). The churches offer each other the possibility of eucharistic hospitality, but since a full interchangeability of ministries does not yet exist, concelebration is excluded, as is the laying on of hands by an Anglican bishop or priest during a German Protestant ordination. (It will be interesting to note, towards the end of this article, the similarities and differences between the Meissen Declaration and the Porvoo Declaration between certain churches of the Anglican Communion and the Nordic and Baltic Lutheran churches.)

It should be remembered that the Meissen Agreement involves churches that are conscious of being, not state churches, but national churches whose history is intimately linked with that of two countries, and which each have a sense of responsibility towards the life of their country. There is a long history of relations between the two churches, notably during the period of Nazi rule in Germany, when Bishop George Bell of Chichester was of considerable importance to German Protestants. One should perhaps also remember that the Evangelical Church in Germany has – like Germany itself – a federal structure, being composed of a series of *Landeskirchen*, of which some are Lutheran, some Reformed, and others United.

---

3 para. 17A(iii).

Rome's Official Response to the Final Report of ARCIC I (December 1991)

So in January 1991 the Meissen Agreement was celebrated. In December of the same year there appeared Rome's Response[4] (called 'official' or 'definitive') to the *Final Report* of the first Anglican–Roman Catholic Commission (ARCIC I).

I hope I will be forgiven if I go back a little at this point. In 1982 the Commission had published its *Final Report* ('final' rather than 'definitive', since no one believed that all of the problems existing between the two churches had been resolved by this report). The Commission believed itself to have reached 'substantial agreement' on two themes (the Eucharist, and Ministry and Ordination) and a solid basis for the construction of a future consensus on the third (Authority in the Church).

In the course of that same year, 1982, during John Paul II's visit to Canterbury, the Pope and the Archbishop of Canterbury signed a Common Declaration which, among other things, began a process of official evaluation of the Commission's conclusions by the competent authorities of the two communions. During an initial period, this process seemed very positive. On the Anglican side, despite the reservations expressed by some (generally, people of either a protestant or a liberal tendency), the 1988 Lambeth Conference (the plenary assembly of all the Anglican bishops, meeting every ten years) was able to conclude, after studying the responses already made by each church of the Anglican Communion, that the Agreed Statements on the Eucharist and on Ministry and Ordination were 'consonant in substance with the faith of Anglicans' and that the texts on Authority in the Church provided a 'firm basis' for further dialogue.[5]

---

4 The Official Roman Catholic Response to the *Final Report* of ARCIC I, in C. Hill and E. Yarnold (eds), *Anglicans and Roman Catholics: The Search for Unity* (London: SPCK/CTS, 1994), pp. 156–66.

5 *The Truth Shall Make You Free: The Lambeth Conference 1988* (London: Church House Publishing, 1988), pp. 210–11: Resolution 8.

On the Roman Catholic side, the process was – at first – equally encouraging, the responses of the bishops' conferences of France, of England and Wales, and of the United States (the only ones to have been published) being very positive. But Rome's official Response was slow in coming – perhaps because the Congregation for the Doctrine of the Faith and the Pontifical Council for Promoting Christian Unity (formerly the Secretariat for Christian Unity) had difficulty in agreeing. When it finally appeared, in December 1991, it was experienced as a 'cold douche' (and not only on the Anglican side). The Response had positive things to say. It tried to make a serious analysis of the dialogue, and some of the questions it asked were fair enough, but it was marred by two great errors (signalled by the bishops of the French Episcopal Commission for Christian Unity in their 'Reactions' to this Response):[6]

❖ A confusion between doctrinal consonance (a word chosen by Anglicans and Roman Catholics as the key word for seeing whether this agreement was recognized by the two sides – the statements are 'consonant', their content is 'consonant' with the faith of Roman Catholics and the faith of Anglicans) and doctrinal identity (or even identity of doctrinal language), which risks fatally undermining the spirit and the method of ecumenical dialogue (and not only between Roman Catholics and Anglicans) – a spirit and method formally approved by two popes. It is this confusion which leads the Response to deny the reality of a substantial agreement realized in this dialogue.

❖ The willingness to pass over in silence the considered responses made by the Catholic bishops' conferences, which shows little regard for the collegiality of the bishops.

---

6 French Roman Catholic Episcopal Commission for Christian Unity, 'Concerning the Holy See's Response to the Final Report of ARCIC I' (1992), in Hill and Yarnold (eds), *Anglicans and Roman Catholics: The Search for Unity*, pp. 171–84.

But if I am commenting quite severely on this Response (albeit no more so than Roman Catholic bishops and theologians have), I must also affirm that the Anglicans were not completely innocent in the matter. The refusal of the 1988 Lambeth Conference to adopt a position, at the international level, on the admission of women to the episcopate, and the recognition that in consequence there would be an impaired communion between the churches of the Anglican Communion (and within those churches), a refusal based on the principle of the complete autonomy of each church or province of the Communion, did not encourage the Roman Catholic Church to consider the Anglican Communion a coherent and responsible partner in an international dialogue.

The Church of England's Decision to Open the Ministerial Priesthood to Women (November 1992)

The year 1992 was dominated by the Church of England's decision to open the ministerial priesthood to women. It was a case, it should be noted, only of admission to the presbyterate, women having already been admitted to the diaconate for a few years and the episcopate being excluded (for the moment) from the draft legislation submitted to the General Synod of the Church of England. It is not my intention to go in detail into the theological question posed by the admission of women to the priesthood; the French public is not ignorant of this debate, which is at the same time passionate, delicate and complex. But, in order to understand it and follow it well, one must take account of the following points.

❖ The debate within the Church of England and the Anglican Communion (of which certain churches had already opened the presbyterate and even the episcopate to women, while others had refused to do so) had been very long (it had lasted at least twenty years) and had been conducted at all levels of the Church (in parishes, deaneries, and dioceses, before the definitive vote in the General Synod).

❖ The legislation on which the Synod had to vote was very complicated. While permitting the ordination of women to the presbyterate, it also permitted bishops already in post to prevent such ordinations in their dioceses, and parishes and other communities to vote to exclude women priests from ministering in their community. The legislation also envisaged financial compensation for priests who, unable to accept this legislation, resigned for reasons of conscience.

❖ The final voting on 11 November 1992 was unexpected. Preliminary voting, during the Synod's July sessions, had indicated that the two-thirds majority required in each house (bishops, clergy and laity) was lacking in the House of Laity. But in fact, on 11 November, the legislation was carried in the House of Laity by two votes, with a majority of 67.3% in favour. Twelve bishops (ten diocesans and two suffragans) voted against. The result left the episcopate in great disarray, without very clear ideas to offer as to what should follow.

❖ It was not possible for women to be ordained immediately, because the *nihil obstat* of the two Houses of Parliament and that of the Queen were needed, and then the promulgation of the canons by the Synod. The first female priestly ordinations had to wait until March 1994.

Finally, a word should be said about the motivation of those who voted against. First of all, there were among them some 'impossibilists' (above all, of the conservative evangelical tendency): for them, this initiative was manifestly excluded by the Word of God. Then, on the catholic wing, there were those who were (and remain) 'agnostic' on the question of principle but who, being convinced that the 'historic' ministry of bishops, priests and deacons was part of the inheritance of the universal Church and not only of the Church of England, could not accept the competence of the churches of the Anglican

Communion to determine, at the national level, a question that could only be resolved at the international (and, in truth, ecumenical) level. For them, this question posed itself all the more because (officially, at least) the Roman Catholic and Orthodox Churches did not accept the validity of such an innovation and had given solemn warnings as to the obstacles it would place in the way of the reconciliation of the Roman Catholic and Orthodox Churches with the Church of England. Finally, there were those who thought that the time was not ripe for such an innovation, given that the Church of England itself had not reached a consensus but only a majority (and majority and consensus are not the same thing). This third group voted against but have subsequently, for the most part, accepted the decision.

The Church of England Getting to Grips with the Consequences of the Vote (1993)

The year 1993 saw the Church of England getting to grips with the consequences of the vote. The bishops looked for a compromise that would prevent schism. Not without difficulties or affronts, they finally drew up a document entitled 'Bonds of Peace' and secured the passage of its essentials in an Act of Synod that was approved on 11 November 1993 (exactly one year after the vote on the ordination of women to the priesthood). Three elements of this Act of Synod seem to me to require attention:

❖ The underlying theology of the Act of Synod treats the ordination of women to the priesthood as being a formal and canonical position adopted by the Church of England, yet one that is submitted to the faithful for *reception* (a process of reception, neither the length nor the outcome of which can be determined in advance). Previously, the notion of reception had never been applied to sacramental practice, but in this text it is frankly and explicitly affirmed that the integrity of those who cannot accept these ordinations but continue 'to hold a legitimate and recognized position within the Church of England' is respected.[7] For the bishops, it is also clear that the process of reception is not limited to Anglicans: the discernment of the legitimacy of the Synod's decision has to take account of the reactions of our partners in ecumenical dialogue. It is for them also to receive or to refuse this new practice.

❖ Practically, it is proposed that these '*two integrities*' co-exist in each of the dioceses of the Church of England. A bishop who belongs to the majority (in favour of the ordination of women) will accept that, in certain parishes, he will no longer be able to preside at the Eucharist and he will delegate that immediate pastoral ministry to one of the Provincial Episcopal Visitors who are explicitly appointed with that eventuality in mind. A bishop who belongs to the minority (against the ordination of women) will not be obliged to preside himself at such ordinations or to license women priests, but he will have to accept that another bishop, delegated by the archbishop of his province, will do so within his diocese.

❖ Provincial Episcopal Visitors were proposed (suffragan bishops serving a whole province and themselves opposed to the ordination of women to the priesthood), with a mandate to exercise pastoral oversight over 'minority' parishes in dioceses with a 'majority' bishop. Following the passing of the Act of Synod, two episcopal visitors were nominated, one for the Province of Canterbury and one for the Province of York. There is now discussion of appointing a third (who would be the second Visitor in the Province of Canterbury). This situation points, evidently, to communion within the Church of England being severely diminished – not to say broken.

---

7 '"Bonds of Peace": Arrangements for Pastoral Care following the Ordination of Women to the Priesthood in the Church of England', para. 4: *Ordination of Women to the Priesthood: Pastoral Arrangements. Report by the House of Bishops* (GS 1074), p. 7.

The Position of Patriarch Bartholomew I
(November 1993)

During its 1993 sessions, the Synod received a particularly distinguished visitor, the remarkable current occupant of the See of Constantinople, Patriarch Bartholomew I. In the course of the address he gave on that occasion, he declared notably:

> With such good omens, certainly we would have proceeded in still more substantial theological rapprochement . . . if the major problem of the ordination of women, which suddenly emerged, had not intervened as it ought not to have. This, as was to be expected, became a great obstacle . . .

But he immediately went on to say, 'However, we were not discouraged nor did we halt the dialogue . . . With . . . godly optimism we continue this official theological dialogue with you.'[8]

Therefore, neither from the Orthodox nor from the Roman Catholic side is there a question of abandoning the official dialogue. Recording the existence of an obstacle, even a very grave one, is one thing; suspending the dialogue is another.

The First Female Ordinations (1994)

As already mentioned, 1994 saw the first priestly ordinations of women in the Church of England and the consecration of the Provincial Episcopal Visitors. It also saw the start of a haemorrhage in the body of the Church of England. Significant figures were received into the Roman Catholic Church: the Duchess of Kent, two serving government ministers and three retired bishops: the former Bishops of London (Graham Leonard), Leicester (Richard Rutt) and Dorchester (Conrad Meyer). Around three hundred active priests (not counting those who are retired) have

---

8 General Synod, *Report of Proceedings*, 10 November 1993, p. 838.

already left the Church of England's ministry – half of them to enter the Roman Catholic Church, others planning to so do, and others still in order to become Orthodox. There will certainly be more defections in the years that follow. This of course raises the question of the invalidity of Anglican Orders. Mgr Leonard, the former Bishop of London, was ordained priest *sub conditione* (there was no question of his being ordained bishop); if one could do that for him (and it seems that it was also done in other cases), it is difficult to understand why this is not practised more generally. Another question arises: that of the destiny of the married Anglican priests who enter the Roman Catholic Church. The Bishops' Conference of England and Wales addressed itself to this question in April 1995. These 'movements' – it should be noted that one avoids calling them 'conversions' – could have had a negative effect on relations between Roman Catholics and Anglicans in England. Care has been taken, on both sides, to avoid this: both parties have displayed discretion, pastoral solicitude, respect for conscience and refusal of any triumphalism, together with extensive collaboration between the two episcopates.

On the other hand, what seriously risked aggravating the situation was the Apostolic Letter *Ordinatio Sacerdotalis* of Pope John Paul II on reserving priestly ordination to men alone, issued in May 1994, and the immediate, sharp and curt response of the Archbishop of Canterbury. This exchange prompted serious journalists to say that relations between Rome and Lambeth had not fallen so low for years. The Apostolic Letter posed problems for Roman Catholic theologians: what is the degree of authority attached to a judgement that is described as definitive but not as infallible (*ex cathedra*)? The Archbishop of Canterbury's response would lead one to imagine that all Anglicans reject the Pope's argument. Taken together, the two texts give the impression of an absolute and monolithic division between two churches: the Roman Catholic Church and all of its members are against, while the Anglican Communion and all of its members are in favour. As is well known, the situation is much less simple . . .

Other Events of 1994

Three other developments in the course of the year 1994 should be added.

In July ARCIC published *Clarifications*,[9] in an attempt to reassure Rome and respond to the criticisms made of the *Final Report* in the Roman *Response* of 1991. Cardinal Cassidy gave these *Clarifications* a warm welcome.[10] But, before adopting his opinion one hundred per cent, I think that it is necessary to ask two questions. Can Rome now, in the light of these *Clarifications*, accept the reality and the legitimacy of a substantial agreement between our two churches, at least on the Eucharist and on the ordained ministry and the meaning of ordination? Is there not a great risk, to the extent that ARCIC strives to give satisfaction to Rome by going back to the classical language of Roman theology, that it will induce Evangelical Anglicans to reject the Report? At present one can do no more than pose these questions, but there are reasons to be uneasy.

Secondly, in 1994 the Anglican Diocese of Sydney, Australia, voted in favour of the possibility of laypeople presiding at the Eucharist, though the vote was not subsequently ratified. Evangelical pressure made itself felt in other Anglican churches (including the Church of England) and the General Synod of the Church of England went on to debate this subject in July 1994. This church flatly rejected the idea, but it is not certain that the Diocese of Sydney will refrain from ratifying its vote; it is no more certain that, if it does, it will be excluded from the Anglican Communion. The principle of provincial (or even diocesan) autonomy is in play here, and this matter could give rise to a crisis as grave – or even more grave – than that caused by the question of women priests and women bishops.

---

9 ARCIC II, 'Requested Clarifications on Eucharist and Ministry' (1993), in Hill and Yarnold (eds), *Anglicans and Roman Catholics: The Search for Unity*, pp. 197–206.

10 Cardinal E. Cassidy, Letter to the Co-Chairmen of ARCIC II (1994), in Hill and Yarnold (eds), *Anglicans and Roman Catholics: The Search for Unity*, pp. 206–7.

Thirdly, July 1994 the General Synod gave provisional approval to the Porvoo Declaration, the central and chief text of the Porvoo Common Statement. This declaration goes much further than the Meissen Declaration. It is even a case of something quite different: a relationship of communion – which extends almost to full communion – between the four Anglican churches of the British Isles and the eight Lutheran churches of the Nordic and Baltic countries (from Iceland to Lithuania). The dialogue forms part of a dialogue at the world level between Anglicans and Lutherans, but it benefits from the fact that all of the Lutheran churches in question are episcopal. It is precisely this that poses a problem, because, among these churches, there are those that have retained or regained the historic succession (e.g. Sweden) and others that, while retaining a succession of bishops in the historic sees, lost the sacramental succession – that is to say, at a crucial moment in the sixteenth century episcopal ordination was conferred by a presbyter rather than by bishops (e.g. in Denmark). This problem – experienced as such by the Anglicans rather than by the Lutherans – has occasioned a theological reflection on the meaning and nature of the apostolic succession, a discussion which has profited from the distinction made, some years ago now, by the French Groupe des Dombes between the 'reality' of the succession and 'the fullness of the sign' of that succession. The Anglicans must agree to enter into communion with all these churches, and after (rather than before) this sign of recognition, agree to participate in the laying on of hands at future episcopal ordinations (that is to say, that the restoration of the sign will follow a recognition).

If there is a debate within the Church of England about Porvoo, it exists only among those who share a catholic understanding of ministry and of the apostolic succession. Some of them ask themselves whether this agreement could not allow doubt to arise as to the theological consonance between the agreements on ministry between Anglicans and Roman Catholics and Anglicans and Orthodox on the one hand and between Anglicans and Lutherans on the other; others emphasize the fact that there is now a real desire, on the part of Danish Lutherans and others, to accept the fullness of the sign of the historic succession, as long as this sign is not made a precondition for mutual recognition.

Towards a Conclusion (1995)

We come now, after that long voyage (complicated and tedious, at least in its narration), to the present year 1995 and to the time to attempt to draw some conclusions. Among the events of this year, I will leave on one side the Church of England's financial crisis (resulting from imprudent investments by the Church Commissioners) and the threats made by the Conservative Evangelicals – above all on the part of the movement called 'Reform' – to leave the Church of England and make another schism. I will do no more than mention the very recent nomination of David Hope, the Bishop of London and leading opponent of the ordination of women to the priesthood, to the second position in the Church of England, the See of York – an astonishing nomination (almost as if the Pope made Mgr Gaillot, who was removed as Bishop of Evreux in January 1995, a cardinal).

The Church of England is today a church that has been severely shaken. For a time, one had the impression that it was almost paralysed by a decision that had been hoped for and dreaded (sometimes by the same individuals). Its ecumenical relations are difficult, but there is determination on all sides not to break them off. It experiences, paradoxically, both tragic new limits to communion in its internal life and promises of growing communion with some of its ecumenical partners. But the phenomenon which is in danger of having the most serious consequences is that which I would like to call the change in the physiognomy of the Church of England and of Anglicanism. Despite the nomination of Bishop Hope, which is an encouraging sign for the Catholic tradition within Anglicanism, the most clear-sighted observers ask themselves whether the undeniable weakening of the Catholic movement will not inevitably result in its extinction. Are we seeing the end of the Oxford Movement (and will the Oxford Movement be under the sign of Newman, who left, rather than that of Pusey, who stayed)? And what will be the consequences, for Anglicanism and for its ecumenical role?

But if it is a question of a change in the physiognomy of the Church of England, there is also a question of a change in the physiognomy of the Roman Catholic Church in England. What will be the consequences, for the life of the latter, of such a massive Anglican 'blood transfusion', bringing with it a whole spiritual, cultural and theological inheritance, and the experience of married priests? I ask the questions; I do not claim to have the answers.

Two analyses of the current crisis are possible. Is the traditional comprehensiveness of Anglicanism, made possible hitherto by a common structure and boundaries that were recognized and accepted on all sides, on the point of cracking under the weight of a growing incoherence? Or is Anglicanism once more following its ecumenical vocation by accepting all the pain of an uneasy coexistence, within its own life, of apparently contradictory positions and trying to overcome the pain and to resolve the difficulties by its determination to remain united?

19

The Need for Roots in the
Apostolic Faith:
Letter to the *Church Times*
(3 November 1995)

Introduction (2013)

In the autumn of 1995 a new General Synod was elected. On 27
October the *Church Times* reported that the Catholic Group,
which had had 170 members in the previous General Synod
(elected in 1990) – about one third of the Synod's total membership – had suffered heavy losses in the elections and was
reduced to about 70 members. In many dioceses there had been
a 10–15 per cent swing to (mainly conservative) Evangelicals,
but overall, liberals looked set to predominate.

Representatives of the various groups were interviewed.
Comments by Canon David Hutt of Westminster Abbey,[1] who
until earlier that year had been Vicar of All Saints, Margaret
Street, one of London's leading Anglo-Catholic churches, were
reported as follows:

There is no party ticket for Affirming Catholicism . . . and its

---

1 David Hutt (b. 1938) was Vicar of All Saints, Margaret Street (1986–95)
and a Canon of Westminster Abbey (1995–2005) – latterly as Sub-Dean (1999–
2005). In 1990 he was one of the founders of 'Affirming Catholicism'. He was a
member of the Steering Committee, gave an address at the original day conference held on 9 June 1990, and in August 1990 was a signatory, with Richard
Holloway and Victor Stock, of the first Newsletter.

members stood as independents. They are not in the Catholic Group. 'But there is a lively spirit abroad which can certainly claim to be Catholic, and we can fill a shortfall by strengthening the sacramental presence,' said Canon David Hutt, a leader of the Affirmers. 'Lay people were very pleased with the support they received at the hustings. If there is a difference in the composition of the Synod it is a positive thing. The writing is on the wall for a certain sort of Anglo-Catholic. Catholicism cannot be rooted, static and unchanging.'[2]

This prompted Roger to write the following Letter to the Editor.[3]

The Need for Roots in the Apostolic Faith

From Canon R. T. Greenacre

Sir, 'The writing is on the wall', says Canon David Hutt, commenting exultantly on the General Synod election results, 'for a certain sort of Anglo-Catholic' (News, 27 October).

I think he has people like me in mind, but I am intrigued when he goes on to say that 'Catholicism cannot be rooted, static and unchanging'. People like me have never believed or taught that Catholicism should be 'static and unchanging', but we do argue strongly for the need for roots, which he apparently denies. A Church cannot claim to be part of the apostolic Church unless it is rooted in the apostolic faith; there cannot be catholicity without apostolicity.

Is Canon Hutt expressing a personal conviction, or is he speaking on behalf of Affirming Catholicism?

Roger Greenacre

---

2 *Church Times*, 27 October 1995, p. 1.
3 *Church Times*, 3 November 1995, p. 9.

20

Difference, Divergence and Division: Sermon at Evensong for the Glastonbury Pilgrimage (June 1997)[1]

In one sense it has not been easy for me to know what to say to you this afternoon – or how to say it. The Bishop of Sodor and Man[2] is a hard act to follow at any time, and earlier today I was wondering nervously whether he would steal all my best lines and all my most telling points and whether I would have to spend the lunch break starting all over again from scratch. There is also the heavy disadvantage that I come to you with almost no previous experience of the mood and ethos of this great annual celebration and with no clear idea of your expectations.

But in another sense, my theme is handed to me on a plate, since this Year of Grace, 1997, is a year of significant anniversaries. It is, as you know, the fourteenth centenary both of the arrival in Kent of the Roman missionary S. Augustine and his companions and of the death at the monastery of Iona in Scotland, which he had founded, of the Irish missionary S. Columba. Of all the appropriate settings for a joint celebration, surely Glastonbury, this Holy Place dedicated to the Holy Mother of God and marked by both traditions, one which we might call English, Roman and Benedictine and the other British and Celtic, can effortlessly claim the first place. For we are

1 Published in *The Server: The Quarterly Magazine of the Guild of the Servants of the Sanctuary*, vol. 17, no. 11 (Autumn, 1997), pp. 13–16.

2 The Rt Revd Noël Jones (1932–2009), Bishop of Sodor and Man (1989–2003).

here at a meeting point of the 'Augustinian' and 'Columban' traditions, a place where the two have been allowed to fuse and interpenetrate fruitfully and harmoniously. Since today we are honouring not only Augustine and Columba but all those saints of England and Wales (not forgetting those of Scotland and Ireland either – nor those of the Isle of Man) who preached the Gospel to our forebears and built up the Church in this island, perhaps you will allow me to paraphrase the reading from the Letter to the Hebrews, which was read to us as the Second Lesson:[3]

> And what more shall I say? For time would fail me to tell of Augustine and Columba, of Patrick and David, of Aidan, Chad, Theodore, Cuthbert, Wilfrid, Willibrord, Bede, Boniface, Alfred, Dunstan, Anselm, of Richard Whiting and many others, who through faith conquered kingdoms, enforced justice, received promises, stopped the mouths of lions, quenched raging fire, escaped the edge of the sword, won strength out of weakness, became mighty in war, put foreign armies to flight. Women – let us not forget the women, for some of them were quite outstanding – like that Mother in Israel, S. Hilda of Whitby, and that heroine company of Anglo-Saxon nuns, most of them with unpronounceable names, who accompanied S. Boniface on his mission to Germany. Some of this great company suffered mocking and scourging and even chains and imprisonment. They were stoned, they were sawn in two, they were killed with the sword, they were hanged, drawn and quartered. Of them the world was not worthy.

There is no time to tell their stories and I am not the person to do this. Those of you who come here regularly and faithfully year after year will know them – especially those of S. Dunstan and of the Blessed Richard Whiting – better than a callow newcomer like myself! What we do need to do together is not only

---

3 Hebrews 11.32–38.

to celebrate and give thanks for this great cloud of witnesses which now surrounds us but also to reflect together on some of the lessons for us today of that enriching but not always easy or comfortable encounter between the two traditions represented by Augustine and Columba.

I

Pope John Paul II once said (and Archbishop Runcie underlined his agreement with him by quoting it back to him): 'Unity not only embraces diversity but is verified in diversity.'[4] In other words, unity is not uniformity; it is a wide and mutually enriching, mutually correcting, diversity held together in unity and communion, and catholicity (universality) is precisely unity-in-diversity in the image of the Blessed Trinity. To make the point clearer, let me talk for a moment about three 'd's; difference, divergence and division. *Difference* is sometimes seen as threatening and can certainly lead to tension, but we have, both at the human level and at the Christian level, to rejoice in and celebrate those differences of culture, language, interest, personality and style that make for the best of friendships, the best of marriages, the best of communities. The Church in this island has been enormously enriched by two very different traditions, the Celtic and the Roman. Co-existence was not always easy but we would all be impoverished if one of the two had simply been eliminated. *Divergence* is less easy to live with, because it implies that two parties are travelling down roads which are growing further apart, whereas convergence (which we had seen at work a generation or two ago both within Anglicanism and in ecumenical dialogue) implies two roads which are gradually growing closer together. Divergence is not yet a catastrophe but is a kind of amber light, warning of the red light of division. *Division* occurs when two friends quarrel and never speak to each other again, when a marriage ends in divorce, when two countries go to war, when a church

---

4 See p. 86 above.

is split by schism. Which of these three 'd's best represents the situation of the Church of England or the Church in Wales today?

And what can we learn from the past? There were many differences between the Celtic and Roman traditions of Columba and Augustine. That wise pastor Pope S. Gregory was no stickler for uniformity and he advised Augustine to have a relaxed attitude to liturgical diversity. Augustine was perplexed by the different customs he found in different churches but Gregory wrote to him:

> If you have found customs, whether in the Roman, Gallican or any other churches, that may be more acceptable to God, I wish you to make a careful selection of them and teach the Church of the English, which is still young in the Faith, whatever you can profitably learn from the various churches.[5]

The difference, however, between the Celtic and Roman traditions over the date of Easter was to prove more serious and threatened the ability of Christians of the two traditions to live together in full communion. An earlier difference between Rome and Asia in the second century over the observance of Easter had, at one point, almost led to schism then – this threat was only averted by the great saint whose memorial day it is today, S. Irenaeus of Lyon. But the strain of this particular divergence in our own land was found to be intolerable – not a difference that enriched unity but one that threatened it – and in the year 664 the Synod of Whitby, under the influence of S. Wilfrid, opted decisively for the Roman Easter, preferring the universal to the provincial – a wisdom not always followed by modern synods! Wilfrid was a real hard liner; he crossed the Channel to be consecrated by Frankish bishops, unwilling to have anything to do with bishops in this country who were not sound on the date of Easter. Is this the first appearance in our history of the theory of 'tainted hands'?

---

5 Bede, *Historia ecclesiastica gentis Anglorum*, I. 27.

II

Our problems today are not about calculating Easter. The ordination of women to the priesthood is far from being the only divisive issue we are confronted with, but it is one which, like the Easter controversy, threatens our ability to live together in unimpaired communion and, like the Easter controversy, it comes down in the end to a question about authority. Who, if anyone, has authority to make which kinds of decision?

We meet today on the Eve of the Solemnity of SS. Peter and Paul, whose martyrdom in Rome has given such particular authority to the apostolic church of that city and that see. Celtic Christians were neither closet protestants nor old fashioned 'high and dry' anti-Roman Anglicans; they were ready to acknowledge the primacy of the See of Rome as it was then understood and practised. But it was the influence of Pope S. Gregory that was crucial, the man who was to be called by the English 'our father Gregory' and hailed by Bede and others as 'our own apostle', the Apostle of the English.

Those of us who have had a particular responsibility for Anglican–Roman Catholic dialogue cannot help noting with deep regret the set-back in the relations of mutual trust, ease and confidence that had been growing up between our two communions since the Second Vatican Council. This set-back applies even to us in the Catholic Anglican tradition; among us some have become rather stridently anti-Roman in an understandable reaction to the fact that so many who used to walk with us have felt impelled by their conscience to leave us; and some of them (but not all) have in turn become rather stridently anti-Anglican. The temptation is understandable, *but it must be firmly resisted*.

S. Gregory chose for himself the title 'Servant of the Servants of God' and this vision of the Petrine office as one of service, not of domination, has been revived in our own days, though not without some pressures in the opposite direction. In 1995 Pope John Paul II issued a wonderful and very positive letter on unity, *Ut Unum Sint*. In it he took the courageous but very risky step of inviting the help of the other churches in finding a way of exercising the primacy which, 'while in no way renouncing what is essential to its mission, is nonetheless open to a new situation'. 'This is an immense task' and one, he says 'which I cannot carry out by myself.'[6] The response of the House of Bishops of the Church of England to this invitation is due to be published this summer;[7] let us hope and pray that it will be a positive one and let us try to make sure that it does not just suffer the fate of so many reports – greeted with a yawn and thrown into the wastepaper basket. So much hangs on it and it is vital that the dialogue on this issue should continue.

III

Augustine and Columba were both monks, as was S. Gregory (the first monastic pope) and as were so many of the saints of England and Wales whom we commemorate today. In this time of crisis for Anglicanism, when we find it difficult to know where its true identity lies, we have a desperate need of the values of the Benedictine tradition, the values to which Glastonbury witnessed so powerfully in its greatest days. Life on this planet is threatened if we destroy our forests; the life of the Church is similarly threatened if spiritual deforestation deprives it of what can superficially seem to be the unproductive forest of the monastic life. On this day and in this place we need to pray for and encourage vocations among men and women to the monastic life. S. Benedict died at Monte Casino, a monastery which has been destroyed more than once in its turbulent history. Its motto is a telling one: '*Succisa virescit*' – the felled tree flourishes again. May that motto prove true once more both for the monastic life and for our own church.

6 *Ut Unum Sint: Encyclical Letter of the Holy Father John Paul II on Commitment to Ecumenism* (London: CTS, 1995), pp. 106–7: paras 96–6.

7 *May They All Be One: A Response of the House of Bishops of the Church of England to Ut Unum Sint* (GS Misc 495) (London: General Synod, 1997).

IV

And lastly, I believe we need to recover for the Catholic move-ment in Anglicanism two values. The first is that of toughness and perseverance. Today our church is in danger of many things, but a more real and subtle danger than the total vic-tory of Evangelical or Liberal theology is that of our splitting up into a number of ghettoes – each going its own way and being content to let others go their own way. We are living in a temporary calm while the Act of Synod still operates and while the period of 'Reception' is still, in principle, open. But this is no time for complacency, for the time left to us to make our distinctive witness may be shorter than we think. Vigilance and toughness are essential, not just for our own survival, but for our Christian mission to the people of England and Wales. The need for the effective pursuit of that mission is as urgent now as it was in the age of Columba and Augustine. As we walked through the streets in procession to the Abbey this afternoon we only had to raise our eyes occasionally from our service paper to observe that neo-paganism is alive and well today – not least in Glastonbury. We have a Gospel to proclaim, but a church that is not united in faith has no cutting edge; it is salt that has lost its savour.

But the second value we need to recapture is that of humility. Bede records that it was Augustine's lack of humility, his fail-ure to rise when the Celtic bishops came to meet him, that lost him the chance of winning them over. We must let the bitter blows of the last five years chasten and humble us. There was a lot of laxity, triviality, complacency and lack of theological seriousness in the Catholic tradition in Anglicanism and we have, perhaps, deserved to be brought low. Let our model here be the humble handmaid of the Lord, 'Our Lady S. Mary of Glastonbury', and our inspiration the words of her *Magnifi-cat*. If in our pride we have been brought low, may we now be exalted with the humble and meek and now, as those who hunger for the Gospel, be filled with good things and not sent empty away.

21

Snakes and Ladders:
A Threat to Church Unity
(November 1997)[1]

*Having spoken to sixth-form theologians at Worth School about
the ordination of women to the priesthood, Roger developed his
thinking further in this article for the school magazine.*

**Why did you oppose the legislation for the ordination of
women to the priesthood in the Church of England and
why do you still do so?**

I am not an 'impossibilist' with regard to the ordination of
women to the priesthood. In other words, although the theological case against this innovation is undoubtedly serious, I do
not think that either side has yet provided an overwhelmingly
convincing and conclusive case. It is possible, therefore, that at
some point in the future (not, admittedly, the very near future)
both the Roman Catholic Church and the Eastern Orthodox
churches may decide (perhaps even jointly) that the Church's
practice may be changed without betraying the teaching of
Scripture and Tradition. I do not say that I think this probable,
only possible.

On the other hand I was – and remain – totally and absolutely opposed to the decision of the Church of England and of

---

1 Published in *Identity* (Worth School), 4 (November 1997), pp. 14–15.

196

other churches of the Anglican Communion to proceed to the ordination of women to the priesthood and, in the case of some other of those churches, to the episcopate. In consequence, although I respect and admire many of the women ordained to the priesthood since 1994, I cannot 'recognize' their priesthood by concelebrating with them or receiving Holy Communion at a Eucharist which they are celebrating.

My basic objection is ecclesiological; that is, it arises from my understanding of the nature of the Church, of the place of the churches of the Anglican Communion within it, and of the structures of authority within it.

The Church of England claims to hold the Catholic Faith, and by this it understands the historic faith of the Undivided Church of East and West. Problems arise if changes of fundamental questions of Faith and Order are claimed to be legitimate developments from this original deposit. Can one part of the Church make a unilateral decision – especially if other major churches of East and West disagree with that judgement and point out that, if put into action, it will be a serious obstacle to that unity which we are pledged to seek with them? This is particularly acute in the present case, since one of the foundations on which our church bases its claim to catholic continuity is its faithful maintenance of the historic threefold ministry of bishop, priest and deacon. A claim to possess a common currency should carry with it the corollary that it cannot be changed unilaterally. A distinction does, of course, need to be made between differences of discipline (such as the marriage of the clergy), which are compatible with the principle of diversity in unity, and dogmatic differences, which undermine the ability of one church to recognize the ministry of another church.

How would you asses the present uneasy compromise between the 'two integrities' (as they are sometimes called) inside the Church of England?

I would like to make three points in reply to this question.

First, the Act of Synod of 1993 was a formal recognition by the Church of England that the decision to proceed to the ordination of women priests was neither definitive nor binding on all its members. Since a sizeable minority of clergy and laity (including a number of bishops) was opposed to it and since the *whole* Church (and especially some of those churches with which we were in formal dialogue) had not accepted this practice, there was a certain 'provisionality' about this decision. Officially, therefore, the Church of England is now in a period of 'open reception' and during this time both those in favour and those opposed are, in theory, supposed to be members of the Church of England in equally good standing and to be accepted as such. It is to this official but precarious co-existence that the phrase 'the two integrities' refers.

Secondly, the 'provisionality' of this decision and the continued existence (despite many departures for other churches) of a strong and articulate opposition mean that the Act of Synod will have to remain in force for some time. This, in turn, means that it is difficult to envisage how the Church of England can proceed to legislate for the ordination of women to the episcopate, since this would totally destroy the basis of the Act of Synod. At present there is a kind of uneasy stalemate; the House of Bishops is clearly anxious not to see legislation for women bishops introduced in the foreseeable future.

If people like myself can take some comfort from these first two points, the third is infinitely more worrying. According to the tradition held in common by Roman Catholics, Orthodox or Anglicans, the 'local church' is always the diocese; the present situation has now, of course, gravely undermined the unity of the diocese around its bishop. In the Diocese of Chichester, for example, there are women priests, although neither ordained nor licensed by the bishop, who has to accept their presence in his diocese although he cannot recognize their priesthood. Conversely, in other dioceses there are parishes which refuse to accept the sacramental ministrations of their diocesan bishop, because he has ordained women priests, and which are under the pastoral care of one of the Provincial

Episcopal Visitors provided for by the Act of Synod. In the past Anglican 'comprehensiveness' could be seen to work because great theological diversity was held together in unimpaired sacramental communion. Now that this is no longer possible, we have to ask whether comprehensiveness has not given way to incoherence.

Are you pessimistic or optimistic about the future of Anglican–Roman Catholic Relations?

I am not sure that pessimism and optimism are the best categories to work with on this issue. The Christian virtue of hope is not identical with optimism, nor is Christian realism to be confused with pessimism. From some perspectives there is real ground for hope; at the local level Anglicans and Roman Catholics are working together and praying together (with other Christians also of course) with far greater commitment and there is an increasing impatience (especially, but not exclusively, among those involved in inter-church marriages) with our continued disunity and our inability to share together in the sacrament of unity, the Eucharist. Liturgically too, our traditions are getting closer and we no longer feel like strangers in each other's churches. But there can be no escape from the hard fact that sacramental unity depends on mutual recognition of ordained ministries and that, whereas twenty years ago it looked as if a way forward on this issue was emerging, a new, very serious, obstacle is now blocking progress on this question.

An even more fundamental problem, of course, is that of authority, and at the heart of this question is that of Roman primacy. I personally was both moved and impressed by *Ut Unum Sint*, Pope John Paul II's Encyclical of May 1995, with its appeal to the leaders of the other churches to help him in his search for a more acceptable way of exercising his office. If the churches of the Anglican Communion are going to respond positively to this invitation, they need help from Rome not only in the form of encouraging words but in the form of positive action which will allow the Petrine ministry to be more clearly perceived as one of service rather than domination. But perhaps the present crisis of authority at the heart of Anglicanism will help us to be more convinced of the need for a universal ministry dedicated to the maintenance of unity and communion between the churches.

22

Rome and Canterbury: Two Dysfunctional Ecclesiologies (October 1998)

This lecture was given on a supplementary post-ordination train-ing conference organized by the Society of the Holy Cross (SSC) and Forward in Faith, held at Holthorpe Hall, Leicestershire, on 20 October 1998. It is published here for the first time.

ARCIC I and the Sharing of Gifts

The *Final Report* of the first Anglican–Roman Catholic Commis-sion (ARCIC I) was published in 1982, but the Agreed Statements which it comprised, one on the Eucharist, one on Ministry and Ordination and two on Authority, appeared at intervals from 1971 onwards, as the Commission proceeded on its task. It was an exciting time for those who believed that nothing was more vital than the success of Anglican–Roman Catholic dialogue to be around and, although the texts caused considerable alarm in conservative quarters in both communions, they generated a cli-mate of enormous hope among those on both sides committed to that dialogue. It seemed to many experienced church leaders and ecumenists, both Anglican and Roman Catholic, that a real breakthrough was being made and that there was definitely light at the end of the tunnel. It might take a bit more time to get there but the end was hardly in doubt.

A significant moment in the history of ARCIC I is marked by the Co-Chairmen's Preface of September 1976 to the first of the two Agreed Statements on Authority in the Church. It is a Preface which radiates a mood of definite, if cautious, confidence. The two Co-Chairmen, Dr Henry McAdoo, then Anglican Archbishop of Dublin, and Alan Clark, then Roman Catholic Bishop of East Anglia, pinpoint authority as *the* crucial issue in the dialogue. Though unresolved questions still remained, they are convinced that the question they had reached at that point would put the remaining areas of disagreement in a new perspective, so they allow themselves a prophetic glimpse as they write:

> The consensus we have reached, if it is to be accepted by our two communities, would have, we insist, important consequences. Common recognition of Roman primacy would bring changes not only to the Anglican Communion but also to the Roman Catholic Church. On both sides the readiness to learn, necessary to the achievement of such a wider *koinonia*, would demand humility and charity. The prospect should be met with faith, not fear. Communion with the see of Rome would bring to the churches of the Anglican Communion not only a wider *koinonia* but also a strengthening of the power to realize its traditional ideal of diversity in unity. Roman Catholics, on their side, would be enriched by the presence of a particular tradition of spirituality and scholarship, the lack of which has deprived the Roman Catholic Church of a precious element in the Christian heritage. The Roman Catholic Church has much to learn from the Anglican synodical tradition of involving the laity in the life and mission of the Church. We are convinced, therefore, that our degree of agreement, which argues for greater communion between our churches, can make a profound contribution to the witness of Christianity in our contemporary society.[1]

Let us look a little more closely at what these words imply. The key is perhaps a phrase from the Common Declaration of Pope

---

1 Anglican–Roman Catholic International Commission, *The Final Report* (London: CTS/SPCK, 1982), p. 50.

John Paul II and Archbishop Robert Runcie, signed in Rome in October 1989: 'The ecumenical journey is not only about the removal of obstacles but also about the sharing of gifts.'[2] The sharing of gifts is precisely what this Co-Chairmen's Preface was all about. The Roman Catholic Church and the Anglican Communion were both incomplete and imperfect through their separation. They lacked wholeness, and wholeness can only come through a unity which removes obstacles and allows for a process of mutual correction and enrichment, an exchange or sharing of gifts. The Anglican Communion lacked communion with the See of Rome, and restoration of that communion would bring to her 'not only a wider *koinonia* but also a strengthening of the power to realize its traditional ideal of diversity in unity'. In other words, communion with Rome would give her a stronger unity which would allow diversity to be diversity in fact as well as in name and not just an uneasy co-existence of threatening divergences. The Roman Catholic Church for her part would not only be 'enriched by the presence of a particular tradition of spirituality and scholarship' but would be able to learn 'from the Anglican synodical tradition of involving the laity in the life and mission of the Church'.

The Reversal of Relations

But what has happened in the 1990s makes so much of what was said in the 1980s to seem as if it was said light years ago, not just a decade ago. In 1991 we had the official Roman Catholic response to the *Final Report* of ARCIC I – a douche of cold water, if ever there was one – and in 1992 we had the vote in the General Synod to authorize the ordination of women to the priesthood in the Church of England.

---

2 Common Declaration of Pope John Paul II and Archbishop Robert Runcie, 2 October 1989, in *One in Hope: Documents of the Visit of the Most Reverend Robert Runcie, Archbishop of Canterbury, to His Holiness John Paul II, Bishop of Rome, 2 September 1989 to 2 October 1989* (London: CHP/CTS, 1989), pp. 5–10 at p. 8.

It disturbs the neatness of the pattern, but I think we need to see the beginnings of the reversal of relations a little earlier – perhaps as early as the first admissions of women to the priesthood in some churches of the Anglican Communion in the 1970s, but certainly as early as 1988, when the Lambeth Conference made a momentous decision – or rather a momentous *non*-decision, when it declared itself unable to make a decision at the international level about the ordination of women to the episcopate, thus leaving the door wide open to two new developments: the introduction of women bishops in a number of the churches of the Anglican Communion and the realization that the Anglican Communion had within itself no authority to prevent its own disintegration or at least the breakdown of that full communion and interchange of ministries that allows a body of churches to call itself a 'communion'.

This year 1988, I believe, contributed significantly to the climate that made the Roman response of 1991 so disappointing, and 1991, I believe, contributed significantly to the General Synod vote of 1992. Neither side was innocent; both had legitimate grounds for accusing the other of moving the goalposts in the middle of the game. Rome could say to Canterbury: 'You have created a new and serious obstacle to unity during the course of our officially authorized dialogue, in spite of our warnings.' Canterbury could say to Rome after its 1991 Response, 'You asked for Agreed Statements that were consonant with the faith of the Roman Catholic Church: now you require their identity with that faith and – by implication at least – their identity with that faith in its post-Reformation formulation.' The exchange of gifts seems to have turned into the exchange of accusations!

But we have not entirely gone back to Square One, for there are articulate and critical spirits in both communions who have not hesitated to take issue with the official pronouncements or initiatives of their own churches and to challenge the direction in which their church seems to be moving.

Dysfunctional Ecclesiology
in the Roman Catholic Church

So let us look at the Roman Catholic Church. The Second
Vatican Council (Vatican II) introduced two radical innovations into Roman Catholic ecclesiology (self-understanding as
a church): first, the statement that the Church 'subsists in (*sub-
sistit in*) the Catholic Church',[3] and second, the collegiality of
bishops – hence (less clearly) the importance of the local church
and the understanding of the Church as a communion of local
churches.

But Vatican II also reiterated (though in a new context) the
teaching of the First Vatican Council. There was a tension
between the old and the new and its working out has occurred
in the years since the Council closed in 1965. Things moved so
fast that a reaction set in – already under Paul VI (for example,
Humanae Vitae), but more obviously so under John Paul II.
Hence one can speak of the Roman Catholic Church having a
'dysfunctional ecclesiology' – that is, an understanding of the
Church which in its operation functions badly. The dysfunction is due to unresolved tensions in the doctrine of the Church
and to the fact that only *part* of that doctrine is reflected in
practice, while another part is ignored or contradicted.

We are all aware of aspects of that dysfunction. There is a
need to distinguish between the criticisms of way-out liberals
in the Roman Catholic Church, who have been using Vatican
II as a launching pad for an agenda of their own which is not
grounded in the texts of Vatican II, and a more moderate party,
which is faithful to an older tradition which Vatican II had,
in a sense, rediscovered. This moderate party, fundamentally
loyal to Vatican II and the Pope and supportive of many of the
efforts of Popes Paul VI and John Paul II to check excesses (for
example, in political radicalism, abandonment of priestly discipline, and liturgical anarchy), were alarmed at signs of a return

---

3 Dogmatic Constitution on the Church (*Lumen Gentium*), 8: W. M. Abbott
(ed.), *The Documents of Vatican II* (London: Geoffrey Chapman, 1967), p. 23.

to absolutism and to curial control (for example, checks on episcopal conferences and powers given to the Congregation for the Doctrine of the Faith to discipline theologians). Both dysfunction and the role of moderates have been highlighted in certain incidents in the history of Anglican–Roman Catholic dialogue. I will give two examples.[4]

First, the commentary by the French Bishops' Conference on the Roman Response to the *Final Report* of ARCIC I offered clear and forceful criticism on two grounds: the issue of 'consonance' and 'identity'[5] and of the need (approved by successive popes) for ecumenical dialogue to be free to use new language to express a shared faith; and the absence of communication between the Congregation for the Doctrine of the Faith and the episcopal conferences (which merits use of the word 'dysfunction'). With regard to the latter point, it observed:

At the time of the publication of ARCIC I's Final Report, before the episcopal conferences and their doctrinal commissions could make any study of the document, the Congregation saw fit to send to the presidents of episcopal conferences and to publish for the faithful its markedly one-sided *Observations*, expressing 'the hope that the bishops will be willing to give them careful consideration' (letter of 2 April 1982).

The account we have given of the replies made by the French and English episcopal conferences to the Vatican department which then went by the name of 'Secretariat for Christian Unity' suffices to show that the episcopates most directly concerned were unable to adopt the observations which had been publicly sent to them. The 'definitive Response' which has recently appeared, ten years after ARCIC's Final Report was sent to Rome, seems completely to ignore the replies of the episcopal conferences which have been made public. Is this a healthy exercise of the collegiality

---

4 This last part of the third section of the lecture exists only in note form. The text that follows is a reconstruction.

5 See p. 176 above.

and the ecclesiology of communion which form 'the central and fundamental concept' of Vatican II?[6]

Second, whereas Pope John Paul's *Motu Proprio Ad Tuendam Fidem* of 28 May 1998 merely anchored the second of the three paragraphs of the existing Profession of Faith in canon law (as the first and third paragraphs already were), the Doctrinal Commentary issued by the Congregation for the Doctrine of the Faith on 29 June 1998[7] gave as an example of 'truths connected to revelation by historical necessity and which are to be held definitively, but are not able to be declared as divinely revealed' Pope Leo XIII's declaration in the Apostolic Letter *Apostolicae Curae* on the invalidity of Anglican ordinations.

The French Bishops' Commentary on the Roman Response to the *Final Report* of ARCIC I had drawn attention to the apparent contradiction between the many papal declarations and initiatives to promote progress towards Christian unity on the one hand and 'the slow pace of the magisterial acts of "reception" or the innumerable ecumenical statements of agreement, consensus or convergence and the reservations which accompany the acts of reciprocal recognition' (for which the Congregation for the Doctrine of the Faith was responsible) on the other.[8]

Contradictions can also be found within *Ut Unum Sint* (as also in the response to it of the English House of Bishops).

---

6 French Roman Catholic Episcopal Conference, 'Concerning the Holy See's Response to the Final Report of ARCIC I' (1992), in C. Hill and E. Yarnold (eds), *Anglicans and Roman Catholics: The Search for Unity* (London, 1994), pp. 171–84 at p. 180.

7 *The Tablet*, 11 July 1998, pp. 920–2.

8 'Concerning the Holy See's Response to the Final Report of ARCIC I', p. 183.

Dysfunctional Ecclesiology in
the Anglican Communion and the Church of England[9]

If the Roman Catholic Church can be said to have a 'dysfunctional ecclesiology', the same is certainly true of the Anglican Communion and of the Church of England; I will give one example for each.

As regards the Anglican Communion, I need refer only to the Lambeth Conference of 1988. As I wrote back in 1989:

It is, to put it mildly, ecclesiologically odd that the Anglican Communion can feel empowered to give a verdict on the legitimacy of the Final Report of ARCIC but unable as a communion to give a verdict on the legitimacy of the ordination of women as priests and bishops.[10]

Instead, by leaving that decision to each member church of the Communion, it confirmed and underlined the principle of provincial autonomy.[11] The crucial failure of the 1988 Lambeth Conference lay not in its refusal to give an authoritative ruling on the question of the ordination of women to the priesthood and the episcopate, but in the reason given for that refusal. It could (and should) have appealed to the need for consensus among the churches and, more particularly, within the universal episcopate of the Church Catholic (not the same thing as the episcopate of the Anglican Communion); instead it left each autonomous province to resolve the question for itself.[12]

Within the Church of England, a dysfunctional ecclesiology is the consequence of the General Synod's decision on 11 November 1992 to approve the Priests (Ordination of Women) Measure and then on 11 November 1993 to approve

---

9 Only headings exist for this fourth section of the lecture. The text that follows is a reconstruction, where possible quoting from Roger's earlier writings.

10 See p. 66 above.

11 *Cf.* pp. 81–2 above.

12 *Cf.* p. 93 above.

the Episcopal Ministry Act of Synod. The communion within each diocese of the Church of England is impaired, in that there are priests in some parishes of each diocese who are excluded by law from ministering as priests in other parishes of the same diocese. The impairment of communion extends in practice to the episcopal level: bishops who ordain women have to accept that they are no longer able to preside at the Eucharist in certain parishes of their dioceses, while bishops who are opposed to the ordination of women to the priest-hood have to accept that priests whose priestly ministry they cannot themselves accept will minister in some parishes of their dioceses.[13] This breakdown of the internal communion and unity of the Church of England's dioceses certainly manifests dysfunction. What is true at the diocesan level is true at the national level and that of the whole Anglican Communion: the membership of the 1998 Lambeth Conference included bishops who were unable to recognize other members of the Conference as bishops.

What will this impairment of communion within the Church of England do to its traditional comprehensiveness? Will the Church of England be able to maintain its unity, or is the impairment of communion part of a gradual disintegration? Is it a grievous hurt (but not more than that)? Or is it an incurable wound?

Towards a Conclusion[14]

Failure to act on the vision of authority in the Church set out in the *Final Report* of ARCIC I has accentuated the differences between our two churches and made more acute the existing dysfunction within each of them. This can be seen in three fields:

---

13 *Cf.* p. 140 above.

14 This final section of the lecture exists only in note form. The text that follows is a reconstruction.

❖ Unity in diversity:

Here the two churches have displayed opposite failures. The Roman Catholic Church has often found it difficult to tolerate diversity – despite Pope John Paul II's comment in a homily given in Sweden in June 1989 that the Church's unity 'is a unity that embraces diversity and that is verified in diversity'.[15] The Anglican Communion, by contrast, has struggled to maintain its unity in the face of growing diversity.

❖ Subsidiarity:

Again, the two churches have displayed opposite failures – excessive centralism on the part of Rome and a lack of central authority within the Anglican Communion.

❖ Clarity and comprehensiveness:

Here, it is a case of opposite values taken to excess. As Fr Jean-Marc Laporte SJ has remarked, the Roman Catholic Church prizes clarity, whereas the Anglican tradition values comprehensiveness. He writes:

> What authentic institutional value is each Church prone to affirm in a disordered way?. . . One of the advantages of ecumenical dialogue is that honesty enables each side to lay bare its own weakness in these matters and to receive with compassion the other's confession of weakness . . .
>
> The institutional value Roman Catholics are tempted to cling to appears to be that of clarity. The preference is for doctrines and norms of behaviour stated in an unambiguous and uncompromising way. When this Roman approach works well, persons and groups at a lower level are confident in their right to apply clear principles with *epikeia* and human compassion. When it does not work well, principles grow into detailed regulations and insistent calls for submission in matters which do not threaten the unity of the Church. Outer

---

15 See p. 86 above.

compliance may be achieved but inwardly there will be seething irritation or apathy towards the central authority. The negotiation between unity and plurality which constitutes an essential task of any institution has to that extent failed. The victory of unity is either illusory or pyrrhic.

The corresponding Anglican value . . . seems to be that of comprehensiveness. The preference is for formulations which, whenever possible, will enable individuals and groups with different sensitivities to be at home. When it works well, comprehensiveness is a felicitous approach, English rather than Roman, equally traditional and equally valid, to dealing with the one and the many as it affects institutional life. When it does not work well, it may promote a blurred perception of Church life and discourage the posing of sharp questions on matters of essential moment. Again, the negotiation between unity and plurality has to that extent failed. Their tension has not been allowed to emerge fully.

Clarity and comprehensiveness, in openness to each other, will bring out what is authentically human and perennially valid in our two traditions of dealing with the tensions endemic to all human communities. Together, they can foster a searching and compassionate dialogue between the claims of unity and those of diversity.[16]

There are two ways of looking at the position with regard to the future of dialogue between the Roman Catholic Church and the Anglican Communion. According to the first of these scenarios, ARCIC I aroused unrealistic expectations of euphoric character. It was 'the triumph of hope over reality' – 'a romantic might have been'. New 'obstacles' were already implicit at

---

16 J.-M. Laporte, 'Kenosis and Koinonia: The Path Ahead for Anglican–Roman Catholic Dialogue', *One in Christ*, 21–2 (1985), pp. 102–20 at p. 108.

an early stage of its work and long before publication of its *Final Report*. The Anglican Communion is in dialogue with other world communions (and there is a need for 'consonance' between those dialogues): Rome is one among many. Now the dialogue is on a more realistic footing. There are no quick solutions, but there is a long-term framework for dialogue. An alternative view is that the dialogue has essentially changed. It was the 'flagship' of bilateral dialogues; those who inaugurated it in 1966 were looking for results and, though they wisely avoided specifying a timetable, they were hopeful that there would be substantial progress towards the restoration of communion by 2000.

There has been an apparent *volte face* on the issue of primacy. In receiving the *Final Report* of ARCIC, the Anglican Communion expressed a degree of openness towards a universal primacy, but by ignoring the warnings and pleadings of the Bishop of Rome on an issue which so vitally affects communion between the churches, the Anglican churches have surely rejected the need for a universal primacy or, at the very least, reduced its role to an almost meaningless primacy of honour?[17] And whereas in the past the Church of England accused Rome of innovation, while Rome came to rely on a doctrine of development, now there has been a 'switchover' of concerns – Anglicans have claimed that the ordination of women to the priesthood and episcopate is such a development, whereas Pope John Paul II declared in 1994 that 'the Church has no authority whatsoever to confer priestly ordination of women'.[18]

'Where are we now?' is thus a question to be asked not only of Anglican–Roman Catholic dialogue but also of Anglican identity. The 1998 Lambeth Conference will prove to have been critical for this. In addition to the ordination of women, there are other questions – concerning lay presidency, the

---

17 *Cf.* p. 168 above.

18 Apostolic Letter *Ordinatio Sacerdotalis* to the Bishops of the Catholic Church On Reserving Priestly Ordination to Men Alone, 22 May 1994: http://www.vatican.va/holy_father/john_paul_ii/apost_letters/documents/hf_jp-ii_apl_22051994_ordinatio-sacerdotalis_en.html

Porvoo Agreement, sexual morals, and credal orthodoxy. Does the Anglican Communion still hold to the Lambeth Quadrilateral of the Scriptures, the Creeds, the Dominical Sacraments and the Historic Episcopate?

As the Co-Chairmen of ARCIC I suggested in their Preface to its first Agreed Statement on Authority in the Church back in 1976, the Roman Catholic and Anglican traditions are complementary. The dialogue was commenced because each needed the other:

> Communion with the see of Rome would bring to the churches of the Anglican Communion not only a wider *koinonia* but also a strengthening of the power to realize the traditional ideal of diversity in unity. Roman Catholics, on their side, would be enriched by the presence of a particular tradition of spirituality and scholarship, the lack of which has deprived the Roman Catholic Church of a precious element in the Christian heritage. The Roman Catholic Church has much to learn from the Anglican synodical tradition of involving the laity in the life and mission of the Church.[19]

The Roman Catholic and Anglican Churches need each other in order to achieve a fuller manifestation of unity in diversity and in order to arrive at a better manifestation of subsidiarity. Both churches stand in need of conversion. For Anglicans, this would involve taking seriously the need for authority in the Church and locating it. For Roman Catholics, it would involve taking seriously the need to redress the balance between the Pope and the local churches. So much is at stake: continued dialogue is therefore vital.

---

19 *Final Report*, p. 50.

PART 4

The Gift of Authority

23

A Second Chance or a Last Chance?
(July 1999)

The Gift of Authority, the Second Anglican–Roman Catholic International Commission's report on authority in the Church, was published in May 1999. Roger's criticism of comments about the report in an editorial in New Directions *prompted an invitation to him to write this article setting out his first reactions to it. It appeared in July 1999.*[1]

I would like to structure my remarks around three Old Testament quotations.

> *Lo, the winter is past . . . the flowers appear on the earth, the time of singing has come.*
> *(Song of Solomon 2.11–12)*

While I respect (and indeed share) that recognition of the overriding need for honesty, lucidity and realism which dictated the sceptical tone of last month's editorial comments, I do regret that they were not more welcoming to the Statement. After all, we have for years been lamenting the long 'winter of ecumenism' and deploring the fact that the ARCIC process had been – as many put it graphically – 'relegated to the back burner'. Optimism may be irreconcilable with pessimism, but hope is not the enemy of realism. Were we all perhaps in danger of overlooking the Holy Spirit's unnerving capacity for

1 R. T. Greenacre, 'A Second Chance or a Last Chance?', *New Directions*, vol. 3, no. 50 (July 1999), pp. 15–16.

springing surprises on us and turning the tables? Is it mere coincidence that it was during the Pentecost novena – that period in the Church's year between Ascension and Pentecost devoted to eager, prayerful, expectant waiting upon the Holy Spirit – and in the final months of this millennium (unless, that is, that we still hold to the view that the Third Millennium begins in 2001) that two extraordinary signs of promise (perhaps even of a Second Spring) were revealed to us?

There was, first of all, the visit of Pope John Paul II to Romania. Roman Catholic–Orthodox relations have been suffering in recent years from the same kind of winter as Roman Catholic–Anglican relations; yet on that May Sunday in Bucharest, when the Pope and the Patriarch of Romania appeared together they were given an emotional welcome, with a quarter of a million people roaring out, '*Unitate, unitate!*' And, secondly, on that same weekend the religious press was reporting the 'bombshell' of an ARCIC Agreed Statement on authority, a statement which included agreement on the primacy and magisterial authority of the Bishop of Rome.

There were many immediate reactions, mostly hostile and mostly from the guts rather than the mind, from people who had perhaps read the text but had given themselves little time to mark, learn or inwardly digest it. A visceral hostility from some liberal and some conservative evangelical Anglicans is understandable, but such people need to remember that very few of our own members of ARCIC II could be described as card-carrying Catholic Anglicans and they also need to remember that the published Agreed Statement represents the end (not a full stop, more a semi-colon) of many years of searching and rigorous dialogue, an intellectual pilgrimage that also demands conversion of heart and mind. As I was drafting this response I came across this plea (in *The Tablet* of 12 June) from Anglicanism's soundest and weightiest theologian, Henry Chadwick:[2] 'The Gift of Authority is on any showing a

---

2 Henry Chadwick (1920–2008) was Chaplain (1946–50) and then Dean (1950–59) of Queen's College, Cambridge, Regius Professor of Divinity at Oxford (1959–69), Dean of Christ Church, Oxford (1969–79), Regius Professor of Divinity at Cambridge (1979–83) and Master of Peterhouse, Cambridge (1987–93). He was a member of ARCIC I and, until 1989, of ARCIC II.

deeply serious and impressive document which does not deserve a hasty reaction.' From us it surely deserves a warm and positive – if not uncritical – welcome.

> *And who knows whether you have not come to the kingdom*
> *for such a time as this?*
> *(Esther 4.14)*

I know that I am not the only catholic-minded Anglican who could not in conscience accept the November 1992 decision of the General Synod of the Church of England and who for years has been constantly asking himself the agonizing question whether he should stay in the Church of England or become a Roman Catholic. There was no point in staying in the Church of England if it only meant shutting oneself up in a resentful, bitter and defiant inward-looking ghetto; one could only stay if one could throw what little weight one had into the ongoing process of reception to which the Church of England was officially committed. Our argument all along was not outright rejection of the possibility (I put it no higher than that) that one day Catholic Christendom might reach a universal consensus which saw the ordination of women to the priesthood as a legitimate development of catholic tradition and that this consensus might be confirmed by those with the highest teaching authority in East and West; it was rather a considered and principled rejection of the claim that either the Church of England or the Anglican Communion, which claims to be no more than a part of the Catholic Church, had the authority to make a unilateral decision in this matter in the face of the opposition from Rome or Orthodoxy.

A year ago, in reviewing the Response of the House of Bishops to the Papal Encyclical *Ut Unum Sint*, I drew your readers' attention to the damaging but promising admission by the bishops that the churches 'have sometimes taken decisions which have further deepened their divisions' and that 'other Churches, including the Church of England, have also made unilateral decisions on questions which many consider central matters of faith and order'.[3] This seemed to me at the time to be an implicit recognition of the validity of our stand. This is considerably reinforced in *The Gift of Authority*; to take but one example, in paragraph 37 it is stated: 'The maintenance of communion requires that at every level there is a capacity to take decisions appropriate to that level. When those decisions raise serious questions for the wider communion of churches, synodality must find a wider expression.' What else can one say to that than a very fervent Amen? One might also be tempted to add: 'We told you so' – thinking, for example, of the pamphlet *Lost in the Fog: The Lesson for Ecumenism of Lambeth 1988,* published by the Church Union Theological Committee in 1989,[4] and the warnings it conveyed about the dangers of unlimited 'provincial autonomy' in the Anglican Communion. There is clearly something of a retreat now from this principle among Anglicans (but has it come too late?) and this is reflected very clearly in the summary of Issues Facing Anglicans in paragraph 56 of the Statement. Could it possibly be the case that growing awareness of the increasing incoherence of Anglicanism and the serious impairment of communion within and between its member churches is leading Anglicans to open their eyes to the imperative need in the universal Church for a ministry dedicated to the maintenance in unity and truth of all the churches in one visible communion?

The tragedy is that so many of our fellow Anglicans who shared this fundamental conviction with us have felt impelled to leave our Communion and that the constituency most likely to welcome this Agreed Statement has thereby been weakened. For those of us who remain, the question put by Mordecai to Esther – at least in this slightly modified form – remains acutely pertinent. Who knows whether we have remained in the Church

---

3 *May They All Be One: A Response of the House of Bishops of the Church of England to Ut Unum Sint* (GS Misc 495) (London: General Synod, 1997), quoted in R. T. Greenacre, 'A Response to the Pope', *New Directions*, vol. 2, no. 34 (March 1998), pp. 4–5.

4 See Chapter 7 of this volume.

of England 'for such a time as this'? We must mobilize all our energies to respond to the challenge.

> *Behold, I set before you this day a blessing and a curse: the blessing if you obey the commandments of the Lord your God which I command you this day, and the curse, if you do not obey the commandments of the Lord your God. You shall set the blessing on Mount Gerizim and the curse on Mount Ebal.*
> *(Deuteronomy 11.26–9)*

In one sense we must be careful not to exaggerate the importance or completeness of this Statement. It clearly represents a significant confirmation of, and advance upon, the statements on Authority in the Church in the *Final Report* of ARCIC I, but it does leave a number of key questions not only unresolved but scarcely even articulated – presumably because they belong to the next stage of the process. In particular, when it is affirmed in paragraph 47 that it is 'the wholly reliable teaching of the whole Church that is operative in the judgement of the universal primate', it is not made clear what is meant by 'the whole Church'. It leaves open both the degree of authority to be accorded to papal definitions made since the time of separation between East and West and since the sixteenth-century divisions in the West and also the question of what relation bishops (acknowledged as such by Rome) of churches separated from Rome have to the college of the successors of the Apostles. These issues have been raised in Rome's dialogues with the Eastern Churches, both Chalcedonian and non-Chalcedonian, and notably in that most promising of 'pilot schemes' for Roman Catholic–Eastern Orthodox unity between the two Byzantine-rite Patriarchates of Antioch (Orthodox and Catholic). In this, Catholic Melkite partners in the dialogue have argued (so far unrebuked) that doctrinal definitions made in the West during the second millennium should not be considered binding on the Orthodox.

But I digress! For in another sense it would be hard to exaggerate the importance of this Statement. It surely confronts the Anglican Communion – and, more particularly at this point, the Church of England – with a crucial and irreversible turning point (although I am not suggesting that it does not also challenge the Roman Catholic Church). For us the road ahead now leads to a decisive T-junction marked by a signpost. It points in one direction to Mount Gerizim and in the other to Mount Ebal. Can even Anglicans take refuge in fudge at this juncture? The road to Mount Gerizim represents a clear choice for *The Gift of Authority* and for all that will follow from making such a choice. The road to Mount Ebal represents a choice for revoking the Act of Synod and introducing legislation for the ordination of women to the episcopate. That Act of Synod made it possible for many of us to remain in the Church of England in the immediate aftermath of the 1992 vote; its withdrawal will remove that possibility.

The new situation created by the present set of choices may however involve Catholic Anglicans in something of a reshuffle of alliances. Some who have so far been co-belligerents, if not allies, may see this issue as a parting of the ways, while some others whom we have seen as adversaries may come to realize that affirming Catholicism must mean affirming this latest Agreed Statement. It will be a difficult and confusing time, but for those of us who from the beginning have seen the reception and confirmation of the ARCIC process as our theological priority our present duty will be clear. A rejection of this Statement would be as grave a blow for the Catholic cause in Anglicanism as the 1992 vote, and would we this time have any coherent or honourable excuse for staying where we are? The trumpet is giving a sound that is anything but uncertain and we must prepare ourselves for battle.

24

The Gift of Authority:
An ARCIC Perspective
(October 1999)

On 27 October 1999 Roger gave this lecture to a Sacred Synod convoked by the Bishops of Beverley, Ebbsfleet and Richborough (Provincial Episcopal Visitors) and the Bishop of Fulham in Westminster. It is published here for the first time.

I see my task as one of aiding and leading your reflection on the latest document from ARCIC II, *The Gift of Authority*, launched in May this year, and of trying to discern with you its importance and its relevance to our particular stand and our particular vocation. I shall therefore attempt – in the short time at my disposal – to do three things. First, to say something about the text itself; second, to discuss the challenges and the questions it poses both to the Roman Catholic Church and to the Anglican Communion; third, to try to show its particular and crucial relevance to our own witness.

The Text

So, first of all, let us look at the text itself. If I had been invited to lead a Bible study at a convention of our Evangelical brethren, I would expect you all by now to have your Bibles out, open and at the ready. But though I hope I can be confident that you all have a copy of *The Gift of Authority*, I think I can assume that you have not all got a copy with you now. So perhaps this is not yet the time – though time must be found in the months and years ahead – to make a detailed paragraph by paragraph exploration of the text. Perhaps my job today is to whet your appetite and explain both its main drift and emphasis and also its conclusions.

The first cause both for surprise and for thanksgiving is the very fact that it has appeared at all. After the perceived inability of the 1988 Lambeth Conference of the Anglican Communion (and it is the Anglican Communion, not the Church of England, which is the Anglican partner in ARCIC) to invoke any authority which could pronounce on an issue as divisive and as destructive of its own unity as the ordination of women to the episcopate, after what was perceived as the cold douche of Rome's official response to the *Final Report* of ARCIC I in 1991, and after the vote in the General Synod in 1992 to proceed to the ordination of women to the priesthood in the Church of England, both partners in the dialogue had a case for saying that the other had moved the goalposts since the ground rules of the dialogue had been drawn up and that this constituted a serious threat to its continuance. Relations between Rome and Canterbury plummeted to a new low in the middle years of this decade and, though both partners said they were convinced that the ARCIC dialogue must continue, it did look as though, with the implicit connivance of both sides, it had been relegated to the back burner.

And now it has bounced back to near the top of the agenda – or has it? That is a question we must look at later, for the importance to be given to this document does not depend only on the text itself but also on its post-natal development or, if you prefer, its subsequent trajectory. And we must go back to 1982 when the *Final Report* of ARCIC I was published, containing all the Agreed Statements it had already published together with its second text on Authority in the Church. *The Gift of Authority* is therefore subtitled *Authority in the Church III* and one is irresistibly reminded of Luis de León resuming his lectures at the University of Salamanca after five years in the prisons of the Inquisition: '*Dicebamus hesterna die*' – 'As we were saying yesterday.' So there are two fundamental questions to be asked: to what extent does *Authority III* mark an advance on *Authority I* and *Authority II*, and, given all that has happened in the seventeen intervening years, what are the chances of positive reception on either side?

There was already in *Authority II* an advance on *Authority I*. The latter made the cautious statement: 'It seems *appropriate* that in any future union a universal primacy . . . should be held by (the) see (of Rome)'[1] but five years later *Authority II* could state 'that the primacy of the bishop of Rome can be affirmed as part of God's design for the universal *koinonia*' and in another place that there should be no obstacle to Anglican acceptance of the Roman primacy 'as God's will for his Church'.[2]

Part of the advance marked by *Authority III* is the fact that it restates and reaffirms the arguments of its predecessors in a new way and in a new language. For Christians today who tend to think and speak of authority as a problem there is a radical challenge in the very title of the report, which asks us rather to see and welcome the gift of authority. Authority is indeed seen as a positive gift, an inescapable part of God's self-revelation, essential to the Church's witness and mission in the world. So the key to the whole Statement is a scriptural image from St Paul's Second Letter to the Corinthians which speaks of Christ as God's 'Yes' to humanity and of our response to God as the 'Amen', equally given in and through Christ. The Statement is also extremely positive in its refusal to accept false disjunctives and dichotomies often pressed by controversialists. There is essentially no opposition between freedom and obedience, between the faith of the individual and the faith of the Church, between Scripture and Tradition, between the ordained ministry and the laity, between the local church and the universal Church, between definition and reception, and

---

1 Anglican–Roman Catholic International Commission, *The Final Report* (London: CTS/SPCK, 1982), p. 64: 'Authority in the Church I', para. 23 (italics added).

2 *The Final Report*, pp. 87–8: 'Authority in the Church II', paras 15, 14.

between synodality and primacy. In all these examples it is a case of both-and, not of either/or.

There is also however an advance in content as well as in presentation, and ARCIC II has tried not only to go further in its own thinking but to take on board requests for clarification both from the Vatican and from the Lambeth Conference. I do not have the time (let alone the competence!) to cover the whole ground. I must limit myself here to what is said about the Roman primacy, though in many ways it is unsatisfactory to do this in isolation from the rest of the text. Let us take note of the following affirmations in *Authority III*:

> Para. 37: 'The mutual interdependence of all the churches is integral to the reality of the Church as God wills it to be. No local church that participates in the living Tradition can regard itself as self-sufficient.'[3]
>
> Para. 46: 'The exigencies of church life call for a specific exercise of *episcope* at the service of the whole Church.'[4] The text then goes on to describe this ministry of universal primacy in terms that surely imply that it is of the *esse* and not of the *bene esse* of the Church.

Authority III goes on to speak of papal infallibility – the one area in which *Authority II* and therefore the *Final Report* of ARCIC I acknowledged a remaining and serious disagreement. I quote paragraph 47:

> Within his wider ministry, the Bishop of Rome offers a specific ministry concerning the discernment of truth, as an expression of universal primacy ... Any such definition is pronounced *within* the college of those who exercise *episcope* and not outside that college ... When the faith is articulated in

---

3 *The Gift of Authority. Authority in the Church III: An Agreed Statement by the Anglican–Roman Catholic International Commission* (London, Toronto and New York: CTS, Anglican Book Centre and Church Publishing Incorporated), p. 27.

4 *The Gift of Authority*, p. 32.

this way, the Bishop of Rome proclaims the faith of the local churches. It is thus the wholly reliable teaching of the whole Church that is operative in the judgement of the universal primate . . . The reception of the primacy of the Bishop of Rome entails the recognition of this specific ministry of the universal primate. We believe that this is a gift to be received by all the churches.[5]

And if this were not strong enough:

Para. 60: 'The Commission's work has resulted in sufficient agreement on universal primacy as a gift to be shared, for us to propose that such a primacy could be offered and received even before our churches are in full communion.'[6]

Note the phrase here – 'sufficient agreement', for this is not yet a full and final agreement, nor would it be fair to expect it to be so. There are hints of areas where more work needs to be done – such as in the hope and expectation that Anglicans will be 'open to and desire a recovery and re-reception *under certain clear conditions* of the exercise of universal primacy by the Bishop of Rome'[7] and the absence of any reference in this text to the Marian dogmas of 1854 and 1950, signalled as problem areas in *Authority II*. It would appear to be the case that these are to be looked at again in the near future by ARCIC II.[8] Perhaps the Commission is hoping that what seems to be quite possible in Rome's dialogue with Orthodoxy – i.e. that the Orthodox Churches will not be obliged to accept definitions made in the West in the Second Millennium – will also be applied to the Anglican–Roman Catholic dialogue. It does raise

---

5 *The Gift of Authority*, pp. 33–4 (italics in original).

6 *The Gift of Authority*, p. 42.

7 *The Gift of Authority*, p. 42, para. 62 (italics added).

8 ARCIC II's work eventually resulted in the publication of *Mary: Grace and Hope in Christ, An Agreed Statement* (Harrisburg and London: Morehouse, 2005). See R. T. Greenacre, *Maiden, Mother and Queen: Mary in the Anglican Tradition* (Norwich: Canterbury Press, 2013), chapter 19.

the issue of what the Commission understands by the phrase 'the whole Church' when it speaks of the 'teaching of the whole Church' and the 'faith of the whole Church'.

Challenges and Questions to Our Churches

The Gift of Authority is not an abstract exercise in theology; it also issues challenges and makes practical suggestions. The challenges are of particular importance, because it is fairly clear that both communions are living with internal contradictions and tensions and that both can fairly be described at the moment as 'dysfunctional churches'. In an assembly like this I hardly need to labour the point as far as our own church and our own communion are concerned. But in the Roman Catholic Church there are forces pulling in conflicting directions too – not only, for example, tension between episcopal conferences and the Curia, but even within the Curia between different dicasteries. What is clear, however, is that neither communion at the moment can offer an exemplary model of the exercise of authority and that both communions show serious imbalance in exactly opposite ways. Unity in diversity is, for example, the model held up by both, but Rome has valued unity at the expense of diversity and Anglicans diversity at the expense of unity. How much we have to offer each other and to learn from each other!

But the particular example of dysfunction I need to emphasize today is concerned with levels of authority. The principle of subsidiarity lays down that decisions should be taken at the appropriate level: this certainly means that smaller units – in this case, the local churches – should not have the power of decision making in questions which are of purely local concern taken away from them, but it also means that questions which put at risk the maintenance of universal communion should be dealt with at the universal level. Rome shows herself to be dysfunctional when she fails to respect the authority of local churches; the Anglican Communion shows herself to be dysfunctional when she has no powers of decision making at the international level but has to bow to the principle of provincial autonomy, which has already impaired the integrity of the Anglican Communion. And this now seems to be leading – as some of us warned that it would – to a new principle of diocesan autonomy, as the threat of the authorization of lay presidency in the Diocese of Sydney makes clear. 'When major change occurs within our worldwide Anglican family,' says the Archbishop of Sydney (as quoted in the *Church Times* of 22 October 1999), 'it is usually through one part of the Communion acting unilaterally, and then the Communion follows.'[9] Quite! Doesn't that say it all?

The tragedy of the estrangement of our two communions is in this failure to learn from, enrich and correct each other; instead we drift further away from each other and drift further towards opposite and dangerously unbalanced extremes. But there have been signs of hope. On the Anglican side there has been an increased awareness of the dangers of unlimited provincial autonomy – as the Virginia Report of 1998 (twice cited in *The Gift of Authority*) made clear. On the Roman Catholic side there has been the remarkable breakthrough of Pope John Paul II's 1995 encyclical on ecumenism *Ut Unum Sint*, in which he spoke of heeding the request made to him to find new ways of exercising his primacy, and invited the leaders and theologians of other churches to engage with him in undertaking a task he could not carry out alone. It is signs such as these that have enabled the Commission to submit its work to our two communions, expecting that it will be taken seriously and not laughed out of court as totally unreal.

But let us look for a moment at what *The Gift of Authority* has to say about specific issues facing Anglicans in its crucial paragraph 56. First of all it reminds us that the Anglican Communion is exploring the development of structures of authority among its provinces. It then asks the question:

---

9 Quoted by M. Porter, 'Sydney says lay people can preside', *Church Times*, 22 October 1999, p. 1.

'Is the Communion also open to the acceptance of instruments of oversight which would allow decisions to be reached that, in certain circumstances, would bind the whole Church?' In other words, not only is it a question of stronger structures within Anglicanism but of structures at the universal and ecumenical level, with, at their heart, the primacy of the Bishop of Rome. This leads to a passage to important that I must quote it in full:

> When major new questions arise which, in fidelity to Scripture and Tradition, require a united response, will these structures assist Anglicans to participate in the *sensus fidelium* with all Christians? To what extent does unilateral action by provinces or dioceses in matters concerning the whole Church, even after consultation has taken place, weaken *koinonia*? Anglicans have shown themselves to be willing to tolerate anomalies for the sake of maintaining communion. Yet this has led to the impairment of communion manifesting itself at the Eucharist, in the exercise of *episcope* and in interchangeability of ministry.[10]

Take alongside this a quotation from the Virginia Report in paragraph 4:

> The long history of ecumenical involvement, both locally and internationally, has shown us that Anglican discernment and decision making must take account of the insights into truth and the Spirit-led wisdom of our ecumenical partners. Moreover, any decisions we take must be offered for the discernment of the universal Church.[11]

---

10 *The Gift of Authority*, p. 40.

11 *The Gift of Authority*, p. 11, quoting 'The Virginia Report: The Report of the Inter-Anglican Theological and Doctrinal Commission', in *The Official Report of the Lambeth Conference 1998* (Harrisburg, PA: Morehouse Publising, 1998), pp. 15–68 at p. 63.

Relevance to our own Witness

By now I have moved from my second section – discussing the challenges and questions posed by this report to both our Communions – to the third and final section: the relevance of this Statement to the particular witness to which those of us taking part in this Sacred Synod are called.

It cannot be said loudly, frequently or emphatically enough that, though I do not think that any of the Anglican members of the Commission would identify with our position,[12] yet the Statement totally vindicates the legitimacy of our stand – at least the stand of those of us who have always affirmed that our fundamental objection to the ordination of women to the priesthood and the episcopate is that we cannot accept the authority of a part of the Church (provinces and groups of provinces) to make a unilateral change in the historic ministry of the universal Church of this kind, especially when such changes (and I quote again from the Statement itself) 'raise serious questions for the wider communion of churches'. I am not saying that we should welcome the Statement simply because it backs up what we have been saying for years or simply because it allows us to say 'I told you so' to those who have been trying to dismiss or marginalize us as discredited reactionaries; we should welcome it only because what it says is true. But if it does also vindicate our somewhat lonely stand (not perhaps so lonely a stand in the Diocese of Chichester), that is a bonus for which we must be grateful.

At this point I must register both real disappointment and real anxiety. Disappointment, because Evangelical opposition to the Statement (and I do not want to suggest that all Evangelicals are hostile to it) has been rapidly and effectively mobilized and the case for the opposition put very ably and skilfully by, for example, the Church of England Evangelical Council and in a number of articles in the *Church of England Newspaper*,

12 The members of the second Anglican–Roman Catholic Commission did not include any representatives of traditional Anglo-Catholicism.

notably in a critique by Bishop Colin Buchanan,[13] accusing the Anglican members of ARCIC of letting themselves be hijacked by Rome. What has been the response from the Catholic side? I am grateful to the editors of *New Directions* for printing a short piece of mine in the July issue, but that was wrung out of me by what I considered to be the far too sceptical tone of the previous month's editorial and in the July issue my piece appeared opposite an even more sceptical comment from a Roman Catholic theologian. A more detailed appraisal of the Statement by the Bishop of Basingstoke has been promised by the editors and we eagerly await its publication.[14] Stephen Platten, Dean of Norwich, has written a helpful commentary in the Assumptiontide issue of *The Walsingham Review*,[15] but – as far as I know – that is all, apart from a very mixed bag of comments in the *Church Times* and in *The Tablet*. We really do need to mobilize our forces and our resources and to prepare material for our use in the debate that will soon be initiated in the churches of the Anglican Communion. There is an extremely detailed, thorough and penetrating commentary on the Statement by Fr William Henn, a Capuchin theologian and Professor at the Gregorian University. It takes up twelve pages of issue number 100 of the Pontifical Council for Promoting Christian Unity's Information Service and is also published in French in the May issue of *La Documentation Catholique* – but how many of you have access to either of those publications? We urgently need a volume that will continue the work of Christopher Hill and Edward Yarnold in their first collection of ARCIC documents, *Anglicans and Roman Catholics: The Search for Unity*, published in 1994, and also simpler pamphlet study guide material for use in parishes and deaneries. As a former Chairman of Church Union Theological Committee I

13 The Rt Revd Colin Buchanan (b. 1934) was Bishop of Aston (1985–89), Vicar of Gillingham, Kent (1991–96) and Bishop of Woolwich (1996–2004).

14 D. G. Rowell, 'A Pattern of Primacy', *New Directions*, vol. 3, no. 55 (December 1999), pp. 16–18, no. 56 (January 2000), pp. 6–8.

15 S. Platten, 'The Gift of Authority – ARCIC II', *The Walsingham Review*, 124 (Assumptiontide 1999), pp. 9–12.

have to ask: Where – if anywhere – is its successor? At a time like this we certainly need one.

That is my disappointment; my anxiety is this: that *The Gift of Authority* will become a dead letter not so much because of outright opposition (a public and open debate which we lose) but because it will be smothered by an Anglican agenda that will lead us progressively further away from the challenges and the questions posed in this Statement and make it impossible for us to give a positive response. If I were Screwtape, my advice would be on these lines: 'Don't let people actually get round to reading and discussing it; that's far too dangerous. Don't even work to get it rejected; just let it be forgotten by being relegated to the bottom of the Church's agenda.'

One of the temptations of our minority situation is to opt out of the official structures of the Church of England altogether. It is a temptation we must resist, for, if and when this text is debated in the Church of England in our parishes, our deaneries and our dioceses, we must be here and we must be there to do battle, courteously, but firmly and theologically well-prepared. It is a battle that will demonstrate that what motivates us is a positive conviction about truth, unity and authority and not merely negative opposition to change.

We may be tempted too by a certain weariness. 'What is the point? We have no chance of winning this battle either.' It is here that we need to take to heart the serious warning that God addresses to the watchmen and shepherds of his people through the prophet Ezekiel and which today he addresses to us as priests and pastors in the Church of England:

So you, son of man, I have made a watchman for the house of Israel; whenever you hear a word from my mouth, you shall give them warning from me. If . . . you do not speak to warn them, they will die in their iniquity, but their blood I will require at your hand.[16]

---

16 Ezekiel 3.17–18.

25

Ecumenism and future relations with the Roman Catholic Church (May 2000)

This lecture was given at 'Christ Our Future', a theological and devotional conference commemorating the Jubilee Year 2000, sponsored by the mid-Atlantic catholic rectors of the Episcopal Church and held at St Clement's Church, Philadelphia, on 12 and 13 May 2000. It is published here for the first time.

The title and theme of this Conference is 'Christ our Future'; so this challenges me to look to the future neither with the smooth and easy optimism of the false prophet nor with the deep cynical despair of one who does not believe in Christ's Easter victory, but rather with that Christian virtue of hoping against hope, of believing in the power of the one whom St Paul calls the God of hope to fulfil his promises. But before we can look forward we need to look back: as the French proverb puts it, *reculer pour mieux sauter* – step back in order to take a better jump forward.

Anglican–Roman Catholic Dialogue

The twentieth century was certainly an ecumenical century. From that point of view the most important event in it was the Second Vatican Council in the 1960s, which saw the Roman Catholic Church, which up to that point had either condemned, or at least declared itself unable to join, the Ecumenical Movement, embrace it wholeheartedly. It was no accident that Archbishop Michael Ramsey waited until 1966, when the Council had completed its work, to make a formal visit to Pope Paul VI and to inaugurate with him a serious, official international dialogue which aimed at restoring complete visible unity in faith and order between Rome and Canterbury.

ARCIC I began its work in 1970 and its agenda was devoted to three subjects: the Eucharist, Ministry and Ordination, and Authority in the Church. The logical sequence is clear; if we are to have full communion, we must first of all be sure that we share the same eucharistic faith – not necessarily the same theology, the same language or the same devotional and liturgical framework, but the same faith. Then we must be sure that we have the same faith with regard to the ordained ministry and the meaning of ordination, so as to be able to arrive at a point where we can recognize each other's ordained ministries. On these two subjects the Commission itself judged that it had reached 'substantial agreement' and asked the two Communions to confirm and ratify this judgement. The third and most difficult theme was Authority in the Church, for without agreement on this there can be no full and visible unity. Here the Commission judged that it had not yet had the time to claim substantial agreement on all the points which it had to consider, but at least a converging consensus which would afford a solid basis for further progress. If there was still a gap, this was particularly true of the two overlapping subjects of the infallibility and universal jurisdiction of the Bishop of Rome.

The remarkable progress represented by twelve years of dialogue was celebrated during Pope John Paul II's visit to England in 1982 at a great service in Canterbury Cathedral after which the Pope and the Archbishop of Canterbury committed themselves to the next stage of the dialogue, which involved setting up a new or second ARCIC and launching a process by which the *Final Report* of ARCIC I would be subject to critical evaluation by the authoritative bodies of both communions and to reception by the faithful of both churches.

But already things were turning sour, and the great hopes of an ecumenical Spring were giving way to the more sombre and pessimistic mood of an ecumenical Winter. This came to dominate not only Anglican–Roman Catholic relations but the whole ecumenical scene in the last decades of the twentieth century. To give but one other example, the world of Roman Catholic–Orthodox dialogue became paradoxically that much more difficult with the collapse of the Iron Curtain and the revival, so much feared by the Orthodox, of the Eastern-rite Catholic churches in Eastern Europe.

But let us return now to Anglican–Roman Catholic relations. Here both communions had serious and well founded reasons for accusing the other of creating obstacles to the successful continuation of the dialogue, for accusing the other of 'moving the goal posts' to use a phrase commonly used in the United Kingdom (a football playing nation, or at least a football watching nation).

The Roman Catholic Church could reproach Anglicans for proceeding to the ordination of women to the priesthood and then to the episcopate while a dialogue on the reconciliation of ministries was taking place and in spite of the emphatic and solemn warnings of two popes that this would create a new and very serious obstacle to unity. The Roman Catholic Church could also observe the crisis that this development provoked within the member churches of the Anglican Communion and within the Communion itself and could hardly avoid asking the question: What is the point of having a dialogue with a Communion which is undergoing serious breaches of sacramental communion within its own life and which has no organs of authority at the international level capable of preserving its own unity? And if that is the case, what can it 'deliver' ecumenically?

Meanwhile, Anglicans had a serious problem with Rome's Official Response to the *Final Report*, which after interminable delays, due in part to conflict between two curial bodies in Rome, the Congregation for the Doctrine of the Faith and the Council for Promoting Christian Unity, finally appeared in

1991. This response, which Professor Henry Chadwick described as a 'cold douche' seemed to Anglicans (and indeed to many Roman Catholics) to have two grave defects. First, it totally ignored the official evaluations of the *Final Report* made by a number of Roman Catholic episcopal conferences (including those of the USA, of England and Wales and of France); second, it appeared to undermine a spirit and method of dialogue, formally approved by two popes, based on the principle of going behind the polemical texts of the sixteenth-century period of rupture and confrontation to the shared inheritance of the Gospel and the Tradition of the early Church. The two Churches had agreed to try to answer the same question – 'Are the agreements contained in the *Final Report* consonant with the faith of our Church?' Now the Response was asking 'Is the *Final Report* identical with the teachings of the Roman Catholic Church?' The demand for identity clearly goes beyond the demand for consonance.

ARCIC II bravely continued to meet and to work during this period, but there was a widespread feeling in both churches that – to use a phrase often in use at the time – the Anglican–Roman Catholic dialogue had been 'put on the back burner' and had little, if any, future. Perhaps 1994 marked the lowest point in the drop of temperature, with Pope John Paul II's uncompromising Apostolic Letter on the Ordination of Women and the Archbishop of Canterbury's sharp reply. But last year, at the very end of a century that had seen such brilliant promise and then such bitter disappointment, came an extraordinary surprise.

Signs of Hope

In fact 1999 gave to a tired and jaded ecumenical world three – at least three – signs of hope. In May Pope John Paul II visited Romania, and when he and the Orthodox Patriarch of Romania appeared together at a great open-air liturgical celebration they were greeted by an enormous crowd of between

250 and 300,000 people who shouted out – as if with a single voice – *Unitate, Unitate!* It was at the same time, during the period between Ascension and Pentecost when the Church is praying for a fresh outpouring of the Holy Spirit, that the report of ARCIC II, *The Gift of Authority*, was published – and we will return to this in a moment. And then in the Autumn, on 31 October at Augsburg in Germany (both the date and the place being highly symbolic), there was signed between the Roman Catholic Church and the Lutheran World Federation a Joint Declaration on Justification by Faith – that key doctrine which had polarized Western Europe into two bitterly divided camps during the sixteenth century.

It was a cause for both surprise and thanksgiving that a major document from ARCIC on the key issue of Authority was able to be launched, and it was a document whose subtitle *Authority III* demonstrated that it was picking up precisely where the last two texts of ARCIC I, *Authority I* and *Authority II* had left off. This return to the theme of authority had been made possible by two developments, one from each side of the dialogue, which were evidence of the thaw which was preparing for this Second Spring.

In 1995 Pope John Paul published a remarkable and courageous Encyclical Letter (*Ut Unum Sint*) on ecumenism. In it he took note of the obstacle to unity which seemed to be posed by the Petrine ministry which he exercised and declared himself ready to consider proposals for a reform of that ministry, inviting church leaders and theologians of the other churches to engage with him in dialogue on this subject. This in turn provoked a response from the House of Bishops of the Church of England in which they went so far as to admit that 'other Churches, including the Church of England, have also made unilateral decisions on questions which many consider central matters of faith and order'.[1]

The development on the Anglican side has been an increasing realization of the weakness of both the theology and the structures of authority within Anglicanism and of the need to cut

---

1 See pp. 219–20 above.

through the anarchy and incoherence that inevitably follow from the theory and practice of so called 'provincial autonomy'. The Virginia Report of the Inter-Anglican Theological and Doctrinal Commission, prepared for the Lambeth Conference of 1998, spoke of the urgent need for strengthening what it calls rather obscurely 'instruments of synodality' at the international level.[2] The Conference resolved to pursue this quest and in this context to study 'the issue of a universal ministry in the service of Christian unity' – in other words, the issue of the papacy.[3]

But the crisis only seems to have worsened since then, with storm clouds from Australia and Singapore, bringing with them the threat of lay presidency and the prospect (indeed reality) of further schism over issues of sexual morality. Is this crisis perhaps a *felix culpa* – a 'happy fault' which is forcing many Anglicans to see that the only real choice may be between the total incoherence of a free-for-all and acceptance of the ministry of the Bishop of Rome as one whose essential mission is to safeguard communion and unity between the local churches?

A Vindication of Catholic Anglicans

At this point I think it is important to say that, implicitly at least, *The Gift of Authority* totally vindicates the stand which those of us who have gathered here today have taken. We do need to remind not only ourselves of what is said in this text but also our bishops and synods and theologians, remembering in particular that the new Anglican Co-Chairman of ARCIC II is Presiding Bishop Frank Griswold.[4]

---

2 'The Virginia Report: The Report of the Inter-Anglican Theological and Doctrinal Commission', in *The Official Report of the Lambeth Conference 1998* (Harrisburg, PA: Morehouse Publising, 1998), pp. 15–68.

3 *The Official Report of the Lambeth Conference 1998*, p. 399: Resolution III.8(h).

4 The Rt Revd Frank Tracy Griswold III (b. 1937) was Bishop of Chicago (1987–97) and Presiding Bishop of the Episcopal Church in the USA (1997–2006). He was Co-Chairman of ARCIC II from 1998 until 2003, when he resigned following his consecration of Bishop Vicky Gene Robinson to be Bishop of New Hampshire.

Let me read you three extracts from paragraphs 4, 37 and 56 of *The Gift of Authority*. If you have a copy of the text, underline these; otherwise, as soon as you have acquired a copy make sure you underline these passages:

Para. 4: 'Anglican discernment and decision making must take account of the insights into truth and the Spirit-led wisdom of our ecumenical partners. Moreover, any decisions we take must be offered for the discernment of the universal Church' (The Virginia Report, 6.37).[5]

Para. 37: 'Bishops are, both personally and collegially, at the service of communion and are concerned for synodality in all its expressions. These expressions have included a wide variety of organs, instruments and institutions, notably synods or councils, local, provincial, worldwide, ecumenical. The maintenance of communion requires that at every level there is a capacity to take decisions appropriate to that level. When those decisions raise serious questions for the wider communion of churches, synodality must find a wider expression.'[6]

Para. 56: 'Is the [Anglican] Communion also open to the acceptance of instruments of oversight which would allow decisions to be reached that, in certain circumstances, would bind the whole Church? When major new questions arise which, in fidelity to Scripture and Tradition, require a united response, will these structures assist Anglicans to participate in the *sensus fidelium* with all Christians? To what extent does unilateral action by provinces or dioceses in matters concerning the whole Church, even after consultation has taken place, weaken *koinonia*? Anglicans have shown themselves to be willing to tolerate anomalies for the sake of maintaining communion. Yet this has led to the impairment of communion manifesting itself at the Eucharist, in

---

5 ARCIC II, *The Gift of Authority: Authority in the Church III, An Agreed Statement by the Anglican–Roman Catholic International Commission* (London: CTS; Toronto: Anglican Book Centre; and New York: Church Publishing Incorporated, 1999), p. 11.

6 *The Gift of Authority*, p. 28.

the exercise of *episcope* and in the interchangeability of ministry. What consequences flow from this?'[7]

Surely those of us who have taken our stand on the principle that a 'major question' such as the ordination of women to the priesthood and the episcopate cannot be resolved unilaterally either by a national church or by a communion which sees itself as a part – but only a part – of the One Catholic Church of Christ find that our stand is affirmed and validated by these paragraphs.

The Key Paragraph

It would be foolish of me to try, in the short space of time allotted me, to go through *The Gift of Authority* in detail. The most useful thing I can do is to urge you all to read and study it and to encourage the priests among you to incorporate its insights into your preaching and teaching, for it is a rich and spiritually and theologically rewarding document. Perhaps the key paragraph is paragraph 47 and, though there is a danger in going straight to this paragraph without rehearsing the closely argued sections that lead up to it, it is a danger I must risk taking.

Para. 47: 'Within his wider ministry, the Bishop of Rome offers a specific ministry concerning the discernment of truth, as an expression of universal primacy. This particular service has been the source of difficulties and misunderstandings among the churches. Every solemn definition pronounced from the chair of Peter in the church of Peter and Paul may, however, express only the faith of the Church. Any such definition is pronounced *within* the college of those who exercise episcope and not outside that college. Such authoritative teaching is a particular exercise of the calling and responsibility of the body

7 *The Gift of Authority*, p. 40.

of bishops to teach and affirm the faith. When the faith is articulated in this way, the Bishop of Rome proclaims the faith of the local churches. It is thus the wholly reliable teaching of the whole Church that is operative in the judgement of the universal primate. In solemnly formulating such teaching, the universal primate must discern and declare, with the assured assistance and guidance of the Holy Spirit, in fidelity to Scripture and Tradition, the authentic faith of the whole Church, that is, the faith proclaimed from the beginning. It is this faith, the faith of all the baptized in communion, and this only, that each bishop utters with the body of bishops in council. It is this faith which the Bishop of Rome in certain circumstances has a duty to discern and make explicit. This form of authoritative teaching has no stronger guarantee from the Spirit than have the solemn definitions of ecumenical councils. The reception of the primacy of the Bishop of Rome entails the recognition of this specific ministry of the universal primate. We believe this is a gift to be received by all the churches.'[8]

The Importance of *The Gift of Authority*

'A gift to be received by all the churches'? But what are the chances of this actually happening? Humanly speaking, they are very slim indeed. In the Roman Catholic Church, the way the Petrine ministry is in fact being exercised at the moment will not commend it to other Christians. There will be a lot of pressure within Anglicanism not so much to reject it outright (such directness would not be very characteristically Anglican) but to ensure that it dies the death of a thousand qualifications, to move it to the very bottom of the Anglican agenda and so, because of the nature of some of the other items on that agenda, to reduce even further any chance of its acceptance. But I believe it is our imperative duty to try to keep this issue at the top of the Anglican agenda and to work for its positive acceptance. This conviction is grounded in the following three considerations.

---

8 *The Gift of Authority*, pp. 33–4.

First, at the present moment both the Roman Catholic Church and the Anglican Communion are severely dysfunctional churches and in quite opposite ways, in need of a process of mutual enrichment and of mutual correction. They have trajectories or flightpaths going in opposite directions. If our shared ideal is unity in diversity, then Rome is putting such emphasis on unity that genuine diversity is endangered, while Anglicanism is putting such emphasis on diversity that unity is endangered. When it comes to working out the principle of subsidiarity (that issues should be decided at the appropriate level), Rome is reserving more and more questions to the universal (i.e. the Roman) level, while Anglicanism, unable to learn from the results of 'provincial autonomy', now seems to be moving in places to diocesan or even parochial autonomy. When it comes to the language of theology, Rome is in danger of turning the admirable virtue of clarity into univocal rigidity, while we are in danger of turning our traditional comprehensiveness (which was not without its virtues either) into a dialogue of the deaf.

Second, the future of Anglicanism is bleak; we are now a Communion in which we are no longer in full communion with each other, and every year fresh cracks appear in the structure as we descend into a sea of incoherence. *The Gift of Authority* is perhaps a lifebuoy thrown to us as we thrash about in that sea – a lifebuoy, and the only one in sight.

Third, at the heart of *The Gift of Authority* are two urgent questions which lie at the heart of the Anglican–Roman Catholic dialogue for the present and for the immediate future; they happen to be also two questions that challenge every Christian tradition and all the Christian churches:

1 Who has the authority to decide what constitutes a legitimate development of Christian doctrine – and by what means?

2 Who has the authority to decide what are the acceptable limits of diversity and what are the obstacles to Churches living together in full communion – and by what means?

Postscript

On the day after this paper was delivered an international meeting of Anglican and Roman Catholic bishops, convened by Cardinal Cassidy and the Archbishop of Canterbury, gathered near Toronto. After the end of their meeting, on 20 May, they issued a statement and an action plan. Both of these encouraging texts demand our vigilant, prayerful and sympathetic support. A joint unity commission is proposed and its suggested mandate has no more vitally important item that that which requires it to examine 'ways of ensuring formal consultation prior to one Church making decisions on matters of faith and morals which would affect the other Church, keeping in view the Agreed Statements of ARCIC'.[9]

---

9 The Commission's report was eventually published in 2007: *Growing Together in Unity and Mission: Building on 40 Years of Anglican–Roman Catholic Dialogue. An Agreed Statement of the Anglican–Roman Catholic Commission for Unity in Mission* (London: SPCK, 2007).

Index

McCowan, Lord Justice 149
Meyer, Conrad 181
Mirfield xxiv, xxxv, 24n, 111, 129
Montefiore, Hugh xxx

Neale, John Mason 28
New Directions 217, 220n, 232
Newman, John Henry xi, 6, 7, 38, 46, 52, 78, 109, 153, 156, 186
Norris, Richard 61

Old Catholic churches 25–7, 29, 111
Ordinal (1662) xxxi, 45, 122, 123, 169
Ordinariate xxxv, xli, 10
ordination 9, 41, 58, 59–60, 123, 235, *see also* diaconate, episcopate, Orders
Oriental Orthodox churches 13, 82, 115, 129, 131
orthodoxy, credal 142, 213
Orthodoxy, Orthodox churches xvi, xxii, xlii, 10, 20, 21, 25, 27, 28, 29, 58, 82, 111, 115, 117, 127, 158, 163, 167, 179, 181, 182, 185, 196, 198, 219
dialogue with Rome 11, 48, 131, 218, 221, 227, 236, 237
oversight 124, 126, 140, 180, 230, *see also episcope*
Oxford Movement xliii, 27, 28, 38, 43, 186, *see also* Catholic Revival, Tractarians

papacy xii, xxvii, 158, 129, *see also* Petrine ministry
Papalism (Anglican) 113, 154, 157
'semi-papalism' 11, 131, 157

Patey, Edward 19, 20
Patrick, Simon 73
patrimony, Anglican 10, 48–51
Paul IV 118
Paul VI 115, 129, 157n, 166, 205
and Michael Ramsey 12, 50, 118, 166, 235, *see also* common declaration
and the Anglican Church 47–50, 158, 166
Humanae Vitae 205
on women priests 17, 18, 162
perseverance 195
Petrine ministry/office 10, 83, 117, 193, 200, 238, 242
Pius XI 90, 91
Quadragesimo Anno 90
Pius XII 83, 91
Platten, Stephen 232
Porvoo churches 9
Porvoo Declaration 169, 174, 184, 213
Prayer Book 3, 30, 43, 45, 68, *see also* Book of Common Prayer, Ordinal
presidency of the Eucharist 21, 61, 167, 169, 183, 212, 229, 239
priesthood 56, 60, 122, 154, 163
ordination of women to *passim*
primacy xxvi, xl, 0, 111, 52, 53, 63, 68, 77, 101, 113, 114, 130, 131, 154, 157, 167, 168, 193, 194, 199, 202, 212, 218, 225–7, 229, 230, 241, 242
primates, Anglican 12, 65
Primitive Church, 73, 116, 154, *see also* antiquity, Early Church